ECONOMICS AND SOCIOLOGY OF INDUSTRY
A Realistic Analysis of Development

ECONOMICS
AND SOCIOLOGY
OF INDUSTRY

A Realistic Analysis of Development

BY

P. SARGANT FLORENCE

*Professor Emeritus, sometime Dean
of the Faculty of Commerce and Social Science
University of Birmingham*

LONDON
C. A. WATTS & CO. LTD.

First published 1964

Printed in Great Britain by Richard Clay and Company, Ltd.,
Bungay, Suffolk
36/430

THOUGH such reprinting is fashionable today, this book is not an assemblage of the essays and articles that I have written in the past. It is, however, an attempt to review and bring up to date the realistic analysis of industry, which has over several years been undertaken by a number of us, mostly working independently, though quite a proportion of the authors quoted in my bibliography have been pupils or colleagues at Birmingham. This bibliography includes a few classics, but otherwise is very much an integral part of my review, and its entries, placed in alphabetical order, are referred to in numbers inserted in the text instead of in repetitive footnotes. These references and the review presented in my text match up, I trust, with my title and subtitle.

By the *realistic analysis* of my subtitle I refer, as the phrase was used at Cambridge, to an approach based on observation and records of the real facts, but proceeding beyond mere description and empiricism to comprehensive measurement and causal interpretation and a hunt for some possible underlying logic.

My own hunting has brought out work being done (including its technology, markets catered for, and sources of supply drawn from) as a main factor determining the characteristics of different industries—even their form of government. The pervasiveness of this "ergological" interpretation will, no doubt, be disputed. Be that as it may, the nature of realistic analysis can be brought into relief by contrast with an opposite practice, that of building elaborately upon unverifiable or unfalsifiable assumptions often taken over from "authoritative" writers. Galbraith has quite recently written (209) of the "varied interpretation" to which Marx (and Keynes too!) have lent themselves. "Marx is the only writer since biblical times for whom reinterpretation is not a scholarly pursuit but a profession." When I was a Cambridge undergraduate we learned to worry *not* about what X or Y said, but about the truth; and thanks to the labours of census-takers, registrars of companies, statistical divisions of ministries, and fieldwork of research institutions, the truth, and often the exactly measured truth, can now be

obtained about a great number of industries and their characteristics. These characteristics are shown in the final Table
(XV) of this book. Beside measures of technique, such as capital intensity, and of markets and sources of supply measures
include the size, siting and scope of industries' plants, their
growth and fluctuation, and the concentration of control in
their larger firms. Testing trends and possible correlations in
these measures needs painstaking spade-work without the
glamour and status of abstract and pure theory such as deduc-
tions from economic man. The economic motive is powerful
and is far from ignored in this book, but it should be treated as a
plausible hypothesis to be tested rather than assumed as an
axiom, as do so many economists—Malthus in his population
theory, honourably excepted.

"Painstaking" reads in many critical reviews almost as a
term of contempt, but taking pains is not just a matter of observing and calculating accurately; realistic analysis includes
being careful to use appropriate indicators of the point *really* at
issue and not just some slick, easily handled average measure of
the data, and it means, also, checking hypotheses exhaustively.
Pain, indeed, comes with increasing cost when all relevant cases
have to be comprehensively measured and accounted for, and
not just (as "realistic" is often interpreted) some few actual
cases cited as neat illustrations. In spite of contempt, this painstaking research has been the approach bringing success to the
physical and biological sciences in contrast to the barren results
of medieval scholasticism, however fascinating.

Increasing pain has, I suspect, deterred quite a galaxy of
economists from realistic research. For one of the most remarkable phenomena is the continuous preaching of what I am
preaching by established economists and publicists with so little
subsequent practice. Dr. Keynes (107, p. 17) pointed out that
Mill, Cairnes, and Bagehot "all insist that the appeal to observation and experience must come in, before the hypothetical laws
of the science can be applied to the interpretation and explanation of concrete industrial facts." He himself maintained (107,
p. 172) "it is only by the unprejudiced combination of the two
methods" that any complete development of economics is possible.
Unfortunately those able and willing to carry out induction are,
here and now, comparatively scarce, nor is university training

adequate for any large additional supplies of social researchers. If I may use the economist's own apparatus of thought, induction should have, at present, greater marginal utility than deduction. Analysis must solve not only statistical problems now being brilliantly tackled in social accounting and econometrics but the "peristatistical" problems involved in research design (64, pp. 205–9). Though some contemporary reviewers seem to think only statistical method and "intuition" to be involved, there is still a role for a combination of non-statistical and statistical reasoning in the realistic analysis of practical problems, such as (below, pp. 10 and 200) the effects of science upon industry, or the population explosion consequent upon successful public hygiene.

Modern industry with its complex structure and government ramifies in many directions and, if it is to be analysed realistically and fully, requires the co-operation and co-ordination of a number of social sciences besides economics—hence *sociology* in my title. Sociology, following the pioneering of modern Universities such as London and Birmingham, has now become an accepted discipline in English Universities, however ancient. And I write in the hope that sociology will not set itself up against economics in becoming exclusive, even snobbish, and clearing its skirts of the no doubt sordid but socially important sociology of the joint-stock company, of business motivation and of industrial management. Is it really too much to hope, in the words of J. H. Smith (218, p. 104), "that the older Universities whose interest is in social behaviour and Hottentots rather than on Hawthorne and human relations, should immediately appreciate the social aspects of the management function?"

Industrial economics has now to deal more and more with large organizations or institutions and realistic economists like Farrell (208) and Gordon in his second edition preface (89) recognize as one of the main types of practical problem the effect of social structure, including process of government, upon economic behaviour; the effect, for instance, of control by salaried managers upon pricing or dividends. Recent investigators like Barna (10) or Mackintosh (125) have brought out the importance of the attitude as well as the abilities of those in control of firms. Nowhere is this more evident than in the risks and uncertainty that have to be faced when planning capital investment, or exports, or pricing generally, in relation to costs and to the demand curve. The controversies still unresolved here might perhaps come nearer resolution if more attention were paid to the bodies and types of persons whose attitude is so important to the growth of the national economy. If the characteristics of an industry are, as suggested, largely ergological, those of the single firm within an industry are largely to be interpreted by sociology and social psychology. To quote Barna (10, p. 48), "Investigation . . . brought to light differences in the attitude of managements, underlying behaviour in basically similar situations. The speed and energy with which firms seized a given opportunity, and the efficiency with which they exploited it, varied enormously and appear to have been associated with the character of the firm."

Some correlation has been established between rates of investment of different countries and their increase in national product, but admittedly material investment does not explain all growth. Indeed, modern input and output analyses have shown that increase in inputs of capital and of labour are quite insufficient to account for the whole increase in output of developed countries, such as the United States. The residual can probably be attributed to increase in the efficiency of an educated management in organizing and using capital and labour. Certainly education and training for management must be considered an investment; growth of staff (the third trend in development noted in my first chapter) has been, in fact, almost as marked as mechanization and investment in capital (my second trend) in all developing countries. The all-round study of management and managers is particularly important in the British economy, where, as I have long maintained, peculiar sociological institutions, hold sway. The Public Schools and the "character" they "build" and attitudes they foster toward individual enterprise and trading certainly develop a "pluralistic" system, with conflicting attitudes and goals in industry.

My subtitle's *development* needs no introduction in these days of "dynamic economics." If institutions and social conventions are important in the developed countries, how much greater are their influence on development in the poor but populous underdeveloped portion of the world! Here the most urgent trend in development, apart from the population explosion that underlies it, is the rapid urbanization which I have particularly considered in Chapter III—an urbanization unfortunately not always supported by sufficient industrialization. It is in fact becoming a sociological rather than an economic trend due to the insufficiency of tribal or peasant agriculture to support the growth of the rural population rather than any positive industrial attraction. But city custom, breaking down tribal or peasant society, will certainly have its economic, as it is having its political, effect.

Much of the contents of the book were first given as the Charles Beard lectures at Ruskin College, Oxford, sponsored by the Rationalist Press Association; subsequently brought up to date for lectures at Johns Hopkins University, Baltimore, in 1959 and the Leverhulme Lectures at the Royal University of Malta in 1962 and in 1963 for final publication. Where the last dates that I cite are not up to the minute, the slow process of publication, official or otherwise must be borne in mind; also the fact that many of the more relevant intensive inquiries are conducted only occasionally. But delay in publication is less serious when measuring, as in this book, the structural characteristics and long-term trends than when measuring short-term fluctuations. In fact, the text demonstrates repeatedly the relative stability of industrial structure.

I received much help in writing Chapter IV from Dr. Leslie Smyth of Keele University and in revising Chapters VI and VII from my colleague, Dr. David Wightman. I am deeply grateful, too, to Miss Irene Bowyer for proof reading, indexing and supervising the bibliography (pp. 245–53) which takes the place of footnotes.

P. SARGANT FLORENCE

Birmingham 1964

CONTENTS

LIST OF TABLES

xiii

CHAPTER I

ECONOMIC TRENDS IN INDUSTRIAL DEVELOPMENT

1. NINE MEASURABLE TRENDS

THE aim of this book as its subtitle implies is to analyse the important economic and sociological factors in the real world of industry. With a view to practical action, we may then discover the circumstances favouring and limiting industrial development in countries developed and underdeveloped.

Industry refers, as in common usage, to the manufacturing sector and excludes agriculture and mining and most services; but may, when so stated, include building and public utilities. Industrial development is important to all persons except the purely aesthetic or ascetic—keen, perhaps, on the "simple life" —because it appears to have brought with it higher standards of living and ultimately the relief of abject poverty. A realistic measured analysis of the conditions favouring industrialization and the consequential higher standards must begin, to put it alliteratively, by tracing the main *trends, traits* and *trains of events* appearing in the past and present development of the currently industrialized countries.

Development is a continuing dynamic process. The trend of events should be traced first, quantitatively if possible, before the traits or characteristics are laid down that are found at any one stage of the process. J. A. Hobson in his *Evolution of Capitalism* (96) was a pioneer in this quantitative tracing of trends, but since his day the greatly increased statistical data allow more certain and more exact conclusions to be established. When trends and traits are established we are in a position to suggest and, again perhaps quantitatively, to test the causal train of events and the relationships between trait and trait, trend and trend, trait and trend.

In the historical development of modern economies nine

1

more or less independent industrial trends can be fairly reliably disentangled and measured—

1. The growing importance of industrial and service as against agricultural activities.

2. The application of science (such as in mechanization or chemical treatment) to agriculture, mining, transport, and industry itself, involving investment of capital.

3. The growing proportion of organizers, managers, and research, technical, and administrative staff compared to actual working operatives in industry.

4. Largely as a result of science applied to transport and communication, the widening of the market and sources of supply, especially for manufacturing industries, and the localizing of particular industries as between countries or regions within countries.

5. Partly as a consequence, the differentiation of certain manufacturing industries with distinct characteristics.

6. Urbanization: the growth of industrial cities and conurbations faster than the population generally.

7. Enlargement of the size of industrial organizations such as factories and firms.

8. Emergence of a governing hierarchy of top managers in industry who, even in a capitalist economy, do not necessarily own the capital.

9. Though subject to fluctuations, higher standards of living of the total population.

The nine trends fall into four classes. The first five trends can be studied without reference to any organization of persons. They state some changing relations between individual persons and their activities, occupations, techniques or markets, in short, some change in the "activity structure" of a society, and are mainly economic trends.

The sixth, seventh, and eighth trends, on the other hand, immediately involve bodies and organizations of people and are (in the sense discussed later) largely sociological. There is, however, a further distinction between the sixth and seventh trends, which refer to changes in the "organic" *structure* of industry (particularly the size of its firms, plants, and cities) and the eighth trend, which refers to changes in the *government* of industry, in, as it were, its physiological processes. As we shall see, the distinction is important because all developing countries, Communist as well as Western, follow a certain pattern in the anatomy of their industry in the sixth and seventh as they do for the first five trends, but their trend in the form of government follows no single pattern. A particular example of this is that, though control by management has emerged, the Russians have not, since their Revolution, developed the joint-stock company or corporation now so characteristic a form of Western industrial government.

The ninth trend, the rise in standards of living is largely the consequence of the other eight. Like the eighth a class by itself, it is the aim of policy in developed and underdeveloped countries, and its achievement is thought of as "progress." Three significant features in this progress have been established by statistical measurement. The first is that the countries at present rich are in a sense *nouveaux riches* and have advanced rapidly in income-a-head during the course of the last half-century—a result that may give hope to the countries at present poor. In Britain (151) national income-a-head has risen in terms of constant prices (level of 1900) from an average of £25·7 in the five years 1870 to 1874 to £41·5 in 1900–4 (a rise of 61 per cent in the thirty years) and to £56·0 in 1934–8 (a rise of 34 per cent in the thirty-four years). Since then, till quite recently, the trend has accelerated again and the rise may be reckoned at almost 75 per cent for the last half-century.

The second feature in progress, statistically established, is that the year-to-year course of the trend was by no means smooth, and it is for this reason that five-year periods have just been compared. Apart from the years of war, falls in income-a-head in one year of over 2 per cent (associated with the slump phase of the trade cycle) occurred, for instance, in 1879, 1892, 1903, 1908 and again in 1921. This instability exposed all persons engaged in industry to financial loss or to unemployment and is, possibly, a price to be paid for the rapid long-run trend due to the application of science. Economists differ as to the fact of this possible connexion or the reasons for it, but Schumpeter (172) has made out a strong case for attributing trade cycles under the capitalist system to a concentration of scientific innovations at certain times.

B

TABLE I

COMPARISON OF DEVELOPED AND UNDERDEVELOPED COUNTRIES

in respect of Income-a-head, Percentage in Agriculture, Birth-rates and Life Expectation

Countries	Income-a-head		Percentage Change Relative to World 1949–57	Percentage in Agriculture 1957 or nearest year	Birth-rate (crude) per 1,000 Population 1957 or nearest year	Male Expectation of Life, at 0 Life-table previous to 1957
	$ 1957	$ 1949				
	(1)	(2)	(3)	(4)	(5)	(6)
Ten with Lowest Income-a-head						
Burma	48	36	87	69	50·0	N.A.
Pakistan	52	51	67	70	N.A.	N.A.
India	62	57	71	69	39·1	32·4
Nigeria	69	67	67	N.A.	49·2	N.A.
Bolivia	69	55	82	N.A.	34·9	49·7
Congo	74	52	93	N.A.	38·1	37·6
Thailand	85	36	155	75	34·2	48·7
Egypt	112	100	73	73	37·8	35·6
Ceylon	116	67	113	44	37·3	60·3
Peru	123	100	81	54	37·2	46·1
Average	*81·6*	*62·1*	*88·3*	*65*	*41·9*	*44·3*

All (5) Other Countries (with Population over 40 m.)

Brazil	251	112	147	56	43·0	39·3
Japan	252	100	165	33	17·3	65·2
Italy	403	235	112	35	18·1	63·7
W. Germany	741	320	152	12	17·0	64·6
France	847	482	115	20	18·5	65·0
Ten with Highest Income-a-head						
Denmark	869	689	83	19	16·8	69·9
Norway	914	587	102	24	18·0	71·1
Belgium	920	582	103	11	17·0	62·0
United Kingdom	954	773	81	4	16·5	67·6
Australia	1,074	679	103	17	22·9	67·1
New Zealand	1,166	856	88	20	26·2	68·3
Switzerland	1,223	849	94	20	17·7	66·4
Sweden	1,267	780	105	19	14·5	70·9
Canada	1,458	870	110	19	28·3	66·3
U.S.A.	2,101	1,453	95	12	25·0	66·4
Average	*1,190*	*812*	*96·0*	*16½*	*20·3*	*67·7*
THE WORLD	500	327·3	100			

Sources: (1) and (2) Sixty-two countries are listed by Andic and Peacock, *Statistical Journal.* The top and the bottom of this table gives ten now independent countries with the highest and with the lowest income-a-head in 1957. In the middle of the table all other countries (5) with over 40 m. population are listed. Countries in the Communist bloc and all with population below 2 million are omitted.

(3) The world change from 327·3 to 500 is an increase (mainly due to a fall in the purchasing power of the dollar) of 152·6 per cent. This column gives the change in each country as a percentage of the world change.

(4)–(6) *United Nations Demographic and Statistical Yearbooks,* 1955–9.

N.A.   Unavailable

The third and, for us, most significant feature of the rise in living standards statistically measured is the tremendous distance the poorer underdeveloped countries have to travel before they reach the *present* level of the rich or, indeed, any of their very recent past levels. To be sure, national income-a-head is a less satisfactory indicator of differences *between* countries than it is between periods in *one* country, and the deficiencies of this measure are discussed later (VI §1). It will be found far from worthless, however, and Table I gives the measurements published by the United Nations in 1949 and 1957 for the ten richest and poorest countries and five large countries in the middle. The table is the key to much of this book, and its salient features must briefly be surveyed.

The difference between income-a-head in the United States and Burma, the highest and lowest given in the table, was, in 1957, as 100 to 2·3. In this scale Britain came seventh, with about 45 per cent, and India came near the bottom, with 3 per cent of the American income-a-head. The trend since 1949 will be taken up in Chapters VI and VII, which are devoted to the underdeveloped countries. The differences between rich and poor countries seem not to have narrowed; and, certainly, hopes of a rapid rise from poverty have so far been disappointed.

Few countries have had the same amount of research devoted to them as America or Britain and when some of these countries are being dealt with it is not possible to measure rise or fall in income-a-head so exactly. The third column of Table I is thus only a rough index measuring the trend in each country between 1949 and 1957 compared with the "world" total for sixty-two countries where data were available in the two years. This world income-a-head rose between the two years mainly because of inflation, from $327·3 to $500·0 or by 1·53. The proportionate rise in each country's income-a-head is then expressed as a percentage of this ratio. Thus Burma's income-a-head rose from $36 to $48 or by 1·33. This is 87 per cent of 1·53. The advantage of these index numbers, given in column 3, is that, according as they stand below or above 100, they show at a glance whether the income-a-head of a country has fallen or has risen *relatively* to the world.

The fourth column of Table I gives the percentage of the total occupied population that is engaged in agriculture. The close correlation of low income-a-head with high percentage in agriculture will be seen at a glance. None of the ten countries lowest in income-a-head have an agricultural percentage below the 44 per cent of Ceylon, and none of the ten countries highest in income-a-head have an agricultural percentage above Norway's 24 per cent. If all countries with sufficient data are included the correlation of poverty with high agricultural occupation is extremely close.

The significance of the birth-rates and expectation of life in the last column will be discussed later (in Chapter VII) when dealing with sociological limits to economic development.

Income-a-head by which countries are being compared is not the same as productivity-a-worker, particularly where productivity refers only to manufacture. Besides differences in productivity and the rate of change of productivity in different economic activities, divergence is also due to the proportion of heads in a population which are those of workers. One country's working force may per worker be 10 per cent more productive than another's, but if 20 per cent less of its total head of population is at work, that country's standard of living—its average production *per head of population*—will be the lower. Increasing the proportion of the population at work is not one of the clear trends in development. Spreading education and raising the school-leaving age (an index of higher development) will, for instance, lower the proportion at work. This proportion and the factors in its determination will, therefore, be taken up in the next chapter as a question, largely sociological, of economic mobilization.

Anticipating this next chapter and the two Chapters (VI and VII) devoted to the underdeveloped economies, it can be stated that the range of difference between the productivity-a-worker of different countries is narrower than the range of differences in income-a-head. In the underdeveloped countries the workers form a smaller proportion of the total population and more of them are in agriculture. If we confine attention to *manufacturing* productivity-a-worker the range of difference is still narrower. The underdeveloped countries have a particularly low income-a-head because their rather lower manufacturing productivity-a-worker is diluted by a higher proportion of relatively low-value-producing agriculturists and further diluted by a higher proportion of their population being unoccupied. In short, the underdeveloped countries have only a small band of workers engaged in the high-value-producing manufacture, the rest doubly dilute the standard of living by working in low-producing agriculture or not working at all.

2. THE TREND AWAY FROM AGRICULTURE TOWARD INDUSTRIAL AND SERVICE ACTIVITY

The trend away from agriculture and into industrial occupations is so universally measurable that, exceptionally, Russia has been included. Table II traces the trend in England and Wales, the United States, and the U.S.S.R. and reveals that in England agricultural employment in 1960 had been reduced to as low a proportion as 4 per cent of the total employed. At first there was a corresponding rise of the proportion in manufacture, but later a slowing down of this rise.

TABLE II

PERCENTAGES OF OCCUPIED POPULATION ENGAGED IN AGRICULTURE: PAST AND PRESENT IN DEVELOPED COUNTRIES, PRESENT IN UNDERDEVELOPED CONTINENTS

	England and Wales	U.S.A.	Russia	Underdeveloped continents
1821	34			
1841	22			
1861	18			
1880–1	12	49		
1900–1	8	37		
1920–1	7	27		
1930–1	6	21	(1928) 80	
1940–1	—	18	(1937) 56	
1949–51	5	12	(1955) 43	Asia 70 S. America 60
1960	4	8		Africa 74 C. America 67

Sources
Col. 1. Robinson, E. A. G. (160)
Col. 2. *U.S. Statistical Abstract.* (195, p. 293)
Col. 3. U.S.S.R. Economy (190)
Col. 4. Burns, A. R. (29, p. 39) refers to 1949

Mining and building occupied normally only a small percentage of the population and show little trend. The remaining

proportion of the occupied population—occupied in services—
is rising. These facts appear to support the "law of tertiary production" formulated by Fisher (52, pp. 25–31) and developed
by Colin Clark (40, pp. 70–1), to the effect that, under full development, employment in the "tertiary" service industries
increases fastest. How firm is this generalization? During the
1939–45 War and in the years just after, this trend toward employment in the service industries was reversed in Britain and
America. But in more recent years, apart from the virtual disap-
pearance of the domestic servant (a million strong in England
fifty years ago), the trend has been resumed again.

When underdeveloped are being compared with developed
countries, however, the statistics are often deceptive. Before the
trend toward differentiation sets in, persons counted as agriculturists will be mainly pursuing a subsistence economy, but
incidentally transporting and marketing some of their produce,
making their own rough tools, supplies like soap, clothing, and
houses. Thus, as Bauer and Yamey point out (11, pp. 40–2) the
proportion statistically classified as agriculturists will cloak a
certain amount of manufacturing, building, transport, and trading services. And in the later stages of the development trends,
the substitution of machines and processes for persons makes the
relative fall in occupied persons no exact index of a relative fall
in the importance of activities. Measured in the values to which
machines as well as men contributed, manufacturers and agriculturists are not being displaced by services as much as appears
from the proportion of men occupied in each activity.

Though the exact percentage may exaggerate the change in
activities, there is little doubt of the displacement, at the middle
and later stages of development, of a way of life based on
agriculture. Besides the historical trend, shown vertically down-
wards in Table II the proportions based on agriculture of the
total occupied population can be compared laterally, region by
region, as in the toe of this L-shaped table. The poorer underdeveloped continents are seen to be the continents with a
relatively high proportion based on agriculture. While in 1949,
(29, p. 39) Australia (Oceania) had 33, Europe 33, and North
America 20 per cent of their population engaged in agriculture,
Africa had 74, Asia 70, Central America 67, and South America
60 per cent.

3. SCIENCE APPLIED TO INDUSTRY

For some time now I have presented the application of science as a dominating causal factor in modern industry. A simple chart in my *Investment, Location and Size of Plant* (69, p. 73) developed into an elaborate genealogical tree (72, pp. 72–3) distinguishing economic reasoning and statistical correlation as proving parts of the supposed train of causation. Here I reproduce, as Table III, a still later chart (78, p. 23) which

TABLE III

CHART OF CONDITIONS AND RESULTS OF THE
APPLICATION OF SCIENCE

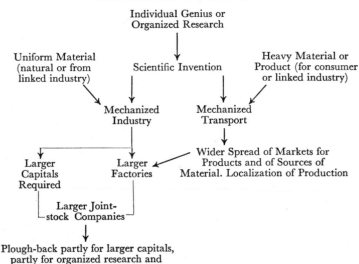

stressed the important self-perpetuating "circular" character of the train of causation, an important element in the take-off. To that chart I add a reference to the material and the product and market conditions necessary for inventive genius or organized research to have affected production, and for scientific inventions to have been applicable as an innovation in industry and transport.

Inventive geniuses certainly existed in all ages and even perhaps among our apelike ancestors, but the application of their inventions to industry is very recent and has not, apparently, happened in history before at anything like the present scale or pace. Many reasons have been put forward why the start of this unique set of events (which is still developing and reaching an extreme form in *automation*) "took off" at the particular time and place that it did, namely, the late eighteenth century, in England. Scientific knowledge was not enough. As Blackett said in his Presidental Address to the British Association in 1957 (19)—

> During the first two hundred years of modern science, from 1600 to 1800, science learnt much from technology, but taught it relatively little. . . . Despite the interest of the Royal Society in the "useful arts," it was not until the last quarter of the eighteenth century that the impact of science on technology began to be decisively important.

In the countries now developed and, as we shall find, in the underdeveloped countries, it is the *application* of science in society that is the stumbling-block. Particular social conditions are necessary. To quote the chapter headings of Arthur Lewis's *Theory of Economic Growth* (121), they are not only Knowledge and Training but Will to "economize" and certain economic Institutions (such as economic freedom and the right to reward for work), the formation of Capital, and Wise Government.

The will to economize and the reward for work have in the historical past been overlaid by the will to "conspicuous waste," to military power and glory, or to provision for the next world; the institution of true freedom of thought and religious tolerance only just preceded the Industrial Revolution in England.

Even now, not all business leaders or even the majority of them have the will to economize or make the effort to maximize profits; nor does freedom of thought necessarily give them useful thoughts. They are often driven to innovation by sheer need, substituting capital for labour to avoid loss through higher wage demands (138, pp. 64–6), or having to match the innovations of competitors. Certainly those who do not innovate or imitate the innovators are liable to be driven out of business and may fail to survive.

These innovators (Schumpeter (172) confusingly calls them entrepreneurs) might be the owner-managers of a business (entrepreneurs as defined later, p. 123) or just managers, inventors or promoters, or a bit of each. Many empirical studies have recently been published of the way innovation gradually percolates through the firms and plants of an industry. Carter and Williams have shown in successive chapters of their *Investment in Innovation* (33), the variety of business motives (IV) and the grounds for investing (V) or not investing (VI). Much is found to depend on the opportunity offered by available funds obtained, as will be seen (V, §3), by plough-back of sporadically large profits. My genealogical tree (Table III) is, however, meant as a model of the way not only sociological and psychological, but material and market factors may affect industrial development and how, once the development is thus "primed," it may "take off" on its own through plough-back of profits, particularly by large organizations and the research they often undertake.

It is unnecessary further to elaborate the importance of science to industrial development, since this thesis of a dynamic economy has now been generally accepted and built upon as an assumption. But if economic analysis is to be realistic it must try to measure fairly exactly the speed with which science is being applied in various industries and in various countries, developed and underdeveloped.

To the economist, the main consequence of applying physical science is the growth, compared to the labour employed, of the value of the capital investment and physical capacity, normally appearing as fixed assets in the balance sheet. The growth of capital investment in industry (to avoid confusion with investment in stocks and shares it may be referred to as equipment or mechanization) appears particularly strongly in manufactures, transport, and communication, fairly strongly in mining and agriculture, where conditions of work are less uniform, but only weakly in building, trading, and other services. As already suggested, the tapering off in the proportion of workers in manufacturing, compared to services (referred to in the "law of tertiary production") does not necessarily indicate a relative fall in manufacturing production, but rather the growing substitution of machines for men in the manufacturing process.

The amount of the fixed capital investment relative to labour, or more generally, but vaguely, the degree of "capital intensity," is indicated most readily, simply, and without recourse to fluctuating monetary values by the industry's horse-power capacity per worker (69, pp. 90–3). Other indicators (frequently referred to, but seldom actually measured for specific industries) are the capital/output or the capital/labour ratios. The wide range of mechanization even within the manufacturing sector shown by these and one or two other indicators is illustrated from a number of industries in the Appendix. Cement-making, in Britain, 1957, had a horse-power per worker of 25·4, tailoring and dressmaking only 0·2; china and earthenware fixed assets per worker of £590, mineral oil refinery of £12,680. These differences in the capital intensity of different manufactures illustrate the complex factors explaining the application of science. As lawyers say, it is not only a question of motive, but of the opportunity offered by the material and market situation. If materials are uniform and a uniform product can be sold, like cement or petrol, then mass-producing machines and processing are the easier to apply.

In Table IV, L-shaped like Table II, the upward trend of horse-power-a-worker in manufacture is seen to be continuous

TABLE IV

HORSE-POWER-A-WORKER IN USE IN MANUFACTURE: PAST AND PRESENT IN DEVELOPED; 1939–54 IN UNDERDEVELOPED COUNTRIES

	U.S.A.	Britain				
1869	1·1	—				
1889	1·4	—				
1909	2·9	(1907) 1·6*				
1929	4·9	(1930) 2·4				
1939	6·5	—	Brazil	1·4	Mexico	2·1
1951	—	3·1	Brazil (1949)	2·0	Argentine	2·1
1954	9·6		Nicaragua	0·9	Taiwan	1·4
			Guatemala	0·6	Greece	1·0

* Available: in use approximately 1·3
Sources: U.S. Census of Manufactures, U.K. Census of Production, United Nations (184) Part II

for Britain and America, though at a lower level in Britain. Other developed countries show the same trend. But the underdeveloped countries, shown at the toe of the L, appear, for the same recent dates, at an altogether lower level.

Horse-power-a-worker, though accurate enough for comparison between particular industries at the same time and place, greatly understates the increase in total power put at the disposal of industrial operation as a whole, because factories used to rely mainly on their own power-houses, applying steam power direct to machines. Now they have largely "disintegrated" power generation and rely on specialized electrical power-stations, appropriately localized in big cities or on water, or if nuclear, at the sea-shore. The increase from 2·4 to 3·1, shown in rated horse-power a British factory worker in the twenty-seven years 1924–51, amounts to an increase of 20 per cent per decade. But the power purchased by industry from central electricity supply undertakings, about half the total used in 1930, has in recent years about doubled per decade.

4. The Increase in Staff

The third trend refers not, like the first, to a measurable relation between industries or economic activities generally, but to one within an industry between its occupations. The distinction between industry and occupation is that a man's industry depends on whom he works for, his occupation on what he works at. A bench-hand and a factory manager are different occupations both in some manufacturing industry; a professor and a college porter are different occupations both in the educational industry.

The trend now to be noticed is the increase within manufacturing industries of the ratio of administrative, scientific, and technical (including clerical) staff, usually paid a salary, to the operative producers, usually paid a wage. If these administrative occupations are considered "services" this trend reinforces the law of tertiary (i.e. service) production mentioned earlier.

This increase in the staff ratio is confirmed by the census taken in various years in all the major countries already industrialized, though it is not easy to obtain data on the ratio in underdeveloped countries. A further difficulty, apart from the poverty of statistics, is that in the early stages of development, with small firms producing the bulk of output, the owner-manager or entrepreneur prevails, and if he is counted as "staff" the staff–operative ratio appears high. In fact, he may, like the "dirt-farmer," be both staff and operative (76) as well as capitalist.

The ratio of staff to operatives in British manufactures has advanced from 11·8 per cent in 1924 to 15·1 in 1935, 20·0 in 1948, and 26·1 in 1957; in the United States from 11·9 in 1909 (about fifteen years in advance of the United Kingdom) to 20·0 in 1939 (nine years in advance) to 26·5 per cent in 1954, little more than the United Kingdom's 26·1 per cent in 1957. This trend, in which the United Kingdom seems to be overtaking the United States, is sometimes deplored as an unnecessary growth of overhead cost and an example of Parkinson's Law (146). With more forward planning of productive operations, however, the increase of staff per operative may well not be just "empire-building." American evidence (138, p. 147) is that staff has increased less than the rise in productivity level. In Britain, too, it is probably (72, pp. 139–40) a natural consequence of increased output due to the use of machines which displace the operative, but add to the work of staff, thus increasing the numerator but diminishing the denominator of the staff ratio. In many industries, notably chemicals and electrical engineering, the staff is "scientific" as well as technical and administrative and not wholly concerned, directly, in coping with output. Subtracting scientific staff, the ratio of staff to *output* has in fact probably fallen in England and in America.

Though increase in the staff ratio and increase in size of organization are both apparent trends, it does not appear to be true, as often assumed, that staff ratios are greater where the size of plant is greater, measured in total employed. Many British industries with, typically, large plants such as shipbuilding, motor and cycle, iron and steel, and marine engineering have low staff ratios, and it can be said that the staff ratio of an industry is fairly independent of the size of its plants.

Who precisely compose the staff? A survey by the Ministry of Labour (113) discloses that in manufacturing industries the number of women on the staff is about half that of men, a rather higher proportion than among operatives. Of the men 44 per cent are paid their salary monthly, not weekly; of the women only 15 per cent. The staff thus consists largely of office clerks and typists. This is confirmed by an analysis of all the employees of Imperial Chemical Industries in 1956; 30 per cent were male or female staff and nearly 50 per cent of this staff, clerical workers. Nevertheless, the increasing proportion of staff as a whole is a measure of the need for considerable secondary education. And the growth of the scale of management, varying with industry, is reflected in the 44 per cent among staff of monthly paid males, ranging from 21 per cent in shipbuilding and marine engineering to 74 in chemicals and allied trades. In Imperial Chemicals, indeed, 30 per cent of the male staff hold the rank of manager. This excludes foremen—another 9 per cent of male staff.

This trend toward higher staff ratios is likely to continue with continued application of science and greater forward planning, budgeting, and other management procedures; and it has sociological as well as economic implications for the under-developed as well as the developed countries. A cadre of men and also women literates educated at school up to at least sixteen must, for full development, be supplied side by side with the semi-skilled and skilled workers operating, tending, and maintaining the new machines.

5. WIDENING OF MARKETS AND SUPPLY SOURCES

The fourth trend, the widening of markets and sources of supply, and thus the possibility of localizing manufacture, is more difficult to measure and test quantitatively than the trend away from agriculture, the trend to mechanize, or the increasing ratio of staff. Within a single country, measurement of markets is possible only if that country keeps records of economic activities and structures separately for separate regions. Thanks to the "check-points" that custom-houses present and the detailed publication of imports and exports, quantitative measurement is made easier, however, *between* countries. It is, in fact, possible to measure a common line of development whereby some countries will increasingly import supplies from other countries for their manufacturing industries and will widen their sales of manufactures by export to markets abroad. They thus become differentiated as manufacturing countries—as "workshops of the world."

The process can be traced in detail, for instance, from the United Kingdom's annual summaries of imports of "raw materials and articles mainly unmanufactured" and exports of articles "wholly or mainly manufactured." Both these imports and exports greatly increased *in volume* per head of population as the United Kingdom developed its industries, particularly after 1830.

Apart from coal, British visible exports were—and are—almost wholly manufactured products. In the forty years between 1830 and 1870 exports rose in declared money value from £38·3m. to £199·6m. or just over fivefold, and in real values per head of population about three and one-third times. The growth in the (money) value of exports after 1870 was much less rapid, but in the thirty years up to 1900 prices were falling and the real value of exports per head of population rose about 50 per cent. The total rise in this simple real indicator of widening foreign markets was, therefore, from 1830 to 1900 about fivefold.

The expansion of exports which has been so frequently described must be seen as only a part of the analysis and measurement of widening markets and sources of supply. Apart from "invisible" services, about a quarter the value of its exports, Britain must export manufactures to import food, and also the raw materials for the manufacturers; hers may be called a "through-putting" economy in which materials and food from abroad are "put through" her factories, and her factory workers' stomachs, in order that factories and workers may produce for a high standard of living at home *and* for importing the necessary foreign materials and food. It is possible to measure the degree of through-put from official foreign-trade statistics by a summary coefficient which would average the percentages (with a possible range of 0–100) of total rawstuffs and food used that was imported and of all foods manufactured that was exported. A coefficient of 100 would measure complete through-put in which, as in a city state with no rural environs, all food and rawstuffs used were imported and, to pay for them, practically all manufactures had to be exported. The coefficient would be nil in an agricultural and mineral-sufficient country, where no food or materials need be imported and no manufactures exported. Such a coefficient, that I calculated (81) from summary data given by the 1907 *Census of Production* gives Britain 33. The summary data were not repeated in subsequent *Censuses*, but the British coefficient of visible through-put has certainly gone still higher since, probably to near 50, owing to increased imports of materials, fuel, and food. Saunders (171) considers that nearly all the expansion in industrial output between 1851 and 1950 has been fed from the increase in imports. Since 1907 *fuel* has been imported in the form of oil in place of the home-mined coal; and with the increase of population the need for food imports has not diminished, even though home agriculture has been heavily subsidized. This does not mean that Britain imports a greater proportion compared to her national income. Robinson (160) makes that proportion about the same in 1951–3 as in 1870–80. It means that Britain imports more of the foods and materials that are essential to her life and industry. To that extent, the British economy has become increasingly differentiated and specialized as a manufacturing unit. Belgium, Holland, and Japan, like Britain, increased raw material and food imports and manufactured exports rapidly since 1850 and have a high coefficient of through-put, and such almost completely urbanized areas as Hong Kong, Singapore, or Malta have coefficients still higher, well over Britain's probable 50.

Dependence on foreign trade makes national planning much more difficult, since the demands of foreigners to whom exports are to be sold cannot be planned. Is there a risk in overdevelopment?

This process of differentiation and specialization in manufactures (much of them exported) by countries of relatively small area is associated with high densities of population. Contrary to common opinion, it is not India nor China that has the highest population per square mile, but Great Britain (particularly England), Holland, Belgium, Western Germany, and Japan. All of these countries had by 1957 a density of more than five hundred to the square mile. The increase in density of these smaller countries has outrun their natural resources for food, raw materials, and fuel production and they must rely increasingly on imports. For the world as a whole, trade between countries has, partly in consequence, been measurably increasing. The *United Nations Yearbooks* (185) give certain index numbers tracing the growth of aggregate international trade since *1938*. It appears that in terms of volume total world exports rose between 1938 and 1961 from 53 to 116 per cent of the 1957 volume, though population increased only from 75 to 104 per cent and total production from 67 to 104 per cent.

In Britain and the similar through-putting countries, home markets were also widening. But in countries with a large area and a variety of natural conditions, such as America and Russia, these internal markets and also the internal sources of supply are of chief importance. For the United States the coefficient of visible through-put is low. Except for tropical products, such as coffee, sugar, rubber, and for minerals, including oil, not found in large enough amounts within its own boundaries, the United States imports relatively little rawstuff, and exports only a small proportion of its manufactures. It is a self-sustaining, not a through-putting economy.

In such countries of wide area certain regions or districts tend to develop as industrial centres differentiated from the mainly undeveloped regions. This differentiation can be quantitatively traced only if regional statistics are published, as they are in the United States. Here, the New England States had by 1950 38·5 per cent of their total man-power employed in manufacture but only 3·7 per cent of it in agriculture and mining; the Mountain States of the West, on the other hand, had only 9·5 per cent in manufacturing (a quarter of the New England proportion) and 21·8 per cent in agriculture and mining, six times the New England proportion. This "localization" and regional development of industries within countries is an important element in development and, in Chapter III, will be analysed further.

Whether a particular industry localizes regionally within a nation or internationally, a developed transport is essential. As early as the Canal Age, Adam Smith realized that markets widened largely because of greater transport facilities. A relevant indicator, therefore, which fits into and verifies the argument pictured in Table III, is the increase in the proportion of the occupied population engaged in transport and communication and the growth of mechanical equipment for transport and communication.

In England and Wales the proportion of the occupied population in transport and communication rose (160, p. 459) from 3·0 per cent in 1841 and 6·2 in 1861 to 7·6 in 1881 and 9·7 in 1901. In the United States the number so engaged rose

c

from 4·7 per cent of the total occupied in 1880 to 6·6 in 1900 and to 7·5 in 1950. In Russia the proportion engaged in "transport and posts" has risen from 2·0 per cent in 1938 to 6·0 in 1955 (190). With the increasing proportion of transport going by road not rail, workers constructing and maintaining roads should be included in the transport force, as workers building and maintaining railways are automatically included when employed by the railways. Further evidence of the development of transport is that, recently, the net output of transport and communication equipment has outstripped considerably the net output of manufacturing generally. In the United States transport and communication equipment formed, in 1937, 8 per cent of the total value added in manufactures, in 1957, 12 per cent. In Britain "vehicles" formed, in 1935, 8 per cent of the total net output of manufactures, in 1957, 11 per cent. These are inclusive figures, from which vehicles used purely for pleasure, if the figures were available, ought to be subtracted and also the *net* export of vehicles to be used for business; but the proportion of total vehicles directed in these different ways did not vary greatly.

A factor that has widened markets almost as much as transport is the art of preservation—of overcoming the perishability which I have singled out (60, pp. 338–41) as a physical quality of materials or products equal with portability and gradability (avoiding the need of personal inspection), in basic economic importance. Industries particularly affected are canning and slaughtering, which can now be localized far from their markets.

Before concluding it must be said that this trend toward widening markets internationally has in the last decades been greatly hindered by tariffs, quotas, and other national, not to say nationalistic, restrictions. To quote Myrdal (143, p. 32)—

> International trade was increasing not only absolutely but also in comparison with total production. . . . Beginning with the First World War, however, . . . and more definitely with the onset of the Great Depression—all international movements were securely curtailed by national policies.

The Second World War caused a further set-back, but since 1948 the trend has set in again in general, though not in every trade—not, for instance, in textiles, where production for the home market has increased, while exports and imports have decreased.

6. The Persistent Differentiation of Manufacturing Industries

Widening markets and sources of supply, together with the application of science, bring in their train a differentiation of industries. The traits of separate industries are elaborated and illustrated in the Appendix, but the process of separation and the relation of separation to width of market is not easy to measure by any one indicator. This relation has been recognized at least since the days of Adam Smith, who devoted a whole chapter (173, Book I, iii) to the proposition that the division of labour is limited by the extent of the market. In a small market there can be little specialization—

> It is impossible there should be such a trade as even that of nailer in the remote and inland parts of the highlands of Scotland. Such a workman, at the rate of a thousand nails a day, and three hundred working days in the year, will make three hundred thousand nails in the year. But in such a situation, it would be impossible to dispose of one thousand, that is, of one day's work in the year.

Without splitting up the work of a smith even as finely as to differentiate nailmaking, the British *Census of Production* was able in 1951 to differentiate forty-one metal industries; and the American *Census of Manufactures* differentiated in 1954 one hundred and twenty-seven metal industries. Though, occasionally, industries coalesce and integrate, increase in manufacture, together with the new applications of science and widening markets has on balance resulted in persistent differentiation between manufactures.

The first four trends: the flight from agriculture, the application of science, increased staff, and widening of markets, have occurred, whatever the system of *industrial* government, whether Communist or capitalist. At this point, however, one of the main characteristics of capitalism must be distinguished—a characteristic not, like control by capital owner, implicit in the word *capitalism*, but conveyed in the phrase free enterprise. Any one capitalist organization in fact controls only a small

part of industry; and capitalist industry *as a whole* is not controlled
by any single authority but is *controlled*, if that is the right word,
by the balance of prices and costs on the market. Under this
"market control" if a capitalist firm sees a profit in the difference between revenue from the prices charged and costs in *any*
line of product, or process, it is free to take up that line in its
plants or, if the firm sees a loss in any line, to drop that line.
If enough firms in one established industry take over the products or processes of another, as steel has iron-making, the two
industries may coalesce or integrate; if enough drop a product
or process a separate industry may be formed from the activities
dropped. As Allyn Young pointed out (206), the progressive
division and specialization of industries is an essential part of
the process by which increasing returns are realized.

Industries are not in fact preordained. Instead, freedom of
enterprise has allowed each firm or plant to develop a set of
lines (products or processes) apparently arbitrarily, but
usually with technical characteristics which fit together
logically and which are adapted to the general work to be performed on the particular materials for the particular market.
One may thus discern an economic logic of events underlying
the "mix" within the firms or plants of an industry, and the
differentiation between industries. The whole process of converting materials into final products is usually split vertically
(72, p. 9) by a "Great Divide" into at least two stages: that of
refining or producing a uniform substance or stuff out of the
raw material; and that of making up or assembling the stuff.
Thus, smelting and rolling iron ore, to make the stuff steel, is
differentiated from engineering, working on, or assembling steel
and stuffs from other industries. For steelmaking is most
economically carried on near, or accessibly to, the sources of
its heavy and intransportable raw materials, while engineering
is most economically carried on near the markets for its products, most of which are of awkward shape and relatively costly
to transport and whose producers and customers require frequently to consult together. Industries differentiated similarly
to steel and engineering are textile and clothing; grain-milling
and bread; sawmilling and furniture.

This logic of events accounts for the fact that though industries are formed by the policy of single firms, the ultimate

scope of the different industries is so similar in different countries that British productivity teams have had little difficulty in finding their opposite numbers in America; and that Censuses in the two countries use a very similar industrial classification.

It is important for our purposes to define *an industry*; and since an industry is the result of a trend—sometimes a quasi-biological, trial-and-error, fight-for-survival trend—this task may appear difficult. We can accept, however, the official standard census classification of industries as corresponding sufficiently to current usage, yet covering all manufacturing without overlapping. Its basic principle is to assign all establishments (i.e. plants) to one industry or another according to their principal products. Few, if any, industries make only one product, as economists sometimes still assume, but they usually make similar kinds of products. The definition I have adopted (63, p. 5, 72, p. 17) for an industry is *any kind of transactions* (e.g. products or processes) *usually specialized in by a number of plants who do not usually perform much of any other kind of transaction.* This definition can, of course, more appropriately for sociology, be put another way round that "an industry is a group of workers in a number of plants usually specializing in any kind of transactions not usually performed by other plants." To the sociologist, an industry is a *community* of persons, which the persons themselves recognize and to which the employers, at least, may feel a certain loyalty. An industry, however, unless nationalized or a complete private monopoly, is not, as expounded later, an *association* with an organization and government for general purposes.

Exactly how usual or not usual the specialization may be is a question now answered statistically by the Census (182, p. 22–5 and 69, pp. 2–5). The Census now gives the proportion in which the plants of any one industry (*a*) *specialize* on their principal products, e.g. how far grain is only milled in grain mills, and (*b*) are *exclusive* and do not make other products, e.g. how far grain mills only mill grain. It is surprising how little most industries' plants engage in products or processes not usual to that industry and how few plants in other industries engage in the products and processes which are usual to that industry. Firms, however, as we shall see (pp. 90–2), often integrate plants in different industries and cross the usual boundaries more frequently.

My definition of industry is perfectly in keeping with that of Joan Robinson (162), though, to agree with the Census, her *firm* should read *plant*—

> In ordinary language, when we speak of (any industry) we are thinking of a group of firms engaged in a certain type of pro-duction, governed by the kinds of object produced and the materials of which they are made.

Later in the article, she adds—

> there are often certain basic processes required for the pro-duction of the most diverse commodities (tennis balls, motor tyres and mattresses) and economies in the utilization of by-products under one roof.

It is a great help to definition that industries, even manu-facturing industries, differ so widely one from another in their characteristics. The Appendix illustrates the extent of the range by citing from the *Census* those industries which have the most extreme measured characteristics—with their precise measure. These characteristics have, moreover, tended to persist for each industry over several years. In 1931 the cement industry had 150 times the horse-power-a-worker of the tailoring and dress-making industry, and in 1951 it still had over 125 times as much. The six British industries with the highest horse-power-a-worker in 1951, given in the Appendix (Table XV p. 241) all with above 9·8 had been among the nine industries with highest horse-power in 1930. The same persistence appears in size-of-plant differentiation. The three industries with the smallest and the three with the largest representative size of plant are the same industries in 1930 as in 1951. There is little, if any, general tendency for industries to draw closer together in their characteristics, for instance for high mechanization or larger plants to spread from one to another industry till all industries are equally mechanized or large-scaled. This per-sistence of differentiation is particularly significant in the degree of localization. The Appendix gives the seven industries with the highest coefficient of localization in 1951. They were all among the eight most localized comparable industries in 1930.

As well as persistence and stability for different periods in the same country, these contrasts in the characteristics of the different industries show a certain ubiquity if tested by similarity in different countries. Elsewhere, I have demonstrated (72, 79) the measurable similarity of the inter-industry contrasts in size of plant, power-a-worker, and degree of localization between British and American industries. The United Nations has brought out the similarity of the contrast, even between developed and underdeveloped countries, in net output (i.e. value added) per worker, for wide industry groups. Here are the data for the seven manufacturing groups that are complete for all continental regions—

TABLE V

VALUE ADDED PER PERSON (IN 1,000 1948 U.S. DOLLARS) IN FOUR REGIONS 1953

	Asia, E. and S.E.	Latin America	Europe	N. America
Chemicals	1·4	3·0	4·0	9·8
Basic metals	1·1	2·4	2·8	5·9
Paper	1·0	1·3	2·8	7·4
Metal products	0·6	1·1	2·1	6·3
Food	0·5	1·4	2·5	5·8
Textiles	0·4	1·0	1·8	4·4
Non-metal mineral products	0·4	1·0	1·9	5·9
All manufacturing 1953	0·5	1·3	2·1	5·9

Sources: United Nations (184, pp. 120 *et seq.*)

The seven industry groups are listed in order of their value added per employee in East and South-East Asia; but the ranking is much the same in the other continental regions. None of the first six industry-groups is ranked more than two places differently in any continent! The ubiquity of their relative differences in net output a worker is evident enough.

7. FURTHER TRENDS AND CAUSAL RELATION BETWEEN TRENDS

The five trends traced in detail in the last few sections are mainly economic. They describe changes in the kind of work, industry, or occupation which individual persons *exchange for pay*, and changes in the technical processes and location of production for exchange. More people were drawn out of agriculture and into manufacturing industries and within those industries into staff occupations, and industries are mechanized and localized nationally, and otherwise differentiated. But the next four trends: urbanization, larger-scale organization, government by manager, and higher living standards are as much sociological as they are economic and will be taken up in later chapters.

Though partially so, the nine trends are not completely independent of one another. Some of them have been statistically correlated, mechanization and location pattern, for instance, with scale of organization. But before the correlation tests are applied unthinkingly, hit or miss, it is important to put forward, for testing, some theory or hypothesis about the lines of causation, which has some logical probability or plausibility.

The chief train of causation which I put forward as a possible logical sequence of industrial events has already appeared in the genealogical tree model of Table III, and is followed in the sectional arrangement of Table XV (in the Appendix). The four main "generations" of this tree may, by holding the page horizontally, bottom next to the eyes, be viewed in perspective as, back first, hinterland, background, middle-ground, and foreground. The hinterland (i and ii in Table XV) is the type of external work done, the nature, especially uniformity and weight, of the materials used and products made for various markets that are served, and the linkage with the work of other industries, including input and output relations. No word that is ordinarily used covers the study of all these hinterland factors of work done, and I am compelled reluctantly to introduce one of my few technical terms. The Greek for work is *ergon*, so the study of these characteristics will, on the analogy of *erg* and *ergograph*, be called *ergology* and the train of causation I put forward called the *ergological* interpretation of industrial characteristics. Nearer than the hinterland, the background (iii and iv in Table XV) is technological; its outstanding feature is the trend toward mechanization of industry, transport, and communication. The middle-ground of the suggested causal train (v and vii in Table XV) is largely sociological— one of social or "organic" structure: the trends (soon to be traced) toward the larger-scale organization with, for many industries, localization and urbanization.

This whole perspective is put forward as a "visual aid" in tracing trains of causation. Many such trains have already been explored by economic sociologists notably Adolf Weber and Karl Marx.

Adolf Weber in his *Standortstheorie* associated location pattern with the physical properties of an industry's materials and products, especially their weight and intransportability. Avoiding the jargon of material or market "orientation" we can say that intransportable *materials* keep an industry like cement-making "rooted" near the source of materials. According to the scatter or concentration of materials, so will the industry be distributed. Heavy and intransportable *products*, on the other hand, keep an industry like brewing "tied" near the consumer. There are at least two sorts of consumer. The final consumer, such as the beer-drinker, is presumably dispersed among the population; but the *producer*-consumers may be localized. Industries, like machine building, providing the producer with products awkward to transport will probably conform to the producers' location pattern. Where both materials and products are heavy, the industry may be near the source of materials *or* the market. Where neither materials nor products are heavy the industry may be considered "footloose" and various plans for location are feasible; but as we shall see (Chapter III) loose feet often lead to high localization owing to the economies, external to the plants of their "flocking together."

Marx's "extension of materialism to the domain of social phenomena," as Lenin put it (119, p. 544), is based less on the hinterland of work than on the technological background. It is summed up in his dictum that the hand mill will give you society with the feudal lord; the steam mill, society with the industrial capitalist. The ergological includes, and is wider than, a technological interpretation, comprising the type-of-work hinterland, as well as the technological background.

The association between the external work being performed together with the techniques used, and the internal characteristics of the various industries within the manufacturing sector, is brought out even more clearly when comparing manufacturing with other sectors of economic activity in respect

of their location pattern and size of plant. Unlike manufacturing, mining and agriculture have intransportable material
and building has an intransportable product. Services do not
work on materials or for a product at all and except for transport
and communication are not heavily mechanized. It would
be interesting, but take us beyond industrial development, to
analyse how these fundamental differences in the work they
perform and techniques they use, affect not only different
sectors' location and size of plant patterns but go beyond that in
effecting differences in their organization and government.
Mining and building, for instance, have distinctly lower,
transport and trade distinctly higher staff ratios than manufacturing. Mining, rail and air transport, communications, and
public utilities are nationalized; at the other end of the scale,
building, retailing, and, above all, agriculture retain the small-
scale entrepreneur to a far greater extent than manufacturing.

The effect of the hinterland of the work done is also evident in
the time incidence of the occurrence of risk. The risks of an
industry are high if the products it markets are fashionable
luxuries, or durable goods not wanted day by day, and if the
material supplied depends on the weather. Seasonal fluctuation
can be measured and to some extent the different amplitudes of
boom and slump likely to be experienced by plants in the
several industries (high, for instance, for *capital* goods) during
trade cycles. But uncertainty remains when both nature and
human nature are so unpredictable. Where, as in extractive industries, weather or geology affect supplies and where, in
industries at large, consumers' and rival traders' behaviour is
not planned or predictable beforehand, the cost of wrong prediction will be particularly heavy if much capital has been sunk
in special equipment for the enterprise and a slump leads to idle
capacity. Social loss will also occur in the form of concentrated
unemployment if the industry involved is localized in any one
area. To guard against the risk of putting all eggs into one
industrial basket, more integration is undertaken by firms than
is justified by the economies of *specializing* in large-scale processes or products. Plants and the firm, the unit of government,
tend for this reason to be the larger, as we shall see, and large
industrial cities are justified by specializing in several industries
offering alternative employment.

In the train of events, so far, the capitalist and Communist economies show much the same ergological development from the particular work to be done through technology to structure. But in the foreground where I place government (VIII in Table XV) the two systems part company. If the firm is small it is, under the capitalist economy, usually governed by an owner-manager (or entrepreneur) risking his own capital. If the firm is large its government will probably be of joint-stock company form, in which the largest capitalist shareholders may or may not be in control. If the firm is large, not just absolutely but relatively to the size of the whole industry, the result may be a narrow concentration of the control of the industry's production in a few firms, if not a single firm, i.e. an oligopoly, if not monopoly. Even if there are many firms, these may have some agreement and the government of the whole industry may be "confederate" by cartelization.

Thus, a train of causation can be held to extend all the way through from the hinterland of the materials and markets through applied science, and the technical background, to the social relations of industry, both the structural middle-ground and the government foreground. A *uniform material* like cotton or wool can, for instance, be spun and woven into a uniform cloth for the market. This uniformity accounts partly for the early technical mechanization of the textile industry in England and other countries, developed and underdeveloped. The technology of mechanization led to medium and large plants, and they in turn to joint-stock-company government. On the other hand, clothing, duly differentiated from textile industries, cannot, except for the army, be uniformly produced for its market, and, technically, mechanization is slight. This in turn leads to small plants and the survival of the owner-manager entrepreneur. This train of causation from work to government is seen, again, in metals. Fairly uniform materials such as iron ore and coal are put through high-power blast furnaces and smelted accessibly to the material to form a uniform product such as steel billets. The high mechanization in a "material-oriented" location leads to very large plants and joint-stock companies, so large as to threaten monopoly of the market and to call for State control either, as now through the Iron and Steel Board, or as under the Labour Government through full nationalization. Thus the work done largely determines not only industrial structure but the form of government of an industry; and, indeed, in considering which industries are ripe for nationalization and which suited rather for the various forms of capitalism, I have elsewhere (73, pp. 151–9) listed a number of conditions pertaining to the work hinterland.

8. The Scope of Future Chapters

The chapters that follow have three main themes: that to forecast the future of the underdeveloped countries, the trends and trains of causation must be studied in countries already developed; that industrial development can and should be analysed empirically and statistically to a greater extent than hitherto; and finally, that the findings of such a study can only be properly understood if sociological is joined to the economic interpretation of industrial organization and behaviour. The first and second themes have already appeared in tracing five of the nine measurable trends and trains of causation experienced in the developed countries. They will appear again when tracing the other trends and trains: urbanization and localization of industries in Chapter III; large-scale industrial organization in Chapter IV; the Managerial Revolution in Chapter V. The bearing of these trends upon the underdeveloped countries is taken up in Chapter VI.

The third theme, the importance of joining sociology to economics, will appear immediately in Chapter II with the limits imposed on the full mobilization and mobility of workers and hence on productivity per head of population; it will appear again with the labour problems of the large organization in Chapter IV, with the sociology of joint-stock companies in Chapter V, and finally, in Chapter VII with the sociological limits to economic progress in underdeveloped countries.

Until recently these themes have been unduly neglected with unfortunate consequences. In many of their hopes and plans, underdeveloped countries have not studied the past lessons of the developed countries; forecasts have been based on theory rather than observed and measured facts; and economists and sociologists have worked in separate compartments. Marx expressed my first theme in the words (131, p. 13) "the country that is more developed industrially only shows to the less developed the image of its own future." He was a bold forecaster and, in collecting facts from Blue Books, a macro-economic empiricist. As Lenin wrote in 1914 (119, p. 555), "an immense advance in economic science is this that Marx conducts his analysis from the point of view of mass economic phenomena and not the point of view of individual cases." But Marx forecast wrongly when foretelling a fall in profits (119, p. 556) and the increase in the mass of poverty (132, p. 836). More recently, unorthodox theories have indeed proved no more accurate than orthodox. Thorstein Veblen's theory that the control of industry was falling under the control of financiers (192, 193) has, generally speaking, been belied by the Managerial Revolution which has brought the engineers nearer to the control which Veblen imagined as a possibility (193, Chapters IV and V) but did not expect. The theory of Burnham, who first publicized that Revolution, has been belied, in so far as he expected ownership of capital to fall to the State (27, Chapter IX). Of the reasons why facts have belied the Marxian prophecies (particularly that industry would bring mass misery) four, perhaps, can be picked out as the chief: the growth of trade unions, not revolutionary in aim but, to quote Lenin (120, p. 708), with the "bourgeoisification of part of the proletariat," trying for the best bargain out of capitalism; the institution of industrial joint-stock companies; State policy establishing a national minimum of living and of industrial standards; and, finally, the spread of birth control. All these trends, as we shall see, can be measured empirically and need a sociological as well as an economic approach.

My final chapter will draw together the themes of integrated empirical measurement with the practical plans for raising standards of living in the future in all countries, particularly in preventing vicious circles from lowering their standards or causing them to stagnate.

CHAPTER II

ECONOMICS AND SOCIOLOGY OF
MOBILIZATION AND MOBILITY

1. GENERAL ECONOMIC MOBILIZATION: THE RECRUITMENT OF WOMEN

OF the nine main trends in industrial development the last, the trend toward higher standards of living, is the "end" trend which leaders of the underdeveloped as well as the developed countries apparently wish to bring about in their country. The aim of development, indeed almost the very meaning now attached to the word *development*, is progress toward higher standards of living. This aim is primarily economic—to increase the goods and services and consequent real income available to the bulk of the people. Average income-a-head is the crude measure, but the real aim is to ensure that few, if any, fall below a certain standard. The three main factors involved, total national income available, its distribution, and the total population, will be analysed when discussing the critical situation of the underdeveloped countries. It must be realized now, however, that the total available income of a country depends on three sub-elements—

1. The level of productivity-a-worker in its various industries or occupations.
2. The proportion of occupied workers in the population as a whole—its "general economic mobilization."
3. The economic structure or distribution of workers between the different economic occupations or industries, and mobility between these activities, so as to ensure that resources are "deployed" in response to demand.

The level of productivity-a-worker depends largely on the precise economic activity concerned and will be discussed with economic structure, in the next Section; the present Section will deal with general mobilization.

How does the total population to be fed, clothed, and housed compare with the number of workers directly or indirectly feeding, clothing, and housing that population?

The number at work seems an easy matter to find from any occupation census, but there are at least two pitfalls in the way of valid comparisons between times and places.

Occupation to the census-taker means a worker's normal activity and he is "occupied" even though, at the time, unemployed. The effect of unemployment and underemployment will be taken up later.

The second pitfall is deeper. To be occupied economically a worker's activity must be in exchange for pay—must be *gainful*, as the American Census has it. This qualification is particularly important when comparing underdeveloped countries where subsistence farming by "extended" families is the rule. The economic conception of an occupation as an individual's activity for something paid him in exchange cannot always be strictly applied to the sort of communities (studied by sociology or anthropology) in which work is done in common and as part of general community or of family functions.

Aware of these pitfalls, we must take the proportion of the total population gainfully occupied as the gross, *crude* rate of economic mobilization. In 1950–1 this crude measure of economic mobilization was 47·5 per cent in the United Kingdom, 42·5 in the United States, and the percentage is found to vary fairly widely from country to country. Its variation *is only fairly* wide, because of two usual constants—

(i) Adult men up to the age of about 65 are nearly all occupied, though not necessarily fully employed, in most countries, at most times. In Britain the proportion of men between 16 and 64 that was occupied amounted in 1911 to 96·7 per cent, in 1921 96·5, in 1931 96·1.

(ii) The proportion of such men of working age in the general population does not differ very widely from country to country, or time to time.

It is, of course, difficult to lay down the precise ages between which a man can be considered of working age, but 16 to 65 is the standard usually adopted. Now the proportion (i) of men in this range of working age who are occupied varies mainly with the proportion of younger men not at work. In the United States a high proportion of young people between 16 and 24 is still at school or university, and though American economic mobilization appears lower to this extent, the additional education acquired may well pay off and yield a higher standard of productivity and of living for the country later on. But even among developed countries such long education is still exceptional and in a broad comparison of developed and underdeveloped countries we may neglect the variation due to working-age students. The proportion (ii) of the male population that is within the working age-range depends fundamentally on migration and on past birth- and death-rates. Since in Britain both birth- and death-rates have been falling over the last ninety years, the number below the age of 15 has become a lower, and the number above 65 a higher proportion of the total population. The two non-working age groups at either end of the age-scale acting thus in opposite directions tend to keep the proportion at working ages stable. In fact, up to 1945 the number of children in the United Kingdom had fallen faster than that of old men had increased, and the proportion of males of working age (no doubt helped by falling emigration) increased from 56 per cent in 1871 and 62 in 1901 to 67 in 1951 —11 percentage points in 80 years. In most underdeveloped countries, owing to the fall in infant mortality, there is a large increase in the proportion of boys under working age, and here the proportion of males at working age to the total population is falling rather than rising, but again only gradually.

Two ratios that are more variable must be set against these two ratios that are, in practice, fairly constant. We may perhaps neglect (iii) the proportion of men beyond working age who are in fact working, a proportion which though variable involves only a few and hardly affects the aggregate. The other ratio, which does strongly affect the degree of mobilization of different countries is (iv) the proportion of women gainfully occupied.

Long-term and short-term considerations are here again opposed as for secondary school and university students. A high economic mobilization of women might involve children being neglected for the sake of industrial earnings with consequent economic and social loss later on. But not every woman is needed away from industry all her working life. A fair test of the highest proportion of women that could, without long-run loss, be mobilized, occurred in the "combing out" for the British war effort of 1939–45—an effort using combs finer toothed than any other belligerent country. Women in care of children were exempt, and eight million, or about half of the total number of women of working ages, were not mobilized in services or industry even by 1944. Since at working ages the population of men and of women is not very different, an addition of about 50 per cent to the (male) man-power may thus form a rough maximum for the economic mobilization of women in the Western economies. In short, 75 per cent of the total population of working ages can be mobilized.

The deviations from this standard will be discussed later, particularly as they appear in underdeveloped countries. But it must be observed at the outset how non-economic biological as well as sociological factors affect the degree of mobilization. The age structure of both sexes obviously directly determines the proportion that is able-bodied, but biology affects also the occupation of women, directly and indirectly. Where a community has many children compared to adults, a greater proportion of adult women will presumably be caring for them at home or in creches and therefore will not be free for economic mobilization.

Biological family checks to women's economic mobilization are reinforced by the sociological checks of tradition and convention. In developed as well as underdeveloped countries unmarried girls, though of working age, are supposed by the traditional social code to live at home even though in their home town or county there is no work available for women. Thus women workers are less geographically mobile than men workers and may, in consequence, never be gainfully occupied at all. The majority of women workers live as wives or daughters in a family where they are not the main earners. Owing to the cost of living on their own, they have an economic as well as the sociological motive to seek work where their menfolk work and are unlikely to move independently. Thus jobs may in some places remain unfilled and the total mobilized less than it might have been.

An exception to the comparative immobility of women

D

occurs in domestic service. During the English Industrial Revolution country girls appear to have moved into the towns as readily as their brothers who were seeking factory employment in industries where often enough women were not employed. The girls found a "home" as domestics in the homes of the industrial employers, the professional classes, or the idle rich. A somewhat similar mobility appears to be occurring in Russian urbanization today, and accounts for an employment of domestics by professional men to an extent impossible to their counterparts in Western countries.

In manufacturing industry, however, it remains possible for women to be unemployed or unoccupied in one region, yet relatively highly paid and possibly in short supply in a neighbouring region, without supply meeting demand. This "anomaly" or "friction" (as an economist sees it) is quite likely to happen wherever mining and heavy industries not employing women are localized, as in South Wales.

Differences in the proportion of women occupied between different regions of the same developed country occur primarily because the economic forces that would level out occupation (unoccupied women moving where their occupation was demanded) are blocked by sociological forces. It is orthodox economic doctrine that women's wages are less than men's for apparently similar types of work, because (though about the same number of women are supplied by nature) much work demanded in industry is unsuitable for them as too heavy. This view ignores the fact that, on sociological grounds, a large "hard core" of adult women, in Western societies at least half of them, is not in the labour market at all. They are not even part of the potential labour supply. No wage that industry could pay would move them from the care of homes and especially of young children. Between married women *actually* occupied and this core (one might almost write the *home-service corps*) of "no-occupation at any price" there are, however, many marginal cases. Recruitment of married women in industry is increasing and is now likely to occur when they have no children, or their children have grown up, or when part-time work is available. In successive decades beginning in 1890 the percentage of occupied to all married women rose in the United States (135, p. 253) from 4·6 to 5·6, 10·7, 9·0, 11·7 and (in 1940) 15·2 per cent.

Definite sociological limits to women's employment will hold, however, where young children and other family dependants are involved. In fact, it is doubtful whether the admittedly smaller industrial demand for women's than for men's labour is not met by a market supply of women still smaller, relatively, to the supply of men. Interpretation of the lower wage-rates of women should in fact be sought elsewhere than in the economics of their total demand and supply. The sociology of family relationships must be called in (62, pp. 19–37) and also the low degree of solidarity and trade-union "organizability" of women with very different family roles—partially dependent, independent, family supporter—involving very different wage demands.

In underdeveloped countries, as Table VI appears to show, the percentage of occupied women varies even more widely

TABLE VI

	Britain	U.S.A.	
1870		16·6	PERCENTAGE OF WOMEN
1880		17·6	TO MEN OCCUPIED: PAST
1900–1	41·0	22·7	AND PRESENT IN DEVELOP-
1920	41·9	26·6	ED, PRESENT IN UNDERDE-
1940	—	32·1	VELOPED COUNTRIES
1950	44·4	36·8	
1950–5		37·2 {India 42·3 Pakistan 7·0 Brazil 17·0 Mexico 15·7 Egypt 11·3	

Source: United Nations Year Book of Labour Statistics, 1962; last available year.

than in the countries fully developed. Numerous interpretations have been put forward, but before plunging into interpretation and the tracing of causes, we must recall the deep pitfall in comparing occupation statistics where large proportions are working in agriculture on small farms as part of the extended family groups and where women perform work mostly unpaid. Sociological studies, however, show that underdeveloped, apart from the most primitive, countries are less likely than developed countries to mobilize fully their womenpower and to utilize it for the general economy. There are certainly numerous religious taboos. The very low proportion of women shown as occupied in Pakistan may, for instance, be the effect of Mahommedanism.

Hitherto, under the term "crude mobilization," it is the proportion *occupied* that has been considered. *Occupied* indicates persons considering themselves attached or belonging to an industry and so describing their position at the census. It does not necessarily mean that they are fully employed at the time. A further loss in economic mobilization, turning crude into *net* mobilization, will, therefore, appear when we subtract the *unemployed* from the occupied and allow for *underemployment* among the employed.

In most developed countries statistics of unemployment rates are published at frequent intervals, and usually these rates measure unemployment at a given moment of time. Part-time workers appear as employed if the count falls at the time they are employed, otherwise not—on balance, part-time employment is thus accurately recorded. Where *few* people are sub-sistence farmers and almost all work for pay there will be little *under*employment except for this part-time work.

In underdeveloped countries, where much agriculture is carried on by the extended families familiar to the sociologist, the amount of underemployment is harder to assess. Persons occupied may be employed only occasionally (134) or may work ineffectively without sufficient material resources, in-cluding land, at their disposal. We shall have to revert to this situation when dealing in Chapters VI and VII with under-developed countries. At present it is mentioned only as a caution against taking the crude proportion mobilized as an exact measure of the use of human resources. Part of the occupied population may in reality be unused capacity to be subtracted before computing the net mobilization which will reflect the proportion of the population genuinely at work producing goods and services to raise the community's living standard.

2. CHANGING ECONOMIC STRUCTURE AND MOBILITY BETWEEN INDUSTRIES

When the number of workers in each of the economic activities or industries of a country are compared (or any other measure such as input or output of their relative importance), it is common practice to speak of that country's economic or industrial *structure*. To avoid confusion with the *organic structure* of an industry formed by the complex of its firms and plants, I shall, however, speak of the *activity structure*. Usually the total occupied at work is expressed as a hundred, the numbers in each activity as a percentage of the total.

The percentage in agriculture has already been given for various times and places (Table II). Since the value of the productivity-a-worker is usually lower in agriculture than in manufacture, this percentage forms, with a low degree of mobilization, the two elements "double diluting" (as said earlier) the lower productivity in manufacturing activity. The contribution of these two elements in depressing the income of the underdeveloped countries can be roughly measured in comparing continents. Productivity per worker in manufacturing during 1953 was, according to the United Nations (183), about as 5 to 13, to 21, to 59, respectively in East and South-East Asia, Latin America, Europe, and North America; and, unfortunately, these inequalities had been increasing between 1938 and 1953. To make things more unequal still, a much higher proportion of workers were in agriculture compared to manufacture in the Asian and Latin American countries, and as we also know they had fewer workers generally as a proportion of the population.

So much for the importance of the structure of activities at a given point of time. This structure, however, must constantly be changing with industrial development, particularly within the manufacturing order. The record of the recent changes in the percentages in Britain is easily accessible and need not be repeated as a whole. Between 1911 and 1951, as given by Allen (3, p. 219), the most remarkable changes were the fall in agriculture and fishing from 8·1 per cent of the total occupied, to 5·1 per cent, in mining from 7·1 to 3·8 per cent, in textiles and clothing from 13·8 to 7·3 per cent; and the rise in metals from 10·1 to 17·8 per cent and in chemicals from 0·8 to 2·0 per cent. Between 1951 and 1961 these differences widened still further; the chemical and metals percentage was about one-fifth higher, textiles and clothing, agriculture and mining each about one-eighth lower. Services as a whole remained relatively stationary between 1911 and 1951 at 45·5 per cent; though between 1931 and 1951 domestic private service fell precipitously from 8·3 to 2·2 per cent (and about one-third lower in 1961).

In a free economy the importance of the various activities depends chiefly on the market demand for their products or services. The consumer is sovereign. As demands change with changes in fashion, with consumers' income levels, and also with the type of goods supplied and their cost (and here applications of science are influential) so the relative importance of the activities supplying those demands must change. Textiles and clothing have fallen in numbers occupied, mainly because many people in the developed countries have not increased the amount of clothing they wear (rather the opposite for women) and the increase of clothing per body occurring in the under-developed countries is being met by production at home.

Single industries show even greater changes in the total they employ than whole orders of industry. From 1935 to 1951 (as shown in Table XV, Section vi A) the hat and cap industry employed 55 per cent and lace-making 26 per cent fewer. On the other hand, radio and telecommunications, it will be seen, employed 235 per cent more. In fact, it is the greater use of such consumer goods as radio sets not to mention motor-cars and kitchen equipment that has most increased the importance of the metal orders of industry.

Parallel with changes in *consumer* demand, new scientific techniques and new discoveries have changed the demands *producers* make upon different industries. The use of oil and hydroelectricity instead of coal has stopped the large-scale export of British coal and accounts for much of the drop in the percentage of miners. The use of fertilizers by farmers has increased the importance of the chemical industry. Changes in *public* demand have also affected industrial structure. Armaments, for instance, have played a part in increasing the proportion of workers in the metal industries.

The changes in the demands of the private consumer can be substantiated by comparing family budgets in developed countries at different times and at different income levels. Engel's Law is well attested that at any one time families with higher incomes spend a less proportion on food and thus agriculture and food manufactures take up a smaller proportion of income, as the average level of income has risen over time. In Britain today (115) while the standard "index" group of households spent 33 per cent of current consumption on food (excluding drink) and 9 per cent on services and also on transport, the richer group with incomes of the head of the household of £30 or more per week spent only 23 per cent on food, but 20 per cent on services and 12 per cent on transport which includes ownership of a car. At any one time different industries will thus have different intensities of demand for their products by consumers at different income levels, and the degree of this "income elasticity" can be measured. The products with the lowest and with the highest measures of income elasticity in Britain 1937–9 (150, p. 104) appear in the Appendix (p. 241) as an important market "trait."

Not only do the changes continually occurring in the structure of industrial activities require continual adjustment and mobility of labour, but forecasting and planning the future of each differentiated industry is fraught with uncertainties and risks arising from the very trends we traced in the last chapter: the application of science and invention of new goods or cheaper processes, the localization of industry and the need to live by exporting for foreigners in competition with foreigners, and the increases in standards of living. Yet, in spite of all this uncertainty, some help in forecasting and planning can be derived from observed connexions between level of income and consumption patterns such as Engel's Law formulates, and also from certain inherent connexions or linkages between industries, particularly those the economist has named joint demand. Forecasting is here akin to the logistics of army supply. Furniture, wall-paper and paints are in joint demand with housing and, with housing booms, were forecast to prosper and (72, p. 115), in fact, did so. Since fashion spreads, it is also possible to argue from fashion-leading countries such as America today to fashion-following countries. The fall in the textiles and clothing industries and rise in the metal industries seems, indeed, world-wide. The United Nations gives the world proportion of persons out of all manufacturers employed in textiles and clothing as 29·6 per cent in 1938, 23·9 in 1953; in metals as 26·6 per cent in 1938, 32·1 in 1953 (184, p. 113).

Thus, in response to the demand at home and overseas, and in reaction to competition with overseas suppliers, a country's working population not only moves out of agriculture but must

continually change the structure of its manufacturing and service activities. The example in England, switching from
mining, private domestic service and textiles and clothing
manufacture to metal and chemical manufacture is no isolated
case. If changing demand and supply situations are to be met,
no part of the activity structure of any country's economy can
be considered immutable.

This changeability applies not only to whole countries, developed or underdeveloped but also, within countries, to their
several regions wherever particular industries are localized.
The regions such as Lancashire or New England where the
textile industry is localized, threatened with loss of employment
and falling standards of living, are loud in their calls for political
help. Quickest help can be brought by the action of firms
themselves developing, with or without State finance, industries
other than textile, and diversifying the region. Labour is more
capable of mobility from one industry to another when both
industries are in the same place and workers need not change
their homes. If, owing to the difficulty of changing homes or
for other reasons, workers remain immobile when consumers'
demands change, they are liable to become unemployed or
part-time employed. Many a worker before he became
occupied in any new industry may have passed through this
stage in his old occupation, and insecurity of employment rather
than lower earnings may have been the immediate cause of his
change of industry. Correlating increases in employment with
increases in earnings for the several orders of industry, A. J.
Brown (23, pp. 449–63) shows that in the interwar period there
was little correlation between the earnings and employment
changes. The stick of differential unemployment rates rather
than the carrot of wage-rates seems to have operated. In the
post-war inflationary and full-employment period, however, a
differential change in the earnings carrot appeared the chief
stimulus to mobility.

Certainly, if an economy is to develop and raise standards of
living, mobility must be allowed free play either in response to
differences in wages, to unemployment or to other differentials.
It is important, therefore, to analyse the factors for and against
mobility and the persons who are most likely to respond
favourably to differentials.

3. A MODEL FOR FREE MOBILITY ANALYSIS

In time of war, State compulsion was applied to achieve the industrial mobility required for victory. In peace-time, when free societies do not apply compulsion, thought must be given to the complex of interdependent conditions and inducements that influence a worker to act voluntarily. I first developed an analytical model of such a complex in discussing (57, pp. 96 *et seq.*, and 70, p. 26) possible causes and effects of low productivity and unrest. A similar model could usefully be applied to mobility. The original model traced the effect both upon human capacity and willingness, what a man *can* and *will* do—a simple dichotomy, but supported by high psychological authority (45, p. 22). The effect was measured by specified tests of efficiency (such as output, accidents, and lost time) of a number of particular conditions of employment. These multiple conditions are grouped as job characteristics such as type of work and the wages, on the one hand, and, on the other, as man characteristics—the type of worker on whom work and wages impinge. Similarly, mobility analysis would trace the effect of job and man characteristics upon human capacity and willingness measured by degree and direction of mobility (industry to industry, occupation to occupation, place to place) or of migration, country to country. The characteristics of the particular type of worker concerned will be taken up shortly (Section 5) and are particularly interdependent with work traits. Jobs that are attractive or repulsive will not be the same for the intellectual with his characteristic horror of boredom as for most manual workers. It is the intellectual who writes about it, however, and his views about the workers' ranking of jobs must be checked by objective observation.

Just as long hours and intensity of work were shown to cause (a temporary degree of) *incapacity to work* (i.e. fatigue) which was reduced by shorter hours, so *incapacity* to *move* from industry to industry may be caused by cost of travel, lack of housing near the job, ignorance of opportunities (if the receiving industry is distant), or (wherever the industry) by lack of training or the inborn type of capacity required.

In between the work and worker characteristics in this model are put the economic or cash characteristics, including with

MODEL OF TERMS AND CONDITIONS OF EMPLOYMENT INFLUENCING MOBILITY

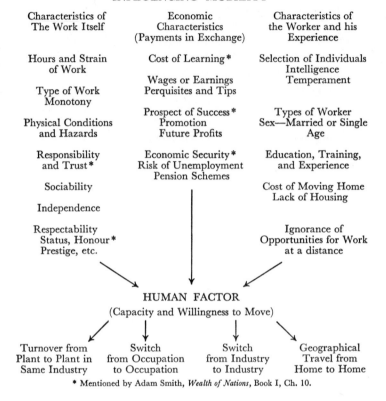

Characteristics of The Work Itself	Economic Characteristics (Payments in Exchange)	Characteristics of the Worker and his Experience
Hours and Strain of Work	Cost of Learning*	Selection of Individuals Intelligence Temperament
Type of Work Monotony	Wages or Earnings Perquisites and Tips	
Physical Conditions and Hazards	Prospect of Success* Promotion Future Profits	Types of Worker Sex—Married or Single Age
Responsibility and Trust*	Economic Security* Risk of Unemployment Pension Schemes	Education, Training, and Experience
Sociability		Cost of Moving Home Lack of Housing
Independence		
Respectability Status, Honour* Prestige, etc.		Ignorance of Opportunities for Work at a distance

HUMAN FACTOR
(Capacity and Willingness to Move)

Turnover from Plant to Plant in Same Industry	Switch from Occupation to Occupation	Switch from Industry to Industry	Geographical Travel from Home to Home

* Mentioned by Adam Smith, *Wealth of Nations*, Book I, Ch. 10.

immediate earnings the cost of learning, if any, and economic prospects and security.

Even if most of the work characteristics cannot, except for hours of labour, easily be changed, many of the man and cash characteristics can. The employer can change rates of wages to attract labour. Many conditions lowering capacity to move again can be, and have been (73, pp. 120, 125, 183), overcome by state control over industry and services for industry; by subsidized housing, for instance, or grants for journeys, by information from employment exchanges and (particularly where the workers are young and not committed to any one industry) by technical colleges and vocational training and guidance.

Unwillingness to work is, by definition, overcome through

"incentives." *Unwillingness to move* from one industry to another can be overcome by appropriate "attractives." Here economists have, for nearly two centuries, suggested besides the economic attractive of wages, other types of attractives and deterrents, many of them sociological; but unlike the parallel case of incentives to work economists have not been helped much by psychologists. Adam Smith (173, I, 10) mentions agreeableness (including honour), easiness of learning, constancy of employment, probability of success and the trust which must be reposed in those who exercise any employment. Marshall (129, VI, iii, 8) put it that to be attractive a trade's *net advantages* must outbalance that of alternative trades. "The attractiveness of a trade depends on other causes besides the difficulty and strain of the work to be done in it on the one hand, and the money earnings to be got in it on the other." "One trade is healthier or cleanlier than another . . . is carried on in a more wholesome or pleasant locality . . . involves a better social position." Marshall proceeds to quote Adam Smith's "well-known remark" that the dishonour in which many people hold the work of a butcher and to some extent the butcher himself raises earnings in the butchers' trade above those in other trades of equal difficulty. Adam Smith, indeed, followed this up with a further illustration of the effect of social disrepute. "The most detestable of all employments, that of public executioner, is, in proportion to the quantity of work done, better paid than any common trade whatever."

Considering the importance always attached by economists to mobility, it is surprising that so little empirical research has been done to test the disadvantageous or advantageous effect upon measures of mobility of these characteristics that form, according to the economic "classics," the conditions of mobility, and to verify or falsify classical theories. It is particularly surprising, when most of these characteristics, like hours of work, as well as their effects, such as labour turnover, are fairly measurable. Of the disadvantages, cost of learning can be audited, insecurity tested by rates of unemployment for the industry, monotony by frequency and regularity of repetition, physical hazards by accident, occupational disease, sickness and mortality rates, physical conditions by thermometer and light meter readings, and so forth. On a modest scale I did once show, for instance (57, p. 164), that at a large American plant, departments with poor air conditions and noise had turnover and requests for transfer at considerably higher rates than average; departments with bad lighting and muscularly strenuous work rates near or below average.

Of the advantages, earnings of occupations are now published, and prospect of success could be indicated by the frequency and extent of promotion. Though less often cited by economists, sociability is certainly important to some people and independence to others, for instance, farmers. One could be measured by the number of contacts with other persons, the other, for a whole industry, by the proportion of persons working on their own account in that industry. Recently, to measure respectability, sociologists have devoted some attention to the way people grade occupations and industrial groupings; and job analysis has tried to measure the strain, and through the time span during which the use of discretion is authorized (102), even the trust and responsibility of a different job. Job analysis has assessed the rewards jobs deserve, but presents little synthesis of all these measures and gradings, giving appropriate points or weights to each, either to explain flights from industries known to have taken place or to foster any movements that are required.

A nice question on flights, and one important to the tourist trade, is why domestic services have, between 1931 and 1951, been depopulated of women. In domestic service, though hours of duty were long and often uncertain, there was less hazard, insecurity, monotony, or need of learning than in women's manufacturing jobs. With board and lodging free, the earnings offered today compare not unfavourably with that of factory work. Few industries offer any economic prospects to women, so the answer probably lay in lack of respectability or status, lack of independence of one's mistress, particularly when "living in," and lack of sociability not only by reason of long working hours but by segregation from fellow servants. Hotels employing many domestics could (and still can) obtain and keep staff more easily than the home employing only one cook-general in close contact with the mistress. The personal touch, said to be lacking in large factories, can apparently be overdone. Questioning girls about why they disliked domestic service though no other jobs then offered employment, Midland interviewers heard the majority explaining without reticence that their mistress "is an old cat" or "an interfering old cat."

More important to industrial development than the deterrents to domestic service are those to business management, and the same question of respectability may again be involved. Among middle-class employments, business enterprise is probably more attractive than the civil services on the score of lower cost of learning, freedom from monotony, chance of financial success and independence; less attractive on the score of insecurity and financial risk and perhaps some physical hazards (particularly gastric ulcers). As to respectability and status, the position varies with the sociological "culture" of a country. In the United States of America business tycoons rank high, but in countries of the Old World, both underdeveloped and developed, trade and particularly manufacture are usually thought rather "low." Their position has risen since the days of Jane Austen or even Ruskin (72, p. 329), but business and works managers are still officially ranked in Britain as of second grade below the first-grade medical officers and country solicitors, and this ranking seems to be supported by popular judgement. Certainly, entries in *Who's Who* of industrialists form a far lower proportion of all entries in Britain than in America, though the proportion of men in industry is higher.

Later, a lack of business and technical enterprise will be found a main obstacle to a country's development. Social gradings, so far as they discourage recruitment into industrial enterprise and management, thus tend to slow down development and the raising of standards of living. This conclusion applies to countries both underdeveloped and developed. One of the main reasons apart from material resources for the success of the United States and other new Anglo-Saxon countries in raising the standard of living is probably the greater prestige and respectability of industrial enterprise and management over other forms of middle-class life such as politics. The distribution of ability at birth may be the same in all countries, but in the new countries the most ambitious, best-educated, and able young men became recruits for business instead of for politics, the civil service, or the professions; and business efficiency flourishes. In older countries, like Great Britain, politics, law, and the civil service have superior prestige, and government is "cleaner" and more ably run, perhaps, in consequence. Whatever natural scarcity of talent may exist for industrial management, sociological factors appear likely to maintain that scarcity for some considerable time. Thus do a country's institutions and scale of values, its sociological pushes and pulls, have great influence on its economic life and development. Indeed, a circle is set up, virtuous or vicious according to circumstances, or to taste. An occupation's respectability status pulls in the abler young, and their ability sheds lustre and adds further status to the occupation, thus giving it a push to be yet more respectable and attractive. This status pull and push has many applications besides occupations, to "crack" schools, for instance, or individual "prestige" firms.

4. The Economics and Sociology of Mobility

The economist puts wages, salaries, and earnings in the centre of the picture because they form the factor most exactly measurable and also because the possibilities of their adjustment upward will reflect the profitability of any industry and thus ultimately the consumers' demand for its products. But neither Adam Smith nor Marshall were, as we have seen, such all-out believers in economic man as Bastiat, who thought that labour betakes itself automatically to the quarter where it is best remunerated. They both believed in net advantages, of which money payment was only one advantage put in the balance. Money payments, however, are the most easily adjustable of the mobility pulls or pushes, and the wage-structure might be expected to be adjusted according to the changing national needs.

Yet no national policy or plan existed in most Western countries until recently, for changes in wage-structure. The determination of the different wage-rates has been left, as the prices of services and goods are left, to the forces of supply and demand on the market. It is not a policy of *laissez faire* for individual bargaining, however, but for collective bargaining. *Laissez collectives faire* describes the situation in three words. Trade unions are pitted, as controlling supply, against the demand of employers' associations; and each industry has its own organized antagonists. The outcome of the struggle will not necessarily depend on the national demand and the available national labour supply and resources, but rather on the relative bargaining strength of the antagonists in each industry. If the two sides in any industry finally call in mediators and arbitrators the tradition is for these outsiders not to impose any principles of political economy or national policy. Employers, trade unions, and mediators all have at the back of their minds somewhat similar "human-value" views (such as sociologists delight to study) of relative wages and of what constitutes a "fair" differential. In developed countries their views of a reasonable wage have largely been built up on a long industrial tradition almost dating back to the guilds—views of the just price often more appropriate to medieval than present conditions of supply and demand.

This sociological rigidity has, however, been modified in two directions. Where piece-wages are paid or overtime is extensively worked, earnings—the take-home pay—may vary greatly from the wage-rate for the standard week, and may actually reflect productivity; and in very low-paid occupations or industries, such as were agricultural labour and mining, wages have, by State action, been raised beyond a minimum living wage. These rational departures from the "reasonable," i.e. the traditional wage, have resulted in a narrowing of the earning differentials between the unskilled and the semi-skilled worker (usually on piece-rates) and the skilled craftsman (156, p. 170). Yet this narrowing runs counter to the economic principle of the marginal utility of scarce resources, since the relatively scarce skilled craftsmen, whose cost of learning by apprenticeship has been high, are being paid a reduced differential over the less-scarce unskilled workers.

If we take a wider view and include among occupations within an industry not only unskilled, semi-skilled, and skilled grades but industrial managers, accountants, salesmen, and quasi-professional specialists, then average wage and salary rates of each occupation are found to differ quite radically. Comparing these grades, one might expect a real test of Adam Smith's dictum that economic attractives make up for non-economic terms and conditions, such as honour. Some basis for the economists' logic can be found in the cost of professional and management training and in the possible scarcity of supply of the inborn talent demanded, yet on the whole, high rates of pay seem *negatively* correlated with disagreeableness of work —its monotony and hazard—and with inconstancy and lack of prospects and above all lack of honour. As Lady Wootton puts it (204, p. 68).

> Nearly all the features of the wage and salary structure . . . which are anomalies from the angle of economic theory become intelligible in a broader frame of reference. It is the social factors which are missed in the economist's interpretation; and what is anomalous to the economist may make perfectly good sense to the sociologist. In a hierarchical society such as ours, large issues of social status are involved in wage and salary scales. Pay and prestige are closely linked; and (in spite of some exceptions) it is the rule that the high-prestige person should be also the highly-paid person; and vice versa. Once this rule is admitted as a factor in its own right, it is remarkable how effectively it explains much that on a purely economic hypothesis, has to be explained away . . . and the same principle explains the importance attached to the rule that those who give orders should be paid more than those to whom their orders are given. Where prestige depends on pay, one cannot be expected to obey, or even, perhaps, to respect, one's economic inferiors. Again, the positive relationship between monetary and non-monetary remuneration, which appears so persistently from top to bottom of our wage and salary structure and squares so badly with the economist's "balance of net advantages," is just what one would expect in a society in which the dirty and disagreeable jobs are left to people whose pay is appropriate to their humble social position.

Economists have, as Lady Wootton says, " explained away " this "anomaly" in their theory by the concept of "non-competing groups" between which, "whether from natural causes or as a result of existing social conditions, the movement of labourers from grade to grade is not free." Non-competing groups or grades, though put forward by such classical economists as F. W. Taussig and Henry Sidgwick, are essentially a sociological concept, and today sociologists are investigating statistically the precise degree of mobility of persons from grade to grade. The question usually asked is how many can "climb the social ladder" beginning, for instance, at the bottom rung where the father was an unskilled labourer and the potential climber attended only a primary school. Demographers in particular, Glass, have shown that in all Western countries, at least, the odds on getting to the top rung are in favour of the man who started fairly high, but the exact odds depends on a particular country's culture, its existing class barriers and system of education. In England (Scotland has another culture) mobility between rungs or grades is made harder by the sociological phenomena of differences in pronunciation and accent, and the differentiated streams of children going either through independent boarding schools, preparatory and public, or else through state-aided day schools, where vast differences in family interests and atmosphere, will affect the next generation. Thanks to local-authority scholarships, many more children of the poorer parents get beyond the primary school into grammar schools and universities. And thanks to the falling birth-rates in the last generation of the rich, and to the greater number of upper-grade jobs (the rising staff ratios are one aspect of this) more of these children have a chance of stepping on to the upper rungs of the ladder. It is customary, therefore, to be optimistic about the trend toward greater class mobility and it is possible that Adam Smith's notion of pay balancing the other terms of employment may yet, after two hundred years, be fulfilled. But, as we shall see, the small self-made business man is less frequent today relatively to company managers. Glass points to the possibility (86)—

> that the introduction of joint stock enterprise and the growth in the size of the industrial unit may even have lowered social mobility as compared with the position at the beginning of the nineteenth century. The gradual entry of university graduates into executive and administrative posts in industry may have tended in that direction.

When a change from one industry to another involves geographical movement from place to place women workers are, for mainly sociological family reasons already discussed, less mobile than men. Young persons of both sexes will, similarly, be restricted in mobility by home ties. On the other hand, the constant biological renewal of the population, youth replacing age, is a factor favouring industrial mobility.

Mobility, after all, is not required of everybody (not *all* textile workers should become metal workers!); and of the number that should move into an industry quite a proportion is

E

represented by young people who have not become (socially or psychologically) committed to any particular industry. Even apart from the number of school-leavers entering industry for the first time, the labour turnover is particularly high among the younger workers. The higher earnings offered by the metal industries, even though only slightly higher, may be enough to attract a youth if he is not tied to some other industry. So, when an ageing textile worker dies or retires, his place may well be taken in the general labour force by a young man attracted to the metal industries. This process may be known as *rejuvenation* rather than mobility, but, by whatever name it is called, it remains an important social process for changing the structure of industrial activity.

Confirmation of the potency of this social process comes from two sources: differences in rates of turnover according to age, and differences in the age composition of workers in the various industries. A number of factories owned by large Midland firms all showed rates of turnover for men aged not more than 29 to be conspicuously higher than the rates of older men, in fact, on average, two or three times as high. For instance, in a firm owning several factories turnover in 1950 (123, pp. 64–70) was as high as 68 per cent among men aged 20–24, but only 44, 34, 18, and 13 per cent among men aged respectively 25–29, 30–39, 40–49, and 50–59.

Evidence that the developing industries have on balance been attracting these younger men who "turn over" quickly is given by comparing age-structures. Some industries, by tradition or due to their technical requirements, use *very* young persons, others do not, but the wide age-range 20-39 may safely be taken as the basis of the comparison. In 1962 (213) this age-range formed a higher proportion of the total male working force in the developing chemical (43 per cent) and metal industries (43 per cent in vehicles, 43 per cent in engineering and 41 per cent in metals not elsewhere specified), than it did in the declining textiles and clothing industries with only 35 and 33 per cent between 20 and 39 years of age.

This social process of "mobility by rejuvenation" is more rapid for women than men workers because of the shorter average industrial life of women. The majority, by social custom, not to speak of physiological and housekeeping necessity, leave full-time employment on marriage or at least on the birth of the first child. In consequence, the age-structure of occupied women does not reflect the age-structure of the female (or male) population at large but over-represents the young. Men up to 29 formed 27 per cent of the total of men occupied in May 1957, for instance, but women of the same ages formed 39 per cent of the total of women occupied. Moreover, within this younger set numbers fell off rapidly the older the women. At 18 and 19 there was an average of 274,000 occupied women at each year of age; between 20 and 24, 212,000; between 25 and 29, only 142,000. The younger girls who enter industry take the place of their marrying sisters, are not tied to their particular industry, and if they can reach it from home may easily choose another industry altogether, thus allowing any required industrial mobility. The particularly rapid rejuvenation of the female working force has been a boon to employers with tender consciences about sacking or as it is now euphemistically called declaring a redundancy. It has made it possible to promise no dismissal because of redundancy and yet have mobility and flexibility. As one employer put it to me, the girls, on marriage, sack themselves.

Another form or direction of mobility, like rejuvenation, connected with age and sex, is that of moving right out of a country, in short, migration. Immigrants will tend to move into the industry or occupation paying most. They are usually men of working age and, once employed, will thus increase the degree of general economic mobilization as well being likely to supply changing economic demands. Emigrants from the home country who had been at work will, contrariwise, diminish general mobilization but many will presumably be in fear of unemployment or underemployed and thus will be leaving an industry less in demand.

We turn now to the observed and measured degrees of mobility. The mere magnitude of the labour turnover generally has not perhaps been sufficiently appreciated in connexion with mobility. A high proportion of the high labour turnover consists in voluntary quitting of jobs by a floating population of workers. Later (IV, 8) it will be shown that most factories are, for these personnel, far from stable institutions, to which they are committed. Men and women workers are certainly accustomed to leaving their jobs in a factory at rates much higher than is necessary to achieve the degree of mobility required by the economy as a whole. Records of labour turnover collected from seventy-five factories in 1948 (123, p. 40) showed annual rates of turnover (defined as number of workers leaving who had to be replaced, divided by total working force) ranging mainly (i.e. in 90 per cent of instances) between 10 per cent and as high as 59 per cent for men, 20 per cent and as high as 89 per cent for women. The average was for about 30 per cent of the men to leave their factory every year and to be replaced, and 40 per cent of the women. A small proportion left because of death, retirement, or, for women, marriage. Of the remaining leavers, the question how many merely transferred to a factory in the same industry, how many changed industries, is more difficult to ascertain. Interviews with nearly four thousand men and two thousand women in 1945–9 by the Social Survey of the Ministry of Labour showed that in the course of the five years the men had been engaged, on average, in 2·6, the women in 2·3 different industries. Most of these changes did not involve a change of geographical region. In fact, only 10 per cent of men changed regions in five years.

Another characteristic of the worker besides sex and age which has been found greatly to affect the magnitude of the turnover is his skill grading. Turnover rates are lowest among the skilled, medium among the semi-skilled, highest among the unskilled. Investigating several Midland factories in 1948, Joyce Long (123, pp. 80–3) found the rates as different, respectively, as 6, 26, and 65 per cent. Certainly, where redundancy occurs it is the skilled men having to change their place of residence who will be least adjustable and will need high compensation. For unskilled and semi-skilled living in towns which possess a variety of localized industries (a condition shortly to be accounted for) mobility is high. And skilled craftsmen find it easy to transfer, if within the same town to the same skilled occupation (for instance, toolmaking) even though in a different industry.

To sum up, except among the skilled workers where a change of home is involved, an effective degree of mobility is not limited by unwillingness to change employment or industries. In fact, the mass of semi-skilled and unskilled workers are uncommitted to their factories and turn over readily. Often enough they move into an industry toward which mobility is nationally not demanded—may one coin the word malmobility? It is economic *incapacity* to move rather than psychological unwillingness that checks the required deployment. Some incapacity may be inherent, but for most workers incapacity to move as required can be overcome by various forms of state action.

5. THE CONFLICTING FORCES IN ADAPTING TO DEVELOPMENT; A SUMMARY

Enough has perhaps been said of economic structure and of industries and industrial mobility to form an adequate background for the realistic analysis and comparison, shortly to be undertaken, of developed and underdeveloped countries. Materials and markets and consequent technological factors have determined economic development and set up a train of events; but so also have sociological factors such as the family, class-distinctions, age distributions, and the growth of cities. The clash of these forces may be represented and summed up with some anticipation of future chapters in the form of thesis, antithesis and synthesis. Theses and antitheses are somewhat monolithic, but syntheses are matters of degree and can best be stated and verified in terms of statistical measures.

The first thesis relates to differentiation of industries traced already as one of the trends of development. This differentiation can be logically planned and administered; but under the free-enterprise aspect of capitalism and the push and pull-back of profit and loss, firms will also tend to reach a logical mix of products, processes and services in their plants. This mix is likely to be similar for a set of plants which will thus according to thesis form a tidy, neat pattern of industries which the Census can distinguish.

The antithesis to this tidy neatness arises from the mobility between industries involved in development. The frontiers between industries are not only fluid according as the plants that constitute the industry integrate differently; but also according to particular attractives, social as well as economic, offered to workers who may move fairly freely (some types more, some less freely) from one industry to another. New industries evolve, old industries coalesce, grow, or decline in numbers, according as supplies of materials and labour vary and as demands of the consumer change with new standards of living, new wants, and new opportunities offered by new discoveries and inventions.

Between the thesis of tidiness and this antithesis of dynamic chaos, there is nevertheless a *synthesis* differentiating industries —but only to some degree.

Not all the activities of plants assigned to an industry by the Census are in fact engaged exclusively in the principal products of that industry. Firms, as already said, cross the Census industry boundaries more frequently than plants, and certainly not all firms can be assigned to one particular industry. Nevertheless, when plants, and particularly firms, cross the neat Census boundaries of industries their activities are usually technologically or, to be more accurate, "ergologically" related. The plants owned by one firm may be in different industries but be performing consecutive processes in a vertical relation like plants in the iron and steel industry and in engineering industries. Or the plants may be laterally "diversified" in different industries, (a) diverging from the same industry supplying the material like plants in the toys or sporting goods, or footwear industries from the rubber industry, or (b) converging on the same market as plants in the batteries and the electric-lighting accessories industries converge upon motor assembly. Or again in diagonal (service) integration some plants may be in the mechanical engineering industry making the machinery for the plants in other industries owned by the same firm.

The second thesis, evidence for which will accumulate later, is that certain distinctive characteristics have developed for each of the more or less differentiated industries in the size of their plants or firms, their capital intensity, and their plants' location pattern.

But the antithesis is that there is no uniformity in these characteristics. Certainly size of firm or plant and location are within all industries, of wide variety, and this variety is largely due to sociological factors. Immobility of labour obviously affects industrial location, tradition the use of capital and the application of science, quasi-political empire building, the size of the firm.

Nevertheless, in synthesis, there is not a completely random variety, and certain distinctive varieties of size, integration, and location peep through for particular industries. Though some industries, like printing, appear to have no typical size of plant at all, and nearly all industries contain plants of nearly all sizes; yet distinct typical size *ranges*, where the majority of the workers are employed, appear in most industries. Statistically measured, there are *deviations* from the average size of plant or firm and from a localized centre, but they are usually not too wide or numerous, and we shall be able to speak of typical ranges of behaviour observed by a majority of plants or firms. The synthesis between no uniform organization of an industry and some distinctive varieties is, in short, a set of *variegated patterns* of location, plant and firm sizes, and integration. Statistics may recognize and compare these patterns expressing words like *most, a little, frequently, majority, minority, some* in more exact numerical terms. Statistical inquiries have discovered trends; but even if these trends change the average values the pattern may stay. Plants in most industries, for instance, are becoming larger on average, and yet they fall into the same pattern of distribution around the average size. A *patterned trend* may best denote the dynamics of the second synthesis.

The third thesis is that these variegated patterns, specific to certain differentiated industries, can usually be logically explained as due ultimately to that industry's technological, material, and market characteristics. A given industry's pattern of organization will take form, persist, and survive when suited to these characteristics. This ergological thesis is particularly evident in the logical train of events set going by mechanization and other technological development based on scientific invention which is applicable (and applied) to yield higher economic efficiency in different industries. This train extends all the way from physical conditions of work and technology, through location and the scale of production and the size of organization, to the form of government and economic policy. It is observable in statistical measures, but it is often obscured by one or other of the multiple factors involved in all human affairs. The need to safeguard against risk is one of these factors, particularly the risk of putting all eggs into one industrial basket. More integration, particularly lateral integration, is thus logically undertaken than the economies of specializing in standard large-scale unit processes or products products.

The antithesis to this third thesis is sociological. It is not a new phenomenon, but with the release of powerful technological forces toward change, it becomes more surprising. It points to the slow lag with which human society adapts itself to the train of causation that should follow logically from scientific invention and its transmission. In the underdeveloped countries the sociological traits retarding economic development are most powerful, and a whole chapter (VII) must be devoted to the sociological limits imposed on economic development. Even in developed countries, as we have seen, workers do not move as soon as higher wages are offered anywhere; their mobility is restricted by a whole complex of physical, psychological, and social conditions.

The synthesis between the economic thesis and the sociological antithesis is, as its title implies, the main interest of this book. The pattern into which industry has actually evolved as a result of the conflicting forces has been discovered less from arm-chair deduction on general assumptions than from observation of the real world and the inductive analysis of the data— along the lines of the natural sciences. Considerable progress along these lines can be, and will be, reported in analysing industrial structure and government, both in developed economies, in the next three chapters, and, later, in underdeveloped countries.

CHAPTER III

ECONOMICS OF INDUSTRIAL LOCATION
AND URBAN SOCIOLOGY

1. Relevance and Measurement of
Industrial Location

In tracing the actual development of industrial countries, and therefore the likely development of countries still underdeveloped, trends were disclosed away from agriculture, toward localization of certain industries and toward urbanization. The three are connected but are basically independent. Urbanization refers in particular to the growth of large towns of, say, over 200,000 inhabitants and is not the inevitable implication of the trend, already discussed, away from agriculture. The industries to which agriculturists switch might very well be conducted in small towns or larger villages. Even if the industries had plants employing, say, up to five thousand, they could still be accommodated in cities of less than 200,000 inhabitants. Urbanization is thus a trend independent from agricultural depopulation, to be separately measured and accounted for. Its relation to industrial differentiation is more complex and requires research.

Research of realistic type, starting with measured traits and trends, has, in developed countries, arisen in response to certain problems that were thought to require solutions. These problems were high unemployment in some localities and areas compared to others; large-scale movement of people between regions, as from the North to the South of England; congestion of large cities, and sprawl of town into country. A landmark was the report, issued in 1940, of the Royal Commission on the Distribution of the Industrial Population, of which Sir Montague Barlow was Chairman. The Commission deals in the second section of its introduction with the "World Phenomenon of Urbanization," and its final conclusion sums up the objectives of national action as the regional dispersal of industries from congested urban areas, the diversification of industry in each region, and the redevelopment and limitation of the congested areas themselves. These objectives have been fairly successfully implemented in New Towns and in development of the old, with Green Belts limiting their sprawl. National policy may thus be summed as the five Ds: dispersal, diversification, decongestion, development, and delimitation.

These economic and social problems and their solution, various as they appear, all involve the location pattern of manufacturing industry. Unemployment is due to lack of industry occurring at a given time; urban congestion and sprawl of people, traffic, and housing are due to too much industry at a given place. The industries whose location is involved in a practical way are not *all* economic activities, but only certain footloose, mainly manufacturing, industries, because few other economic activities have a location pattern that can be altered. Mining and agriculture must take place where the mineral deposits and the soil exist; building, public utilities, and services, with some exceptions, such as the tourist trade, where the population is distributed.

Since it underlies so many practical problems, no apology is required for confining attention to manufacturing location and for beginning with a reference to the exact measurement of the location pattern of different industries. Two measures are required to answer the two separate questions: where, if at all, is an industry concentrated and to what degree, as compared to the general distribution of the population; and what industries, taking areas as a whole, are thus concentrated or not concentrated, and again to what degree. The first question is answered by a series of *location quotients* of any industry in the various areas; the second by one *coefficient of localization* for any industry. The calculation of both these measures has been (69, pp. 34–7, 72, pp. 37–9, 79, p. 9) explained and illustrated very amply in Britain, and America (188). Briefly, the location quotient is the degree to which those occupied in any industry in any place are more or are less numerous than would be expected if industries were evenly distributed among the occupied population of each area of a whole country. In England and Wales there were, in 1951, 1·36 per cent of tailors among all occupied, in Leeds 15·17 per cent. The Leeds location quotient for tailoring is thus $15 \cdot 17 \div 1 \cdot 36 = 11 \cdot 2$. The coefficient of localization is based on the same primary comparison of the distribution of one industry and of the total occupied. So far, the localities used for calculating this coefficient have been the regions into which the Census divides the United Kingdom and, strictly, it is a coefficient of regionalization. The positive (*or* negative) differences of every region in the percentage of *an industry* there located from that of the total occupied are added (positive and negative add up to the same total) and the sum divided by one hundred. If the industry keeps to the same percentage as the total occupied in every region the differences will be nil; if the industry's percentages deviate as widely as possible the deviations will approach a sum of 100 and a coefficient of 1. These summary measurements of the facts will come into use when we trace the effects of particular industries upon urbanization and other developments. Meanwhile, we must confirm the general trend toward large industrial urbanization mentioned at the outset of this book and get some idea of its form and extent.

2. The Trend toward Industrial Urbanization

The earliest known large cities were not particularly industrial. Sociologists (135, p. 314, 98, pp. 164–7) usually attribute their development to the needs for defence, to a surplus of agricultural produce over the demands of the rural population and the funnelling, through the payment of rents and otherwise, of this surplus usually into a capital city of an empire where administrators, priests, courtiers, entertainers, shopkeepers, and merchants congregate, but not necessarily industrial workers. Smaller cities developed at intervals for the marketing of the agricultural produce in exchange for the demands of country folk and also at ports and rivers for the longer distance transport and marketing of produce, and these market and transport towns still persist; but the very large towns that have recently grown did not specialize in these activities. The peculiar development in the last two centuries, first in Britain then in all industrial countries, is that the large cities grew as a result of specializing in some branch or branches of manufacturing industry. The trend toward a greater proportion of the population living in such industrial towns can be shown statistically even in pioneer Britain right up to 1931. The thirteen cities with, in 1891, over 200,000 inhabitants grew in population between 1891 and 1931 by 49 per cent, the rest of Great Britain by only 31 per cent, and in 1931 six more cities had joined the over 200,000 inhabitants class.

In case this British example of the absolute and relative growth of large cities be thought too narrow, United States experience may be quoted, between 1860 and 1940. In 1860 cities of over 250,000 inhabitants numbered three and contained 5·2 per cent of the country's total population. In 1940 they numbered thirty-seven and contained 22·9 per cent of that population, a 4·4-fold rise. The smaller towns, between 2,500 and 250,000 inhabitants, contained in 1861 14·6 per cent of the population, in 1940 33·6 per cent—only a 2·3-fold rise. Most of the larger cities were definitely industrial. By 1950 there were sixteen "metropolitan areas" of over 850,000 inhabitants. Exactly half of these had 33 per cent or more of their occupied population employed in manufacture—had location quotients for manufacture, in short, at least 1·27 times the national average of 25·9 per cent. Only two areas, San Francisco and Washington, had quotients for industry below 0·86; their activity structure is that of the pre-industrial courtly and transport pattern.

English cities over 200,000 or 250,000 are sharply distinguished from market towns (and also resort or tourist towns), which have a high proportion of the total occupied in the distributive order of (service) industries. In the smaller market towns, indeed, this proportion is fairly consistently (198, p. 86) around 25 per cent. But in spite of the fact that many of them are ports, none of the eighteen largest English cities, with one exception, had in 1951 more than 17·5 per cent in distribution and nine of them under 15·0 per cent All of them had, on the other hand, some manufacturing order (usually more than one) twice as great as the national proportion.

After 1931 the populations of the large English industrial cities appear to become stationary or even to fall. But this is an illusion due to the spreading use of the motor-car down the income scale. With the increased transportability of persons the population bursts the bonds of administrative areas to such effect that, whatever extension of administrative boundaries is made, the population is a move ahead. Like a volcano (80, p. 2) a city leaves a hollow low density cone at its centre and spreads houses and factories like lava over its boundaries into the countryside. We must now, therefore, shift attention from large cities with legally defined boundaries to conurbations—continuous built-up areas. In the United States the corresponding urban concentrations are the larger "metropolitan areas." The New York–North-East New Jersey area with its population (in 1950) of 12,912,000 is in fact the largest conurbation in the world.

Six English conurbations were officially recognized in the 1951 Census—respectively Greater London, Birmingham and the Black Country (the West Midlands), Manchester (South-East Lancashire), Liverpool (Merseyside), Leeds and Bradford (West Riding), and Newcastle (Tyneside). By 1961 the new Census made it clear that continuous building was bursting even the Census conurbation boundaries in spite of Green Belt legislation. However, the conurbation is certainly now a unit more realistic and significant to economist and sociologist than the single local-authority industrial city, and (in the next section) we will devote attention mainly to conurbations and their industries.

3. Six Propositions in Modern Urbanization

The original location of any one industrial plant is often the outcome of tradition or of an entrepreneur's or manager's, or even their wives, psychological whim. Nevertheless, associations and correlations have been reliably measured of the surviving plants which can be interpreted fairly logically from economic reasoning.

(i) Different large manufacturing industries are found localized in each of the six English conurbations, at least to the extent of a location quotient of 2. This means that they contain at least twice as many workers in that industry as were to be expected if industries were distributed proportionately with the population. Of the *manufacturing* industries listed in the *Population Census* of 1951 (49, Table A) the quotients over 2 were as given on p. 64 in the six conurbations.

Location Quotients		Location Quotients	
London			
Wireless apparatus	2·3	Dressmaking	2·2
Precision instruments	2·1	Printing and publishing	2·0
South-East Lancashire			
Cotton spinning	11·5	Textile machinery	5·5
Textile finish	5·4	Cotton weaving	4·0
Electrical machinery	2·9	Tailoring	2·4
West Midlands			
Other metal goods	6·0	Vehicles	4·3
Metal manufacturing	3·7	Machine tools	3·2
Aircraft and vehicle parts	2·6		
West Yorkshire			
Wool	18·9	Textile finish	4·7
Textile machinery	4·6	Tailoring	3·9
Machine tools	2·4		
Merseyside			
Shipbuilding	3·9	Chemicals	2·7
Food	2·2		
Tyneside			
Shipbuilding	8·9	Electrical machinery	4·4
Other mechanical engineering	2·1		

(ii) The growth of conurbations—their ecology—is due mainly to the growth, nationally, of the industries localized there. The West Midland conurbation has grown with the metal industries, (199, p. 119), the South-East Lancashire conurbation failed to grow much, as the textiles industry has diminished. This proposition is certain enough to enable forecasts to be made of future growth of conurbations (80, pp. 6–10) based on intelligent extrapolation of the growth of industries nationally.

(iii) Certain service industries and services tend to localize in countries' largest conurbations, such as London, Paris, and New York, and also to a less extent in regional capitals such as, in America, Boston, Chicago, and San Francisco. The wireless apparatus, precision instruments, dressmaking, and printing and publishing, in which the London conurbation has been shown to specialize, form part of the top of an industrial hierarchy in which the largest cities overtop smaller cities in providing at least five types of activity—

(i) Finance, business services, and commercial communication.

(ii) Publishing and printing of books and periodicals.

(iii) Scientific research and instrument making.

(iv) Arts and their materials and supplies.

(v) Applied art and design, e.g. fashionable clothing, luxury goods.

(vi) Entertainment.

Paris, to illustrate (v), (iii), and (vi), had, besides the *haute couture*, far more than the national share of *garçons de café* and also of the less familiar *garçons de laboratoire*.

The highest location quotients for services and industries in London in 1951 were (80, p. 19) 2·3 for wireless apparatus, 2·2 for dressmaking, 2·1 for precision instruments, and also for insurance, banking, and finance, and 2·0 for printing and publishing. Among occupations, the highest London quotients were musical-instrument makers (3·6), painters and sculptors (2·5), actors (2·4). Next in rank down this urban hierarchy are cities which appear from their location quotients to specialize, together with the top city, in wholesaling, in specialist professional and public services—such as specialized hospitals—and in daily newspaper publishing, and in department stores. Manchester, for instance, has a location quotient of 4·6 in wholesale non-food distribution, and Liverpool a quotient of 2·3 in wholesaling foods. At a lower rank are the middling cities or towns that appear to specialize in the more mundane activities, including brewing and bottling and commercial printing. But whatever the rank, the essence of a hierarchy is that the top rank performs, or can perform, all mundane or routine activities down the ranks—as an archbishop can those of a country curate! London retails durables, provides restaurants and general professional services like any middling town, and for that matter bakes and retails food like any village.

The word "hierarchy" has been used loosely by economists to mean just a bundle or variety of things, such as demands for instance, thus wasting a word that describes a particular relation between structures or bodies and functions or activities which is frequently encountered in the real world. This hierarchy can be graphically presented by a number of rods, all firmly planted at ground level to represent the mundane activities of *all* the middling and large cities of a model country here taken for illustration to number sixty-five. Only eight of these rods (large cities of second rank) reach the next level of

MODEL HIERARCHY OF CONURBATIONS AND CITIES

Each line represents one city, its height, the extent of that city's specialization in stated activities

TOP (METROPOLITAN) CONURBATION

(8) LARGE CITIES population 200 to 800 thousand

(56) MIDDLING CITIES population 25 to 200 thousand

ACTIVITIES—
Finance and business services
Book and periodical publishing and printing services
Science and applied science
　(medical and scientific instruments)
Arts and their materials
Applied arts: design
　(fashionable clothing): luxury goods
Entertainment

Wholesaling
Specialized professional and
　public services (e.g.,
　specialized hospitals),
Newspaper publishing
Department stores

Public utilities
Commercial printing
Brewing and bottling
Construction
General professional services
Restaurants
Retailing durables

activities specified in the margin and only one, the metropolis, reaches to the top activities.

(iv) The urban hierarchy is clearly seen *spatially* in countries where industry has not developed and where agriculture is still dominant. A region of fairly homogeneous fertility contains homesteads and villages for the direct producers, market towns for the traders, and a capital or country town for administrators and specialized services. Just such an ideal (almost a sociologist's dream!) was found by the West Midland Group in the county of Hereford as of 1931 (198, p. 203). Still earlier, I pointed (60, p. 116) to the regularly spaced pattern of market towns along lines west and east, south and north of Cambridge at distances of thirteen to seventeen miles. This type of pre-development pattern has been made the basis of the honeycomb location theories of Christaller and Lösch.

The symmetrical pattern of urban spacing is broken, however, by natural features, such as mountains, unfertile areas, or estuaries, and by mining, manufacturing, and also health- or tourist-resort development. Mining develops where the mineral deposits lie, however irregular to the rural pattern; and manufacturing centres which, we have seen, now account for the largest cities and conurbations may not conform to the pattern, either.

Since the sea was for centuries the leading transport "lane" and often still is the cheapest, transport and trading cities develop on navigable estuaries, or harbours. Manufactures are less tied to nature than mining or transport, but are likely to settle where cities, with their labour and markets for them, have already naturally developed. Hence, most, if not all, the large industrial cities are found either at estuarine, lake, or up-river sites, or on large coal or other mine fields. In fact, all the eighteen American metropolitan areas with, in 1951, over 800,000 inhabitants (the minimum size of the English conurbations) have within their boundaries ports on the sea, navigable rivers, or lakes. Of the six English conurbations, five are either at ports or on large minefields; Tyneside, on both. The one exception is the Birmingham conurbation, and even here, though now worked out, there *once* were large coalfields and iron-ore deposits.

Zipf observed (207, pp. 374–5) that if a country's towns are

F

ranked in order of population a peculiar harmonic degression holds, such as, for instance, that the second town has half the population of the first town, the third, a third of the first's, the fourth, a fourth, and so on. Zipf's "law" indeed fits the facts better in the middle and lower ranks than in the first few, but it has been confirmed even to quite a low limit of city populations by H. W. Singer and G. R. Allen (80, p. 17). The law is compatible with the urban service hierarchy, since the several regions served by regional capitals are of varying size, and the largest *sub*-region may be only just a little smaller than the smallest region. Thus the main cities of regions and sub-regions and sub-sub-regions may well form a fairly continuous series of sizes, with a corresponding series for the sizes of their economic and sociological capitals, just as the archdeacon of the largest archdeaconry within the largest diocese may have work only a little less extensive than the bishop of the smallest diocese.

(v) A small town of, say, 20,000 inhabitants could not contain a factory employing 5,000 persons, together with their families, and the shopkeepers and others to serve them and their families; and it might be expected almost mathematically that the larger the town, the larger, on average, would be the manufacturing plants within it. And there does in fact appear some sort of general law, as will be shown shortly, associating wide dispersion (i.e. a low localization) of industries with industries composed of small rather than large plants. But *big* cities, or the cores of sprawling conurbations, show a reversal of this law, both in America and England, and have, on average, the smaller manufacturing plants (99, pp. 49–55). A U.S. Census Table shows that, in 1940, cities of 500,000 and over had plants of an average size of only 30·2 employees, and cities between 200,000 and 500,000 plants averaging 38·3. In cities smaller than that, grouped in ten size-ranges, the average size of plant was never less than 54·2 in any group.

This result is due to two sets of facts. First, within any industry its smaller plants appear to exist in the larger cities. Within the thirteen orders of manufacture available in the *Population Census* of 1951, the London conurbation had, on average, smaller plants than the country as a whole, in ten orders; similarly, of the ten orders available for the Midlands, the Birmingham conurbation, compared to the whole West Midland region, had the same size of plant in one order, a smaller average plant in seven, and a larger only in two (80, p. 13). In the second place the smaller-plant industries are the industries that prefer the city or the core of a very large conurbation. A study of the New York conurbation (97, p. 50) found that in the central core the proportion employed by industries with, on average, small plants (of sixty or fewer employees) was 61·2 per cent; but in the outer ring only 14·1 per cent. An opposite preference was exhibited by the industries with, on average, large plants of over 240 employees. Only 7·7 per cent of their total employees were in the core, 38·2 per cent were in the outer ring.

The calculations of Goodrich *et al.* (88, pp. 704–34) make it possible to measure what proportion of workers in various American industries were employed in 1929 in plants within thirty-three principal cities of the United States. The industries, all with this proportion higher than 65 per cent against 35 per cent for the nation as a whole, i.e. with an "urban quotient" above 1·8, were (highest quotient first): women's clothing, perfumes and cosmetics, men's clothes, gas and electric fixtures, printing and publishing (books and job), and confectionery. Now all these six truly city industries had a much higher proportion of workers in small plants (with one to one hundred workers) than the average of 29 per cent in small plants for manufactures in general, in the order named, 78, 51, 39, 41, 65, and 41 per cent.

The *locus classicus* of urban manufacture by small workshops is medieval Florence, which still has streets named after the highly localized industries that plied there—the Via Calzaioli or Corso dei Tintori, for instance, once given over to shoemakers and dyers. A special set of cases contrary to a general law is usually referred to as an *effect*. I hope I shall not be considered immodest if this current of localized small plants running counter to the main stream of a positive correlation of size of plant and localization is called, for short, the Florence Effect.

(vi) The last few propositions have indicated certain specific economic functions of the large urban centre, quite apart from a favourable natural site. To some extent, the city is a local economic unit providing the economic advantages of a single factory. It provides proximity for activities that should for economy be carried on next one another, and accounts for the major part of the economists' *external economies*. It does not, however, provide for the element of *command* exercised over factory operations controlled by one firm.

Elsewhere (54, p. 90) I have listed systematically the economic advantages and disadvantages of large urban concentrations according to specific criteria: current efficiency, future efficiency, income stability, and the offer of a variety of jobs and services. Here, I will only touch the main pros and cons in the short and the long run. *Currently* the main economic advantages are the short transport and communication (*a*) with a large consumer market, (*b*) between related or 'linked' industries described at length elsewhere (72, p. 87) and the large available pool of labour, management, and finance; the main economic disadvantages are shortage of land at the centre and congestion and hold-ups of goods and of workers, the long and costly journey to work, and, often, distance from raw materials. For *long-run* efficiency, the city has a main advantage of wider intercommunication of designs and inventions. In income stability the large city has the advantage over the smaller one-industry cities by usually including several industries and thus insuring against mass unemployment at any one time; and it certainly offers a wider variety of jobs and services. On the other hand, local taxes ("rates") are high, to pay for the wider services. On balance, the *economic* advantages of an industrial city or conurbation probably outweigh the disadvantages up to that size where the congestion at the centre overwhelms other economic considerations. But the *sociological* disadvantages so graphically put (142, p. 122) by Lewis Mumford, including "man-sewers" taking workers from and to their homes, tip the balance against the industrial city at a smaller size.

Both economic and sociological limits must be set higher, however, when it comes to the single metropolis discussed earlier, at the top of the national or regional hierarchy—the city as an intellectual focus. Dr. Samuel Johnson was emphatic (21, 30th Sept. 1769)—

> The happiness of London is not to be conceived but by those who have been in it. I will venture to say, there is more learning

and science within the circumference of ten miles from where we now sit, than in all the rest of the Kingdom.

BOSWELL: The only disadvantage is the great distance at which people live from one another.

JOHNSON: Yes, Sir; but that is occasioned by the largeness of it, which is the cause of all the other advantages.

BOSWELL: Sometimes I have been in the humour of wishing to retire to a desert.

JOHNSON: Sir, you have desert enough in Scotland!

4. CORRELATES OF INDUSTRIAL LOCATION

Before measuring and discussing the various causes and implications of the trend toward larger-scale production, it is essential to grasp the close interrelation of size of plant (if not of firm) with its location. Though simple enough, the interrelation is often neglected, with consequent confusion when the discussion turns to causes of organization size other than location.

Statistical analysis based on comprehensive census data brings out a main law, to which the Florence Effect forms the exception that the less localized the location of an industry's plants, the less large the representative plant tends to be. Thus in 1951 (79, p. 7) sixteen out of the twenty-five industries with low localization (coefficients below 0·30) had representative small or smallish plants (as defined in the next chapter); and sixteen out of the twenty-five industries with higher localization (coefficients between 0·30 and 0·49) had representative large or largish plants. This law was previously suggested by the 1930–5 British data, and confirmed by the American data in 1939 (69) and also by Bruni (26) in Italy and by later Censuses in Britain and America (79). The form of the law associating industries and representative small plants with industries of dispersed location was carefully worded because of a *second* law not yet fully confirmed (79, pp. 13–14) that industries *with no representative size of plant* tend to be ubiquitous, that is, to be industries with a *particularly* low degree of localization. This *all sites, all sizes* law is logical enough, since industries found in *both* small and large towns might well have plants of all sizes to fit the various sizes of their markets.

The law associating local dispersal with small representative plants extends beyond manufacturing and applies to whole economic sectors. Mining is localized and has large units, building and retailing are dispersed, with, on the whole, small firms and shops; wholesaling is relatively localized, with fairly large warehouses. Banking and insurance are dispersed, with small branches or agents acting as money-collecting services. The professions are dispersed, with (except education) small, often one-man, units.

Of the two characteristics thus found in association, the location pattern is the more fundamental in the sense that it arises more closely than the size-of-plant pattern out of the work involved, especially the weight and transportability generally of the *materials* worked upon and of the product made. These and other "inevitabilities" based on the work in hand were indeed given (Chapter 1, Section 7) as illustrations of the ergology of location patterns. Tariffs act like additional trans-port costs, so that a common market strengthens ergological localization, politically unrestricted. What has not yet been sufficiently stressed is the relative importance of each class of orientation. One would expect market-oriented industries, following the human consumers, to have a low coefficient of localization, but industries oriented to material (usually found concentrated in places not much peopled) to have high co-efficients. Curiously enough, though material-orientation is brought out so assiduously in textbooks, it fails in fact to explain the closest localizations either of British or American industries. Elsewhere I have listed the twenty manufacturing industries of both countries with the highest localization coefficients in 1931. Six were common to both countries: cotton, wool, jewellery, fur, corsets, and fish (canning and curing). Since the American cotton industry was still mainly localized in New England and not the Southern States, only fish treatment out of the six was localized near the material. And I have put forward (72, pp. 85–9) an explanation of high localization that is applicable far more frequently, namely, the need for plants of one industry to "swarm" together because of external economies and to be "linked" for contact locally with certain other industries. Recently it has been recognized that in many industries such links and contact are of vital importance and a category has been newly distinguished of "communication-oriented" indus-tries (97, p. 288).

Besides its correlation with the size-of-plant structure, the location of industries affects sociological structure, particularly the geographical distribution of population. During the Industrial Revolution the North of England grew in population compared to the South. In the last forty years, an opposite trend has set in, and now the population of the South and the Midlands is growing compared to that of Scotland, the North of England, and of Wales. During the double decade 1931–51 the Census was able to make a calculation of the gain or loss by migration alone. The Eastern, Southern, and Midland regions of England gained 18·1, 15, and 5 per cent, the North-Western and Northern lost 2·1 and 6·9 per cent and Wales 6·7 per cent (48). The consequent congestion of the receiving regions and age distribution of the deserted towns, such as Jarrow (losing 20·2 per cent of its population between 1931 and 1951), are of deep sociological interest. But, as in urban development, the causation is mainly economic—the growth and decline of the industries localized in the different regions. The regions losing population relatively are regions where the stagnant or relatively declining heavy iron and steel, coal-mining and textiles industries had localized, the regions gaining population, those where the growing light metal engineering and vehicle industries had localized. The solution is more industrial diversification.

5. Location Measurement as a Tool for Policy

Measurements of the pattern of industrial location have often been applied, together with measures of other traits, in the solution of the national problems already indicated. I will pick out three instances, each with a different practical aim; one to repopulate rural areas that were gradually losing population, another, the opposite, to disperse and decongest a conurbation, and a third where areas have been losing employment in industries in which they had specialized and require a replacement. In all these instances the two main questions, assuming the aims to be accepted, were what industries it was *feasible* and *desirable* to introduce or remove. The desirability or feasibility of any industry depends upon its characteristics; so we fall back upon the measured traits listed and illustrated in the Appendix. But to solve the problem of any given area, the industrial characteristics and the economic activity structure of that area itself must also be measured so that the remedy may fit the disease—and the patient.

The characteristics chiefly differentiating the economic activities of an English rural from other areas, over and above devotion to agriculture, are the low proportion of women and juveniles occupied, the decline of employment generally, and its seasonality. *Desirable* industries that would fit the situation should, therefore, employ a high proportion of women and juveniles; and would be growth industries flourishing more, or at least no less, in winter than summer. Such a fit was found to be satisfied by a number of industries, but not all such rurally desirable industries would be *feasible* in a rural setting, with its low density of population. To be viable they should, if possible, be linked to agriculture, and not be organized into large plants requiring a high population density within reach of the factory. About thirty industries were found to score sufficient marks as desirable *and* feasible (67) on these various tests.

More pressing than rural depopulation, and a problem that has resulted in a series of legislative acts over the past thirty years, is the problem of the areas suffering particularly from unemployment in their existing industries. The survey of Worcester (85, pp. 82–9) had, for instance, to deal with the problem of the loss of employment in the glove industry, which had moved elsewhere. Local resources in agriculture pointed to the feasibility of food-processing; and scenery and architecture of a tourist trade. But if so, undesirable industries giving rise to nuisances such as smell, noise, or unsightliness would have to leave, or be put into a special industrial zone. The nuisances analysed were much the same as those listed recently (97, pp. 73–7) as moving industries from the core of the New York region.

A much larger problem in loss of employment was presented by the depressed areas of the North-East Coast and South Wales. These areas, known officially (and euphemistically) first as the *special*, then as the *development* areas, had been the seat of mining and heavy iron and steel industries. Rich natural resources in coal, iron ore, and harbours had brought great prosperity to these industries localized there, and had made a diversity of industries employing women relatively unnecessary. In 1931 40–45 per cent of adult women were employed in London, Lancashire or Leicestershire; in Glamorgan and Monmouthshire, only 17 or 18 per cent were occupied. But these heavy capital-goods industries have the characteristic of strong cyclical fluctuation and the areas lost heavily in employment during the 1932–5 slump. To prevent abject poverty, it was necessary to diversify by selecting industries that were not subject to slump and employed women hitherto unoccupied. Government location policy has been in fact fairly successful in bringing the development areas' unemployment rate down near to the national level, though not yet the rate of "unoccupation" of women.

Two birds would be killed with one stone if industries could be moved to the development straight from the congested areas. Unfortunately, many of the areas designated by the Government for industrial development, such as Merseyside, are also congested, and planning for the decongestion of a conurbation is difficult and has not hitherto been successful. The chief worry is not to disturb existing linkages and external economies. Industries for removal must not be too closely linked (measured (72, p. 86) where possible by a coefficient of linkage) to the industries staying behind. Nor can plants in the same industries swarming together because of advantages in access to specialized services, be feasibly separated. Small plants and firms, in particular, seem to thrive, as we have seen, in large cities.

In spite of these difficulties, about a dozen specific industries were boldly suggested by Midlanders in 1945 (199, p. 136) for removal from the West Midland conurbation (or at least their local restriction)—industries where local linkages were not essential. But a brief follow-up (80, pp. 22–3) of the situation disclosed, wherever 1951 Census data were available, that these industries had not on the whole diminished in the conurbation when compared to their national growth.

This technique of selecting industries for addition or subtraction in a given area, according as its characteristics do or do not specially fit the economic activities already existing in that area, can be carried, over wider horizons, to the industrialization of whole *underdeveloped* countries. The closest analogy is obviously with the planning of industries desirable and feasible for *rural areas*. Industries can be tested for suitability on the score of characteristics, such as are measured and illustrated in the Appendix. And a full-scale survey must extend from the characteristics of the existing economic activity, mainly agriculture, to the character of the potential material and human resources and markets of the nation as a whole.

The problem of "fit" is not only fitting in with other, possibly linked, economic activities but also with the geology, the geography, the climate, the social structure and institutions, the psychological attitudes and even the very size of the underdeveloped country. Most of a whole chapter (Chapter VI) will be devoted to this problem of "fit" in the industrialization of the underdeveloped countries.

CHAPTER IV

THE SCALE OF ORGANIZATION:
CAPACITIES AND INCENTIVES

1. Measures of the Size of Plant, the Upward Variegated Trend

THE fact of a trend toward larger industrial factories or plants has been abundantly measured, and we need do no more than briefly sum up results, first pointing out, however, certain difficulties in a true measurement.

The major difficulty is the very wide variety of plant sizes. In Britain in 1951, for all industry, 317,000 persons were employed in plants of one to ten, 188,000 in plants of ten thousand and over—roughly ten thousand times as large and about the difference tabulated by Haldane and Huxley in their *Animal Biology* between the volume of a mouse and a cart-horse. Very few single industries, moreover, show any uniformity of size in their plants. The nearest to uniformity, as shown in Table XV are the aircraft, marine engineering, and radio industries with 78, 73, and 71 per cent employees in large plants of over a thousand workers, and cotton-weaving and cotton-spinning, with 70 and 69 per cent in medium-sized plants respectively of 100–499 and of 200–999 workers. For most industries one must be content with a grading shortly to be described, depending (1) on how far the bulk of employees are concentrated in a few consecutive size-ranges and if so (2) which ranges. About a quarter of all industries do not fulfil the first test, and some of them have concentrations of two sizes. These industries must be declared devoid of any representative plant-size. A bare arithmetic mean size calculated by dividing employees by total number of plants can, of course, always be obtained. But it may be quite unrepresentative, though useful for comparing the trend from year to year. The general trend, in view of these facts, can only be described as an upward shift of a variegated pattern. The proportion of persons in each of three wide categories of size of plant for manufacturing as a whole is given in Table VII comparing three years for two countries.

Of the minor difficulties the first is the inadequacy of any one easily available indicator of size. Number employed is mainly used here, for reasons argued elsewhere (69, pp. 12–13), but it understates growth, since the increase in power is ignored.

Occasionally, as in the United States, statisticians have worked out with some trouble a value of output per plant at constant prices. The latest of such inquiries (215) shows that in all but one of the forty-six industries able to be measured between 1904 and 1947, the output per plant rose, and that for the total of these manufacturing industries average rise in size of plant was 15 per cent every five years. In a further list of thirty-five industries measurable over rather shorter time-spans all but three showed a rise, and the (median) average quinquennial rise was, again, 15 per cent. A second minor difficulty also results in understatement of the trend. It is that most countries do not report the number of employees or any other details in plants employing ten or less, and to judge from recent British and also German (100) data, these minute plants have recently lost employees rapidly. Table VII, however, includes all sizes.

From employing in 1935 roughly one-third of all persons in each of the three main sizes of plant, Britain in 1959 employed almost twice as many in the five-hundred-or-more plants than in the less than a hundred strong. The American distribution goes back farther, and thus starts with more wage-earners in the small plants, but its 1954 distribution shows a swing over to the larger plant and falls surprisingly close to half-way between the British 1951 and 1959 distributions.

The variety in size of plant is particularly marked when different industries are compared and forms part of the trend toward differentiation already described. Six industries are given in Table XV employing less than 12 per cent in plants of more than 500, seven that employ more than 74 per cent of persons in plants above that size. And this differentiation tends to persist. Small-plant industries stay small-plant, large-plant industries large-plant. Using the test (79, p. 2) of 50 per cent of employees in at least two consecutive size-ranges out of

TABLE VII

SHIFT IN DISTRIBUTION OF EMPLOYEES AMONG MAIN
SIZE-RANGES OF PLANT (PERCENTAGES)

	Great Britain			U.S.A.		
	1935*	1951*	1959†	1909‡	1939‡	1954*
Plants Employing						
0– 99 Persons	32·5	25·2	24·0	37·8	30·0	25·7
100–499 Persons	35·3	32·4	30·0	34·2	34·8	29·1
500 or more Persons	32·2	42·4	46·0	28·0	35·2	45·2

* 72, Revised ed. pp. 34 and 37
† *Labour Gazette*, Sept., 1959 allowing for plants employing less than eleven
‡ Wage-earners only

seven (60 per cent in the smaller ranges), industries that have a representative size of plant can be divided into grades. Large-plant industries have 50 per cent of all their workers in plants employing a thousand or over. Largish-plant industries are industries other than large-plant that have 50 per cent in plants employing 500 or over. Medium-plant industries have 50 per cent in plants of 100–499 workers. Smallish-plant industries have 50 or 60 per cent respectively in plants employing 50–199 or 25–199. Small-plant industries have 50 or 60 per cent respectively in plants employing less than 50 or less than 100.

In other industries the concentration of workers in plants of certain sizes was not so sharp, and two supplementary grades are added for industries showing "bias toward smaller plants" with 60 per cent of workers in plants of under 200, and "bias toward larger plants" with 75 per cent of workers in plants of over 200. All remaining industries were graded as showing no representative size of plant. An example of each of these *eight* grades is given in Table VIII. Now, of ninety-four British industries thus graded, both in 1930–5 and 1951, fifty-seven persisted in the same rather finely subdivided grade and, of the remainder, all except one industry moved only one grade. Similar persistence is found in other countries, in India, for instance, by Ramanadham (152) between 1929 and 1949.

The *general* upward trend for *all* manufactures is partly due to the persistently *large*-plant industries such as aircraft employing, in 1951, a higher proportion of *all* workers than in

TABLE VIII

DISTRIBUTION IN CERTAIN BRITISH INDUSTRIES OF EMPLOYEES AMONG SIZE-RANGES OF PLANT, 1951; ILLUSTRATING THE SYSTEM OF GRADING

Large Industry within the Grade	Percentage of Persons Employed in Plants Employing Stated Number							Grade of Size of Plant Assigned
	11–24	25–49	50–99	100–199	200–499	500–999	1,000 and over	
Timber	14·0	23·8	24·3	15·6	18·0	4·3*		Small
Brick and Fireclay	5·2	17·2	24·8	21·5	20·1	11·2*		Smallish
Woollen and Worsted	2·3	5·7	13·3	25·0	35·3	11·2	7·2	Medium
Mechanical Engineering	2·5	4·7	7·1	10·5	18·5	16·0	40·7	Largish
Motor Vehicles	1·1	2·7	3·7	5·6	10·2	10·5	66·2	Large
Hardware	6·8	12·5	15·1	14·1	19·7	20·3	11·5	No Type
Tailoring and Dressmaking	9·2	14·8	18·4	18·9	21·1	10·4	7·1	Bias to Smaller
Paper and Board	0·4	1·8	5·8	10·1	35·2	28·4	18·3	Bias to Larger

* 4·3 and 11·2 includes both the two largest size-ranges

Source: FLORENCE, Postwar Investment, Location and Size of Plant

1930–5, persistently small-plant industries such as lace-making, a smaller proportion. Nevertheless (excluding industries with no representative plant-size) wherever a representative size or a bias is perceptible in both years and there is a change of grade, nineteen industries (79, pp. 11–12) showed a rise in the size-grade of their plants, only ten a fall. Moreover, where industries are grouped into their Census orders, Table IX shows that in all orders the arithmetic mean size rose between 1930 and 1951.

At least four salient features displayed by the facts thus require to be explained. Two are seen clearly in Table IX: the trend in all orders of industry for a rise in the persons per plant and the horse-power they use; but in most orders only a slow rise. Two other sets of facts are brought out by Table VIII, the variety of plant sizes *within* each industry; but the distinctly different levels round which variety of size occurs as *between*

TABLE IX

CHANGE IN AVERAGE (ARITHMETIC MEAN) PERSONS
PER PLANT AND H.-P. PER WORKER BY ORDERS OF MANU-
FACTURE 1930 AND 1951

Order		1930		1951	
		Average Persons per Plant	h.-p. per Worker	Average Persons per Plant	h.-p. per Worker
III	Treatment of Non-metal Mining Products, not Coal	37	2·5	56	3·6
IV	Chemicals	48	4·1	94	5·7
VI	Engineering, etc.	63	2·3	128	2·5
VII	Vehicles	43	1·4	127	3·0
V, VIII and IX	Other Metals*	30	3·6†	66	4·1†
X	Textiles	98	2·5	105	2·7
XI	Leather	10	1·6	25	2·4
XII	Clothing	13	0·2	38	0·3
XIII	Food, Drink, Tobacco	15	1·7	30	2·1
XIV	Wood and Cork	10	1·7	23	2·9
XV	Paper	34	2·2	57	3·0
XVI	Miscellaneous	38	2·4	73	3·1
	All Manufacturing ‡	—	2·4	—	3·1

* Orders grouped together to obtain comparability between the two years in spite of changes in official classification of industries.
† Unweighted Arithmetic Mean of the three orders.
‡ Unweighted Arithmetic Mean of all twelve orders tabulated.

Source: FLORENCE, Postwar Investment, Location and Size of Plant Table 7; Census (182, Table 10)

industries, allowing most of them to be graded according to a characteristic size of plant.

2. MEASUREMENT OF THE SIZE OF FIRMS, THE CONCENTRATION OF CONTROL

So far, it is the size of the plant (the unit of continuous physical building) that has been traced. What, however, is the trend in the size of the firm or unit of government? Information on this trend is less abundant and more confused, but certain conclusions can be drawn from Census data and official reports. Information is confused because some data refer to simple concerns or companies, possibly subsidiary, others to composite units of control. Owing to holding companies and other devices, these types of governing body are by no means the same, and caution must be exercised in comparing different series of data, particularly between countries. The simplest and most distinctive word to cover the unit of accounting and of government in industry is *firm*, and *within* each country six conclusions can be stated about the size of firm—

(i) Most of the larger firms own more than one plant, but the smaller firms have only one plant. The average firm is, therefore, larger than the average plant and the dispersion of sizes still wider.

(ii) The plants owned by these multi-plant firms are on average considerably larger than those owned singly by a firm and identical with the firm, and the larger the firm, the larger each of the plants they own tends to be. The plants of the three largest firms are in fact on average for all industries (50, Appendix H), about four and a half times the average size of all other plants. Compared to plants firms are therefore *very* much larger on average and their range of variation in size very much wider. In manufacture *generally* the smallest firms will be no larger than the single plant they own and some will employ only one man, but the largest British manufacturing firm employs over 100,000 workers. If plants range in their sizes wider than mice to cart-horses, firms seem to range in their sizes wider than mice to elephants!

(iii) Comparing single industries, the average size of firm varies more widely than the average size of plants. Evely and Little (50, Appendix H) list 219 British manufacturing trades for 1951. Their arithmetic mean size of plant varies as 1 to 67 from 30 employees (in fish-curing) to 2,010 (in rayon, etc., yarn and staple fibres); the arithmetic mean size of business units or firms was, in these two industries, as 1 to 101—40 employees to 4,030.

(iv) Yet the average size of its plants compared to that of its firms does not diverge very widely between the great majority of manufacturing industries. In the list of 219 trades all except 16 (including rayon, etc., just mentioned) have a business unit with an average employment 1·00 to 1·99 times that of the plant; and only in two trades (lead and coke-ovens) is the ratio above 2·99.

In a comprehensive survey of 433 American manufactures

in 1947 (186, pp. 133–62), 373 or 86 per cent have the number of plants per firm in the narrow range between 1·00 and 1·39. Only beet-sugar and four chemical industries average more than 3·00 plants per firm.

This relative conformity, industry by industry, of the number of plants to firms is by no means a matter of course and does not occur in certain economic activities outside manufacturing. The big five banking firms in England, for instance, each have hundreds of branches and make multi-plant ownership typical of that industry. Multi-plant firms are also very frequent in insurance, in retailing with its chain stores, and in public utilities, whether nationalized or not.

(v) Based on the information just summed up, particularly the fairly low divergence from unity of the total of plants and of firms in each manufacturing industry, it is probable that the four conclusions reached concerning plants also apply to manufacturing firms and often more strongly so. There is (a) a rise in their size but (b) a slow one and (c) a wide variety of size *within* each industry, but yet (d) characteristically different levels (round which the variety occurs) as between industries.

(vi) Any absolute increase in size of firm as well as plant, however, does not necessarily involve an increase of size of the largest few firms *relative to that of the whole industry*, does not, in short, involve a concentration of control over whole industries.

The *absolute* size of both plants or firms is important, as we shall see, in questions of costs and efficiency and also of management and labour relations. For *firms* at least, *relative* size is also important in questions of monopoly or oligopoly control. Where one or a few firms sell practically all the output, and monopoly or oligopoly reigns, these firms' policy on prices and production becomes the policy of the whole industry and their government its government. The concentration of output in a few firms is certainly very high when compared with other well-known concentrations, such as income among individuals. Particular industries differ very widely, however, in this concentration both in America and Britain. In five British industries the largest three firms make, (Table XV, VIII *B*)

G

less than 8 per cent of the output, and in five industries they make more than 85 per cent. On the whole, we shall see, the smaller industries are the more concentrated.

As to the trend, the evidence is (72, p. 124) that concentration of firms is not tending to tighten in America, but is to a slight extent tightening in Britain. Of the 114 American industries where the comparison is possible, between 1935 and 1947–50 (187, pp. 22–49), 11 remained about the same, 47 increased in concentration, 56 diminished In Britain (50, p. 152), out of industries comparable between the two years 1935 and 1951, 27 had increased in concentration, 14 had diminished.

3. CORRELATES OF SIZE OF PLANT AND FIRM

Before advancing theories to interpret the four salient features which appeared when measuring the size of plants and which are equally, if not more, applicable to firms, let us examine other measurable facts and trends that might hypothetically be expected to be correlated with these sizes.

Two characteristics of industries that, unexpectedly, are little correlated with their plant-size are their total size and their staff ratio. It is far from true that the larger industries have the larger plants. Baking and tailoring, for instance, are very large industries, but they have representative small or smallish plants. If the 156 manufacturing industries distinguished in the British Census are ranked in order of their total size and also of the average size of their plants, only eight out of the nineteen *largest-plant* industries are among the top quarter in respect of *total* size. More comprehensively, correlating size of industry with size of business units, Evely and Little (50, p. 107) found a coefficient as low as $+0.24$. This independence is often due to small plants specializing within an industry and producing much less than the whole gamut of products included in the Census definition of the industry. Large firms are often found in small industries or trades. Here considerable concentration of control is indicated and a risk of monopoly arises. Evely and Little (59, p. 109) conclude that "72 per cent of the concentration variance is explained in a statistical sense by variations in trade size and unit size." Again, little agreement, it may be recalled, was disclosed in the staff ratios of the large-plant industries. We should, perhaps, follow up the instances given

(p. 15) more comprehensively. Of the 31 manufactures graded as having large, largish or a "bias towards larger" plants (79, p. 32) 3 differed by less than one-half per cent from average in their staff ratios. Of the rest 15 had ratios above, 13 below average (182, Table 3 Column 3). Closer correlates of plant-size that research has, however, disclosed are localization, already discussed (III, §4), degree of mechanization, and earnings of workers and of capital. For manufacturing as a whole apart from plants employing less than five (and probably with much equipment unused part of the time) the larger plants consistently average in America (72, 2nd ed., p. ix) the higher horse-power as well as net output a worker.

Comparing industries, I have claimed (69, 79) a fair correlation of plant-size and mechanization in British industry in 1930–5, and again in 1951, and in American industry in 1929 and again in 1947. Dr. L. Bruni (26) has found a similar fair degree of correlation in Italian industry. Mechanization was measured by horse-power-a-worker, allowing for the fact that in assembly industries less power is normally required for a given degree of mechanization than in other (particularly process) industries. Considering assembly and non-assembly industries separately, it was found, in these countries and years, that industries, typically with large-size plants, tended to be industries with high horse-power-a-worker. Though a factory with few workers might, as already stated, have machinery idle much of the time and thus show a high horse-power-a-worker, yet industries typically with small plants were found to be low-powered. Steindl (175, p. 22) sums up (and supplies some supporting data) that "there is a good deal of evidence to show that the amount of fixed capital employed, both in relation to output and to number of employees, increases with size of plant (*and* with the size of the firm)."

The correlation of high earnings of labour with larger plants has been observed for some time (72, p. 67). In a recent British comparison, the Ministry of Labour (*Gazette*, April, 1959) has given 86 industries with statistics of average earnings in each of four size-ranges of plant. The highest average hourly earnings were found for the great majority of industries (66 out of the 86) in the largest plants (with 500 or more wage-earners) and for 10 other industries in the next largest plants (with 100–499 wage-earners). In only five industries was the highest average hourly earnings in the next largest plants (25–99) and in another five industries in the smallest plants (with under 25 wage-earners).

Correlation of size with the earnings of capital in the shape of profits can only refer to firms, not plants. Moreover, correlation is not scientifically possible except *within* an industry, since industries differ so widely in their capital intensity and profits cover risks and other factors, not proportionate to the amount of capital. What clear-cut evidence exists points on the whole to higher profit of the larger firms (72, p. 62). In the course of trade fluctuations, however, the profits of smaller firms vary more widely and in the boom phase are often higher than the profits on average of the larger firms. This correlation, apart from slumps and booms, appears as far as the evidence goes also in the newly developing countries. In India, for instance, where the average size of cotton firms was fast increasing between 1905 and 1944, Mehta (137) found the larger size on average the more profitable.

4. INTERPRETATION OF THE FACTS, THE LAW OF INCREASING RETURN

When all the relevant details of the trend itself and of its correlates are measured and assembled, how can this general trend toward large-scale manufacturing plants and firms be interpreted?

The explanation that held the field in the hey-day of classical economics was the Law of Increasing Return. Marshall (129, IV, xiii, 2) worded it "an increase of capital and labour leads generally to an improved organization which increases the efficiency of the work of capital and labour." The correlation we have found of plant size with intensity of capital provides reasons for holding this law to be probable. With increase of capital and labour the possibilities open out of full use of more specialized power-driven machines and greater division of labour. In manufacture (as against agriculture) expanse of land is not important and *all* factors of production can in the long run be increased. Three principles apply (63, pp. 16 *et seq.*) those of bulk transactions, massed reserves, and multiples. The cost of large containers is per contents less than that of small

containers, and the cost of dealing in *bulk* quantities less in
proportion to units; when items are *massed*, deviations are more
likely to cancel out and reduce the risk that the final result will
widely diverge from expectation; and when the capacities, e.g.
of specialized *indivisible* machines, are different, balancing production so that no capacity is idle, requires an output that is a
multiple of the several capacities. These principles have been
found to apply not only in the technology of the plant but
(especially with the disproportionate growth of reputation with
size) in marketing, advertising, and finance by a firm. Indeed,
more agreement is found about the economy of these activities
in a large firm than that about the economies of the large plant
(159, Chapters IV and V) and, as the facts indicate, firms
extend to a larger size than plants. Recently research has been
added as an activity with large-scale economies accruing to the
large firm. Villard (195, p. 360) shows a much higher percentage of larger than smaller American firms undertaking research.

A further point, that has been neglected, is that large firms—
thanks to their marketing and financial strength—can afford
(and take the risk of) setting up large plants often in a location
new to the industry concerned. Thus the correlation of large
plants with large firms may well be interpreted as a two-way
causal train. Large plants are partly the cause of large firms.
But, also, large firms may sometimes be the cause of large
plants.

5. Factors Limiting Increasing Returns in Particular Industries

The law of increasing return can be squared with one of the
four salient features brought out by the facts, the growth in size
of plant in all orders of industry; and with the correlation of
size with greater earnings by labour and capital. But can the
law be squared with the other correlations and the remaining
salient features?

Economists have naturally asked themselves why, if the law
of increasing return is true, do the sizes of manufacturing
organizations, as the statistically measured facts show, change
in the different industries at such diverse rates? Why, in fact,
does not the largest firm in each industry with its supposedly
superior efficiency not overwhelm its rivals completely,

incidentally gaining what additional advantages there may be to itself in a monopoly? As Robertson puts it (158, p. 847)—

> The root difficulty about increasing returns has always been to understand how, while they prevail, equilibrium can exist without the whole supply of the commodity in question becoming concentrated in the hands of one producer.

To resolve that awkward question, we will first inquire into the causes underlying the salient feature of the differences in size of plants and rates of increase in size, *between the different industries*. Here several of the correlations traced earlier will help the inquiry, though correlation by itself cannot determine which correlate is cause, which effect. Why do so many industries still employ so many workers in the smaller plants; and why have so many industries not greatly increased the typical size of their plants?

Discussing the differentiation of industries in the first chapter, weight was attached to the different characteristics, on the supply side, of their markets and on the demand side of their materials—in short, to the external circumstances of his work confronting the producer. These ergological factors were correlated with differences in the location pattern. Heavy materials root an industry near their sources, heavy products tie the industry near the market. In its turn the location pattern, again as demonstrated, affects the size-pattern. The more dispersed that plants have to be, in relation to the population, the smaller their accessible market in areas not urbanized and the smaller their size. Where material and product are transportable, the larger their accessible market and sources of supply and the larger plants can (but not necessarily will) be.

More directly affecting size of plant than this transportability (which in the first place affects location pattern) is the uniformity of the materials and conditions of supply and the uniformity of the product and conditions of demand. Demand may be large extensively because many possible customers live within the area where the product can be transported, and intensively because most customers demand a lot of the product. Thus plants are small when the whole demand for their product is neither extensive nor intensive and (e.g. incandescent mantles or manufactured fuel) the whole industry is small. The lack of correlation of size of plant and size of industry when we considered all industries indicates, however, that this cause, on the demand side, of small plants applies only for very small industries. On the supply side the rule probably goes farther that the less uniform the conditions, the smaller is the plant or firm. The outstanding example is outside the manufacturing sector, namely agriculture, where seasons vary and the behaviour of weather and livestock is not uniform or easily foreseen, and where also, sure enough, the scale of organization is smaller than in manufacture. Uniformity allows *full use* of specialized machines and other technological economies. Agriculture employs high-powered machinery, but most of it has to be idle much of the year.

Summing up a comparison of the characteristics of corresponding American and British industries, I found (79, p. 23) a "stronger international agreement in industries' power-a-worker than in degree of localization." This I attributed "mainly to the wider differences between the geography of the United States and Britain than between the techniques employed in corresponding industries in the two countries. The United States is large, has more varied climates from place to place and weather from season to season, and has a greater variety of minerals." Technology, on the other hand, is transferable from one country to another provided that uniform materials and products are similarly supplied and demanded.

Uniform materials allow for mechanization, uniform standard products for large-scale increasing-return operation, and both mechanization and standardization give some industries big plants. In a free economy the sovereign consumer who wants to be different and special, puts a severe limit on the extent of any uniform market. Producers may either pander to the consumer with special goods made on a small scale; or may try by extensive advertising (63, p. 85; 72, p. 121) to stimulate the consumer to demand the article which by large-scale methods is the most efficiently produced. Either policy is costly and not apparently encouraged in Communist economies, where what people are (or are not) to consume, as well as to produce, is planned on a large scale. My discussion of the limits imposed by the consumer's whims was cut out, as only "of bourgeois relevance," in the Russian translation of my *Logic of British and American Industry*!

It is true that the manufacturer does not deal normally with final consumers, but either (when making capital goods) with another manufacturer or with a wholesaler or retailer. The vagaries of the consumer will still be felt, however, by the retailer and, in his turn, by the wholesaler. Thus fashion goods will tend to present small and short-lived markets, and industries catering for them, like the clothing trades, to be on a smaller scale. Nevertheless, increasing return may make itself felt in large-scale communities or organizations *somewhere* in the whole process of converting materials into goods in use. Large cities have already been noticed in the Florence Effect as allowing small localized plants to flourish. Similarly, if both factories and retailers are small-scale large wholesalers will usually (72, p. 102) be interposed between them. Further research should test the hypothesis that if an industry has small plants, a large-scale stage is usually present somewhere in the whole productive-distributive process.

6. Factors Limiting Increasing Returns in General

So much for the differences and different rates of increase, in size of plant between different industries. The salient statistics bear out the law of increasing return in featuring the growth in size of plant generally. But how can we explain the third salient statistical feature, namely, that this general increase is so slow?

The law, it must be observed, is a long way from saying that large plants or firms are more efficient than small ones. It applies, in the first place, not so much to the size of organization through "internal economies" as to the size of a whole industry through the "external economies," largely of localization, as already described. Such external economies can be obtained even though plants remain small.

In the second place the law applies to the scale on which a single commodity is produced, to its mass-production. Large plants, and still more so, large firms, in fact provide a wide variety of different products, processes, and services, many of them on a small scale. Of the thousand largest American manufacturing companies in 1950, only 118 were confined to one census industry, 480 were in two to five industries, 332 in six to fifteen, and 70 straddled over fifteen industries. Two-thirds of these thousand companies even straddled over several of the twenty wide groups into which all the 450 American census industries are classed, 227 of them over four or more groups of industries. Analysing 111 of the largest American manufacturing corporations in 1959, Gort (210, pp. 13–19 and 23–5) bases several measures of integration, including diversification, on this very straddling. To define an industry in the first chapter we accepted the census assignment of all plants to one industry or another, according to their "principal products." One of Gort's indicators of integration is the proportion of workers in the plants or firms of an industry who are straddling into other than the principal products of that industry— who are, we might say, "poaching." Comparing industry groups, he found (p. 33) that the tobacco group of plants integrated or diversified least, with only 16·8 per cent of its employees at work assigned to other groups; the chemical group, with 39·4 per cent of workers thus poaching, integrated most.

The same tale of "integration" can be learned in Britain from *Who Owns Whom* (166). Here, the grouping of industries is wider and only fourteen groups were distinguished, not all of them manufacturing. Yet one firm (Imperial Chemicals) straddled six of the groups, another (Great Universal Stores) five, another (Courtaulds) four, and sixteen firms straddled three groups each.

Integration, like specialization, is a relation between an organization or structure and an activity or activities or, as Talcott Parsons would say, between actors and acts. In measuring its extent we must be careful to specify the structure —exactly who the actors are—and also the category of activities we are talking about. In the preceding paragraph the reference was to firms not plants. The plants, as already said, stick to one industry and certainly one *group* of industries more closely than do firms owning several plants. It would otherwise not be possible, as the Census does, to assign plants definitely to one industry or another. Nevertheless, there is some degree of deviation from this assignment duly measured in the proportion already mentioned (p. 23) to which plants engage exclusively in specialization in the industries' principal products. This measure of the integration by an industry is set (in Section VII) side by side with the measures in Table XV of other characteristics of different industries. It must be remembered, however, that this particular indicator measures the relatively modest integration by the plants of an industry not by its firms, as measured by Gort. It can be seen in Table XV, all the same, that in conformity with Gort's results three chemical industries have a low specialization and thus high integration, while tobacco has a 100 per cent specialization and thus practically no integration.

Using his statistical measure of integration or diversification, Gort found (210, pp. 65–74) only a modest correlation with the size of the firm. Thus the integrated firms not being significantly larger but straddling several industries may have pursued each industry activity on a smaller scale. In short, size and increasing returns are here not necessarily connected. At present we can only surmise that the connexion often depends on the reasons for integrating. If a firm or plant integrates because it fears to put all its eggs into one basket, then it checks the increasing return of enlarging a single line of activity. In fact, a smaller plant or firm taking the risk of specializing in one line and putting its eggs all in one basket, may provide that line on a larger scale and with increased returns compared with the lines which a large but integrating firm or plant may provide. Some large firms have in fact "disintegrated" (72, p. 74) in order to increase their returns.

On the other hand, (i) a small plant or firm is obviously precluded from providing any one line beyond a scale employing all its resources, and (ii) if integration uses up spare capacity, acting on the principle of multiples, increase in size should go hand-in-hand with increasing return. The fact that some resources useful in producing one product are also useful in producing another extends to resources besides the purely material. These resources, to quote Gort (210, p. 58), "include research and development staff, the availability of experienced salesmen and the requirement of common managerial skills for two or more products." Finally, (iii) aggregation within the same plant of related operations may yield increasing return, for instance cutting out transport and reheating between the vertically related processes of iron and steel making, or working up heavy chemical by-products on the spot.

Pending further statistical correlation, one may conclude that though the law of increasing returns does not necessarily involve the large integrated plants or firms, the law may well have been a factor in the increase, but only slow increase, of the size of plants and firms. Integration will presumably, at the time it is introduced, increase the number employed in any particular plant or firm, but it may not lead to the same increased return that extending one particular line of activity would, and thus to the overwhelming of competitors in that line.

The fourth salient feature of the statistical data still remains to be explained. Why is there such variety of plant-sizes *within* almost every industry?

Two of the factors already used in explanation exercise some influence here. Even within the same industry, as officially distinguished, different plants may integrate different activities to a various extent. And ergological factors of materials, markets, and technology will again affect variety of sizes of plant within a particular industry. Many of the industries listed will include plants with markets somewhat different, extensively and intensively, and somewhat different materials and technology.

Even where an industry is fairly homogeneous in technology, materials, and markets, however, the sizes of plants and firms differ. While differences in scale between industries are largely the result of external ergological causes, such differences within a homogeneous industry are largely humanly caused, and the human decisions involved are in turn largely independent of the particular industry, and internal to the particular plant or firm. They may be conveniently distinguished by the standard four economic categories—

> Land
> Capital
> Labour
> Management

(i) Some plants within any industry are often unable to grow for the simple reason that their site is cramped and the management decides no further suitable land can be found.

(ii) If the firm is a one-man business, a partnership, or a private company no one may be willing to make more capital available, and the smaller public companies also often find difficulty in finance. This is an orthodox explanation (159, pp. 54–63), but, as we shall see, is not in reality so important as assumed.

(iii) Possible labour supplies may be physically too scattered to be available without costly and time-consuming transport. Thus, plants in rural areas with a low density of population are limited in size. It is often stated that labour morale is lower, the larger the plant, and morale is then confused with efficiency and high return; but the evidence is conflicting and will be taken up later.

(iv) The theory still orthodox (at least in elementary textbooks) is that management is the great stumbling-block to larger size. I consider this theory not proven. My reasons, being heretical to textbook dogma, must be elaborated in the following section.

7. MANAGEMENT AS A LIMITING FACTOR

The diagrams of economic textbooks show not a continuously falling curve of costs per unit of output in consonance with the law of increasing return, but, after a point usually placed near the middle of the range of output, a rising cost resulting in a U-shaped curve. This rising cost with size is often offered as an explanation of the persistence of small plants and firms. Troughton (181), inquiring among managers of a number of firms, could, however, find no evidence or grounds for the rising-cost phase of this U-curve, which textbook theory connects with management both in the short and in the long run. *In the short run*, after exceeding a normal output (usually drawn in the middle of the output scale) the well-known textbook he quotes assumes that—

> Management problems will increase and managerial efficiency will decline. The entrepreneur will be unable to deal with the very large output and management problems will get out of hand. There will be too many workers per machine for really efficient production.

But the managers' answers pointed to the contrary of these assumptions. Costs fell as fixed capital and overhead staff became utilized nearer to capacity. Each machine took so many men and no more and there could be no question of overcrowding. In the past the ten-hour working day, often followed by overtime, undoubtedly caused sufficient fatigue to affect costs (57, pp. 231–3). But today, with high machine costs, overtime pay is probably cancelled out by the lowered overhead machine costs *per unit* of this greater output. At worst the cost curve is L-shaped—flattening out at the very high outputs.

In the long run, according to the textbooks, the same U-shaped cost curve with increasing size again appears and again is attributed to increasing difficulties of management—the ultimate incapacity of one man to co-ordinate the multifarious activities of very large firms. It is probably true that the variegated pattern of plant-sizes *within* almost all industries, though largely due to varying size of markets and sources when goods are costly to transport, is partly due to the variegated capacities of managers, some of whom, previously perhaps skilled workers or foremen, may not be able to cope with the accounting, finance, or buying or selling involved. Many an owner-manager entrepreneur starting a business may never get beyond employing more than ten or, say, fifty workers. Most of them eventually go out of business; but meanwhile they appear in the "snapshot" of the Census if the business still survives at the date the Census is taken.

At larger sizes of plant it is incapacity *to delegate* or to adopt new techniques, not all-round incapacity, that might make management limit size. But theory should not deny, or even ignore as it often does, the possibility of delegating co-ordination, capably and successfully. Recognizing that management is divisible, it does not follow that the total cost of all administrators (delegator and legates) would increase more than proportionately with size. And as Andrews points out (5), management is not static, but with increasing output will in the long run change its techniques just as in the long run the type of technical equipment is changed. The U-shaped average cost curves are presented in textbooks as though they were the findings of empirical research, but actually little attempt was ever made by economic theorists to verify what is a mere assumption. The more sophisticated economists now admit that the U-curve was a mere deduction from the unrealistic concept of perfect competition. Empirical research like that of J. Johnston and Joel Dean (46, pp. 292 *et seq.*) has not in fact found any such curve. According to J. S. Bain (7, p. 155) "over the observed range of firm sizes, the largest firms appear not yet to have become big enough to suffer perceptible diseconomies of very large scale." Melman (138) has summed up official American data for 1937 to show *administration* expenses per dollar of sales actually *falling* as the asset size of firms rises. The analysis was repeated for more firms in 1941. Table X compares for both years the proportion of administration expenses to total sales for different sizes of firms.

TABLE X

ADMINISTRATION EXPENSES PER $ OF SALES
ACCORDING TO SIZE

Assets $	1,034 Firms 1937	4,107 Firms in 1941
Under 1 m.	17·8	14·1
1–5	15·8*	12·3
5–10	13·8	10·9
10–100	13·5*	} 10·0
100+	10·5*	
Weighted average	14·7	13·0

Source: S. MELMAN, *Applied Statistics*, Vol. III, 1954, pp. 1–11
* Weighted average of several asset ranges

The *capacity* of management, though its variety results in a variety of sizes of plant and firm within an industry, does not then appear to limit the increase in the general level of size. But there is the other side of management, as of all human activity—a side unduly neglected in economic theory—the manager's *willingness* to expand business. Management may well result in both variety of size and in *slowing down of increases in size*, not from incapacity so much as from unwillingness. Here motivation enters in, and we must be definite about the person whose motives are involved.

In the first chapter a trend in development was discerned (to be detailed in the next chapter) toward the divorce of management from ownership. This trend, popularly known as the Managerial Revolution, is more accurately an evolution and is only slowly being accomplished. Industry in most developed Western countries is still left at present with two main categories of manager: the owner-manager or true entrepreneur risking his own family or friends' capital, and the manager owning little capital and paid mainly by salary. The two categories of manager will have a different motivation, and in considering willingness to expand we must, to be realistic, make a distinction between the two. Several subdivisions of these two categories can and have been (72, pp. 298–315) distinguished. The entrepreneur can be the self-made founder of the business or the head of a family business which he inherited, or simply an influential large shareholder in a company; the salaried executive a promoted employee or a technocrat brought in from outside or a trained administrator. Each type has a different outlook,

TABLE XI

MOTIVES FOR EXPANDING THE SIZE OF FIRMS

Motives	Entrepreneur		Salaried Manager	
	For Expansion	Against Expansion	For Expansion	Against Expansion
Economic A Cash nexus	Maximum profits from increasing return (especially self-made entrepreneur and financier)	Marginal revenue becomes less than marginal cost	Chance of greater salary with expanded business	Not *his* profit maximized
Economic B Real-cost nexus		Desire for ease. Owner has no fixed hours. Long week-ends in country possible (especially family head) Tax burden		Desire for ease, but must show results. If expansion unsuccessful *risk* of sack. But no profit if successful
Psychological Boss nexus Hobby nexus Freeman nexus	Power-seeking Empire building Love of work	Independence, from others' financial control Pre-occupation with *public* work	Power-seeking Love of work	Fear of others' power. Fighting an expansion by takeover
Sociological Name nexus Gang nexus Sport nexus	Prestige Status-seeking in industry	"The gentleman-ideal" "Fair" competition Sportsmanship	Identification with firm (especially old employee) Prestige of expanding firm	Professional loyalty Matey with competitors
Alogical "Drifting"		"His own money to play with"		No initiative or ideas from outside

but for the sake of a simple tabulation only the two main categories will be assigned a separate column in Table XI. Attention will be drawn to the subdivisions (in brackets) when especially relevant.

As great a weight of motive against expansion appears in the Table under the modern entrepreneur as under the salaried manager. This corresponds to the facts and business men's attitudes observed by Mackintosh (125) and Barna (10). The entrepreneur managing his own capital is particularly unwilling to expand if it involves calling in outside capital and possibly sacrificing his own control.

Orthodox theory is probably wrong in the weight it attaches to management incapacity rather than unwillingness to expand; and when it does look at willingness it is wrong, again, in confining attention to just one incentive. Maximization of profit still stands in too many economic textbooks virtually as the only motive for industrial operation. In reality, particularly where the top management is paid not by profit but salary, quite a complex of motives underlies business decisions.

In this complex we may distinguish at least five sets of motive: two types of "profit" or economic motive, psychological motives, sociological motives, and no apparent motive at all!

(i) *Economic Motive A*

Profit maximization with shorter or longer horizons (e.g. to keep goodwill) but regardless of Marshall's "real costs" (129, V, iii, §2) may have been the motive that ruled the founder entrepreneur of Industrial Revolution days who apparently allowed himself (and his workers) no rest and ploughed back nearly all the profit on his capital. But, with the spread of the salaried manager and the inherited business, it is probably rare in Britain today. In America it reputedly still occurs even under management control. Many a manager though not paid by profit apparently identifies himself heart, soul (and duodenum?) with the organization and its profit.

(ii) *Economic Motive B*

Here, profit is considered in some relation to the real costs involved. "A firm may fail to develop" to quote Mackintosh

(125, p. 50) because "the rewards for development are thought to be insufficient." This limit he continues "may be found particularly where the rewards to the firm are identified with rewards to the persons in control, which are subject to income tax, and surtax, and eventually to estate duty." The entrepreneur owner-manager may, in general, balance his profits from expansion against enjoyment of his leisure. He will try to maximize his total happiness, in which monetary profit will no doubt still loom large in his calculations. He will weigh the trouble involved in expansion against the risk and uncertainties of profit and, often, the balancing will point against expansion. The *non-owning* manager has no profit to weigh against trouble and risk and may well prefer ease of mind, and showing results to the shareholders in the shape of balance-sheet strength, security, and liquidity together with a reasonably increased but not necessarily maximum profit. In taking risks he will realize that if unsuccessful he may lose his job, but unlike the entrepreneur, if he achieves success, get no profit from it. Many monopolistic agreements between firms may probably be accounted for not by the desire for a monopoly profit but by the desire to shelter from the worries of competition. The owner-manager *entrepreneur* can go further in taking his ease than the salaried manager, since he is playing with his own money. Examples of a leisured gentlemanly, Public School, attitude which I have given elsewhere (72, pp. 302–4) referred largely to heads of family-owned firms.

(iii) *Psychological Non-economic Motives*

Quite an array of nexi beside the cash nexus (and the cash-minus-real-cost nexus) affects the managers' will to expand. Some nexi affect the entrepreneur, some the salaried manager, and some both of them; but as the entrepreneur is his own master, his *un*willingness to work hard can be carried to greater lengths. The hobby-nexus—the love of work in itself—stimulates both types to expand, and so does the love of power. But the negative form of this power-nexus, the will to be independent and *not* to be in the power of others (the freeman nexus) exerts a particular force on the entrepreneur. Considerable empirical evidence has been collected by Mackintosh (125, pp. 71–5) of the *unwillingness* or lack of ambition of small firms

H

to expand business by bringing in outside capital. Both entrepreneurs and salaried managers will usually fight against a
merger if they are to be the submerged party, even though receiving compensation and the "golden handshake." But in a
merger by take-over the salaried manager (as pointed out in the
next chapter) is likely to be overridden by the holders of the
majority of the voting shares, and loyalty to their management
is not usually up to the strength of shareholders' economic
motives.

The existence of small firms has been interpreted psychologically, also, in terms of a gambling attitude combined with the
freeman-nexus. To quote Steindl (175, pp. 60–1) "small entrepreneurs . . . accept unusually high risks at very low remunera-
tions . . . . The social position of the entrepreneur ('to be his own
master') is valued as such and any small entrepreneur will
struggle to the last to retain it!"

(iv) *Sociological Motives*

Empirical research has been disclosing more and more, how
powerful are these motives, particularly in the large organizations. The nexi involved in social relations are not only the
gang-nexus (so potent, as we shall see, in labour relations) but
the fame and the sporting nexi. Which way these nexi pull the
entrepreneur depends on whether his bond is with industry or
with outside public and social life. If he wants to win a name as
a public figure it is unlikely that the industrial effect will be toward expansion. But for the non-owning manager the important question is how far he identifies himself with the interests
of the firm he serves. If he regards the firm's success (though
not necessarily its profit) as *his* success, then expansion may well
result. This tendency to expand will be supported by any desire
he may have for fame and status, and also for winning in a
sporting capacity.

I have often (e.g. 72, p. 309) stressed this identification of
salaried executives, though shareless, with their firm and their
consequent striving for its increased volume of business. Recently (163, p. 143) Joan Robinson has put the point forcibly—

> The main cause that has falsified Adam Smith's prediction that
> joint-stock enterprise would be impossible, and Marshall's dictum

that limited liability companies stagnate, is this capacity for managers and boards of directors to project their egos into the organization that they happen to belong to and care for it just as much as if it were a family business.

Katona however found (103, p. 233) that top executives of large corporations remembered their own and their competitors' volume of business and share of the markets, rather than the profits. On the other hand, the gang-nexus, connecting the salaried manager by ties of loyalty to his fellow professional managers may well restrain all-out competition, especially price-cutting, to secure business. And the sport-nexus itself may restrain the salaried manager, since sport must abide by certain rules of the game. Indeed, regard for his good name as a sportsman among the gang—his fellow entrepreneurs in the trade—may limit the extension of business even by the entrepreneur owner-manager. He wants to be thought (if English) a gentleman, (if American) a "regular guy" not, respectively, a bounder or a chiseller. A sociological, as against an economic impulse will creep in to share business with potential competitors rather than expand.

(v) *No apparent Motive: "Alogical" behaviour*

It must be recognized that many managers, whether owning capital or not, just follow past tradition. Their outlook, as Carter and Williams (33, pp. 38–53) put it, is parochial and their behaviour does not express any particular desires except to carry on. The entrepreneur feels it's his own money and the salaried manager may have no initiative. Many of the firms thus inefficiently managed, will eventually go out of business; but there is a lag, often due to the goodwill of an equally alogical customer, and as already said these businesses while they survive appear in the "snapshot" of the Census. Gentlemen, or firms run by gentlemen, will continue to deal with gentlemen regardless of "bounders" butting in with better terms. A discussion of prices is often indeed considered unethical. This loyalty among gentlemen is paralleled by the loyalty within the co-operative movement, in buying other co-operatives' products. Lack of motive is likely to hold out longer in owner-manager business, since there is no one in authority to dismiss the manager lacking in motive-power and, anyway, it is the entrepreneur's own money to play with.

Thus, on top of some plants' physical limits of land (particularly within conurbations), on top of costly transport of materials and supplies and of product to market, and on top of costly communication with linked industries, slow expansion is explained by many factors (as Table XI shows graphically) that are not of this ergological type. These factors affect management motives. Some are economic and some psychological and sociological, particularly the ethical principles and general sentiment against too cut-throat a competition by such "low" practices as cutting prices. It is true that a few firms not subject to these psychological and sociological restraints might grow fast; but to raise the general level of size they would have to grow *very* fast, and here, in *rate of growth* rather than a given large size, as Robinson (159, pp. 120–33) and Edith Penrose (148, *passim*) have stressed, there certainly are considerable management limits.

8. LIMITS TO LABOUR COHESION

The supply of labour was considered, in Chapter II, as its adaptability and mobility affects different industries in different countries. Attractives and repulsives, psychological and sociological as well as economic, were considered which would move workers and potential workers into, or out of, jobs, newly demanded, or no longer demanded. The present chapter deals specifically with the larger-scale trend and concentrates on attractives for labour to "cohere" and stay and incentives for labour to work efficiently in the larger manufacturing plants and firms. For the size of his firm, plant, or department of plant probably has more effect on labour than the ultimate control analysed in the next chapter. Certainly the attitude of labour seems not very different in large co-operative, large nationalized, or large capitalist plants or firms.

As organizations become larger it might be expected that cohesion between their members would become more tenuous. Contrasting larger and larger plants, I have pictured (72, pp. 272–6) the gradual loss of "matiness" between employer and employed, of first names and of the team spirit (few teams known to sport have more than fifteen members); and the emergence, often by necessity, of check-numbers, of output records, clocking in, office segregation, and a bureaucratic hierarchy—in short, of "depersonalization," paper-work, and institutionalism. The larger plants and firms of modern industry with their mechanization and minute division of labour have presented the worker with four Rs likely to repel rather than attract him—repetition, routine, red-tape, and risk. The risk of unemployment has to some extent receded, though redundancy in certain factories still rears its head, particularly in declining industries and in prosperous industries that are introducing automation. But the place of unemployment risk is being taken by another R—remote control due to the operation by larger firms of several plants from headquarters office.

Thus the trend to larger-scale industry might be expected to raise (and to be limited by) certain labour losses. In my model of the train of causation of industrial fatigue and unrest mentioned earlier (II, §3) six types of labour losses were distinguished. Two refer to the very constitution of the organization: the turnover of labour, in which labour is lost (either by a worker quitting on his own initiative or the less frequent discharge) and *has to be replaced*; and absence (including strikes). Four, quantity, quality and economy of output, and accidents, refer to the behaviour of members of the organization, once they are mustered.

Losses are constitutional or "organic" in the sense that if every member of a factory left or was absent that body would (temporarily at least) not, in fact, exist. Some minimum absence is unavoidable, due to ill-health, and some minimum turnover, due to death and retirement. Indeed, a certain turnover beyond the minimum is necessary for the economic adjustment and mobility, discussed earlier.

In practice, labour turnover has been found to vary widely from factory to factory, and occasionally the rate rises to fantastic heights. Comparing seventy-one factories owned by the "mammoth" firm (and whose records were kept on a comparable basis) Joyce Long found a range from 7 to 700 per cent. Seven hundred per cent turnover means that in the course of the year seven times as many workers left and had to be replaced as were employed on the average at any time during the year. This particular factory was not large; and in general the expected lower morale in the larger factories was not very evident, at least in the men's labour turnover. Joyce Long's inquiry into the factories of the mammoth *and* other large firms, and a contemporary inquiry by the British Institute of Management did not, in fact, reveal (123, p. 79) any marked or consistent relationship between size and turnover.

An important revelation, however, from these studies of labour turnover in large plants is the extremely high rate among short-service compared to long-service employees, constituting a vicious circle. Turnover is high among newcomers, requiring the hiring of more newcomers, thus leading back to high turnover. "Most industrial organizations seem to consist of a nucleus of tried hands who have served their employer like old family retainers, surrounded by a floating and fleeting population of newcomers. A large factory, indeed, is rather like a boarding-house that takes 'transients'." This conclusion derived from an inquiry I undertook at a large American "tenhour" plant in 1917–18 (57, pp. 166–9) was based on the number of persons leaving after a shorter or a longer service, namely, less than three months or more than a year. This turnover was then compared with the number of persons of similar length of service at work at any given moment during the same period. Thus 53 per cent of those employed had a length of service of over a year, 28 per cent of three months or less. But among the persons leaving the plant only 12·6 per cent had over a year's service; 68 per cent had three months or less. In short, the risk of leaving was far higher among the newcomers than among the older hands, in this case a relatively higher risk of 68/28 to 12·6/53, or about 10 to 1. This experience of a "floater-cum-nucleus" structure intensively investigated in a single large American plant was confirmed at much the same time (57, pp. 169–74) by extensive data from American factories and in two English factories.

Some thirty years later, in 1948, an inquiry I initiated in Birmingham showed the floater-cum-nucleus structure still being reproduced and thus deserving the name of a pattern. In a count at a large factory (123) 663 men were found to have been employed over a year; but only 98 of them left during the year, 131 men were found to have been employed under three months, but during the year 265 in this short-service class had left. The

count also found that 557 women had been employed over a
year and 130 of them left during the year; 148 women had been
employed under three months, but during the year 267 in this
short-service class had left. The greater risk of leaving among
the short as against the long-service class was thus, for the men,
265/131 to 98/663, roughly 13 to 1; for the women, 267/148 to
130/557, roughly 8 to 1.

This floaters-cum-nucleus composition of large plants is a
sociological fact of considerable importance to economic
efficiency. To avoid the high cost in loss of output and in training of the many replacements due to this high "infant mortality"
among newcomers, special care is required immediately after a
worker's enrolment in order to turn them from floaters into
nucleus permanencies. So important is permanence and stability that many employers work out a "stability rate," dividing
the number (possibly forming a nucleus) who have survived a
year by the total originally employed. This stability rate was
first suggested by the Industrial Fatigue Board (57, p. 156), who
found during the First World War that in six factories, excluding night-shifts, the survivors of a year's employment ranged
among single women from 72·2 to as low as 27·6 per cent and
among married women from 58·8, even lower, to 16·7 per cent.

Once persons have joined an organization, the next question
is how far they will always appear at the time and place appointed—in short, their rate of absence. A minimum absence
is unavoidable owing to temporary sickness (say up to six
months), accident, and reasonable leave. Sickness varies with
age, but in manufacturing normally averages five working days
a year for men, equivalent to 1·7 per cent of working time, six
for single and perhaps twelve for married women, equivalent
to 2 and 4 per cent of working time (70, p. 39). Absence from
accidents varies widely from industry to industry, but one day
a year, equivalent to 0·3 per cent of working time, is about the
average level for reportable accidents in factories. In large
plants, absence follows the turnover pattern. Its actual level
usually far exceeds the unavoidable minimum; and some
individuals, or classes of individual, are more prone to be absent
(whether from sickness or otherwise) than others, in particular,
the unskilled and semi-skilled rather than the management or
staff. In ten plants of a large firm absence with no excuse,

damned as "absenteeism," averaged about ten times higher among non-staff than among staff grades.

The costs of absence, though they do not include training new workers, are like those of turnover considerable, particularly if the lost time is not known, and, therefore, not organized for, beforehand. With the mechanization and high staff ratios involved in development, overhead costs of idle equipment and of unused services of overhead staff are particularly heavy. There is also disruption of teamwork, which may in assembly industries reduce the output by far more than the absentee's normal contribution (70, p. 38).

It has been maintained (1) that absence rates show a significant correlation with size, being higher in the larger plants, presumed to be due to lower morale. This thesis is plausible in view of the "depersonalization" of the large plants. To test it, we may again appeal to the many factories owned by the mammoth firm whose records were kept in standard form. Absence records were kept of the men employed in thirty-four factories where their total absence rates ranged (13) from 2·5 to 7·1 per cent in 1947, 2·5 to 5·8 per cent in 1948. Women's absence rates were recorded in twenty-five factories and ranged from 3·1 to 11·0 per cent in 1947 and 2·5 to 9·3 per cent in 1948. Eight of the factories were outstandingly large, each employing a total of men and women over 1,300. But instead of their showing the highest absence rates, many of them had rates among the *lowest* two-thirds: for men, four of the eight in 1948, six in 1947: for women, seven in 1947, six in 1948. One can hardly say that these eight largest plants definitely had the highest absence rates, and the hypothesis certainly requires further evidence in proof.

Whether absence rates are higher in larger than in smaller plants, a more significant fact about absence from large factories is the "Blue Monday Effect." If fatigue was the most prevalent factor in absence one would expect the last day of the working week to show most absence. This seems in fact true of school-teachers. But among unskilled and semi-skilled factory workers on no more than a forty-eight hour week, the reverse is the case. The highest rates of lost time occur not at the end of the working week but at the start, on Mondays. Baldamus (8), who drew attention to this unexpected phenomenon, suggested it may be due to the reluctance of a worker to return to a dull remote-control job after his week-end off. *Skilled* workers, presumably with more interesting jobs, do not show the higher absence rate on Mondays. Possibly the ratio of Monday to Friday absences may be the most handy indicator of morale in large plants, and considerably more reliable than the total absence rate.

The extreme degree of absence, often indeed, bringing the whole plant to a stop, is the strike. A strike is an organized absence, either organized unofficially or organized officially by a trade union, which will then supply strike-pay. The working time lost by strikes in manufactures has been on the whole very much less than that lost by individual absence and has shown little sign of increasing. From official American and British statistics, I calculated (57, p. 191) that from 1881 to 1905 only 0·38 per cent of working time was lost in America and from 1899 to 1913 only 0·23 per cent in Britain. In both countries the percentages rose sharply in the hectic years 1916 to 1921, but since then have returned to one-third per cent or below. In 1949–55, in the seven Western industrial countries reviewed (101) the days lost annually per employee varied in manufacturing between 0·5 and 0·9, or 0·17 and 0·3 per cent of total working time. The heavy cost of strikes to industry arises indeed not directly but indirectly from disorganization of linked occupations and trades.

There is little evidence to show whether industries with the larger plants or firms are more or are less strike-prone than average. Kerr and Siegel (106), examining the actual strike records of eleven countries, conclude that it is location pattern rather than scale of organization that is significant. Industries or sectors highly localized, like textiles, lumbering, mining, and docks, appear more strike-prone than industries, like clothing or food, scattered among the general community.

The phenomenon of strikes or organized absence draws attention to the trade unions who organize official strikes and sustain them by strike-pay. Trade unions, themselves, have been subject to the larger-scale trend. The average (arithmetic mean) membership of British trade unions was in 1939 6,181, and in 1960 15,077 when seven unions out of a total of 650 held almost exactly half (49·5 per cent) of the membership (116).

Trade-union growth was not, however, the consequence of factories getting larger and, in Britain at least, shows traces of origins in an age of small workshops. In contrast to America, the British trade-union branch is not based on membership of a single plant however large, but on the locality, and large plants usually contain members of a number of unions. The growth of large plants, each presenting its own particular labour problems and grievances, has, however, forced large-plant off-shoots of trade unions in the form of shop stewards. Western society is pluralist—and large-scale pluralist. Each large-scale sub-society has different aims: management to obtain, perhaps, more income for a given cost; trade unions to obtain greater equality in incomes. But the two aims do not necessarily clash and, as I shall maintain in a later chapter, development toward a higher standard of living implies both aims. In this chapter I am concerned with groups *within the large plant* blocking its cohesion so far as to agree on restriction of output.

Early in my inquiries into industrial fatigue I noted the restriction of output by whole groups of workers both within large English and large American factories. The output of a group working without imposed restriction should, in view of the distribution of human capacity, naturally fall into a normal distribution curve in which the average output was more frequent than either a low or a high output. I certainly (57, p. 221) found examples of such distribution. But among other groups I found a lop-sided curve when no output appeared above a certain figure and that figure was by far the most frequent. Apparently output was restricted at a stereotyped amount which practically all workers could fairly easily make, an output recognized by the group, and often given a name, such as *doggie* in Newcastle, or *stint* in Connecticut. Recently Kilbridge (110) has used this shape of output frequency curves in testing for the continuing effectiveness of wage incentives. The classic study of informal groups, however, was made by Elton Mayo and his associates in the Western Electric's large plant at Hawthorne, near Chicago (164). Here the group of men bank-wirers were found to have their own code—by no means following the employers' "party line" of maximum possible individual efficiency. The four rules of correct behaviour in this American factory group have been so often quoted and compared to English public school codes (70, p. 82–3) that we need only mention the American and English names, respectively, given to four types of violator—

1. Rate-buster, swot
2. Chiseller, slacker
3. Squealer, sneak
4. Act officious, swank

This etiquette is almost as inviolate as primitive rituals. To break it was taboo, simply not done; or, if done, the violation would lead to social ostracism. The public school slang for ostracize "to send to Coventry" is, indeed, now common usage in English factories,—even in Coventry itself!

Large-scale employers try to strengthen plant or firm cohesion by personnel or labour departments and industrial relations officers, often using techniques suggested by the Mayo experiments. Where they are successful in holding an ever-growing staff together, *Organization Man* (201) is often the consequence; and they have widened the staff conception by giving "staff status" not only to foremen but to long-service operators—the type forming the nucleus in contrast to the high turnover floaters already described.

The informal group attitude among workers in large factories, neutralist to increased productivity, has been contemplated with equanimity by sociologists and they are, of course, playing their legitimate role as scientists in neither praising nor condemning what they observe. But it is difficult to escape the feeling that sociologists realize they are professionally "on to a good thing." Groups are their speciality, and the presence of groups in the midst of industry has certainly been neglected by economists. Elton Mayo, himself, called the economists to task for holding "a rabble hypothesis" of workers in factories as completely atomized individuals. The theory of sociological man in industry appears, in short, to be replacing that of economic man; and the theory, curiously enough, seems, as Peter Drücker notes, to be oblivious of industry (25, p. xv)—

It has been fashionable of late particularly in the human relations school to assume that the actual job, its technology and its mechanical and physical requirements are relatively unimportant compared to the social and psychological situation of men at work.

But as Professor Eric Trist adds in quoting from Drücker—

> good human relations as a management philosophy is giving
> place to what may be called the task approach. In this both in-
> struments and people are considered, but in relation to the work
> that has to be done.

This "novel" approach, which has always been my own, will
be followed up in the next section, dealing with incentives to productivity. But, meanwhile, it must not be thought that sociologists and psychologists, wrapped up in group study, and
economists observing the loss of individual output occasioned
by group behaviour, are utterly segregated or that their several
approaches cannot be integrated. Indeed in case-studies,
recently, of operations in two contrasted English factories,
Lupton (214) has cogently assessed the balance of economic
and sociological forces. He appreciates the "logic" of social
group "norms"; but also the "logic" of the nature of the work
including market conditions (along the lines I have ventured to
call ergological intrepretation). Many psychologists, including
Freud, are quite as critical of groups (83, p. 11) as any economist—and particularly of their intellectual capacity—

> When individuals come together in a group all their individual
> inhibitions fall away and all the cruel, brutal and destructive
> instincts, which lie dormant in individuals as relics of a primitive
> epoch, are stirred up to find free gratification. But under the in-
> fluence of suggestion, groups are also capable of high achieve-
> ments in the shape of abnegation, unselfishness, and devotion to
> an ideal. While with isolated individuals personal interest is
> almost the only motive force, with groups it is very rarely
> prominent. . . . Whereas the intellectual capacity of a group is
> always far below that of an individual, its ethical conduct may
> rise as high above his, as it may sink below it.

Economists, keeping in view the total national income, which
so many psychologists ignore, realize the incompatibility of high
personal incomes with output-restriction and consider the behaviour of many factory groups unintelligent and unrealistic,
indifferent to the interests of fellow workers, and destructive of
the national economy. All three of these economic commen's
on groups agree with the modern pyscho-analytical approach as
propounded by Alix Strachey (176, pp. 194–5)—

> The *dis*value of regressive group-mentality is considerable. In
> the first place, it induces an unrealistic state of mind in the subject

on all matters connected with it, so that the ends he aims at in regard to it are often bad, from being mistaken, and the means he adopts to attain them are inexpedient. In the second place, it makes him indifferent to persons outside his group, since his libidinal impulses are mostly directed to persons within it, and most of his identifications are made with them. Nor has he any sense of duty or compunction about outsiders, since his group super-ego is not concerned with them. Indeed, if he happens to dislike them there is nothing to prevent his wanting to injure them and trying to do so, if he thinks it possible and safe.

This brings us to the third and perhaps the most serious objection to group-mentality. Much of the large amount of libido which a group-member expends . . . is got by withdrawing it from non-members, and that makes him not only indifferent to their welfare and happiness but actually desirous of their destruction and unhappiness.

9. Incentives for Productivity

The study of cohesion and its opposite in many large factories has led on to that of restriction of output, particularly by informal groups of individuals. The failure to achieve possible outputs must now be considered on its own. Any individual worker's quantity and quality of output, and his accident records too, depends broadly on three circumstances: his selection for the job, his training and capacity for the job, and his willingness to work at the job once selected and trained. All three have been separately analysed, but are interdependent. A capable and willing worker *mal-selected* for a repetitive job may suffer acute boredom, have more accidents, and attain a lower output in that job than one less capable and willing than he, but impervious to monotony.

Vocational selection and training is investigated by individual psychology; sociology and economics are involved more in the task of getting workers, once hired, willing to produce reasonably up to their long-run capacities. So, always bearing in mind the possibility of more effective selection and training, we will focus attention on capacity and willingness at work.

Relative physical incapacity may be permanent or, as when fatigue occurs, temporary. Industrial fatigue was important while hours of work were long, and output was found to fall in quantity and quality and accidents to rise as hours got longer. Reliable evidence on this was collected in Britain between 1913, when the British Association for the Advancement of Science set up a Committee on Fatigue from the Economic Standpoint, and 1924, when the Industrial Fatigue Research Board (the successor of the Health of Munition Workers Committee) substituted in its name "Health" for "Fatigue." Evidence was also collected in America, beginning with Josephine Goldmark's *Fatigue and Efficiency* published in 1907, and continuing till 1920 with the U.S. *Public Health Bulletin* No. 106 (189), in which Miss Goldmark with Miss Mary Hopkins presented my own investigations contrasting plants with a ten-hour and an eight-hour working day.

During this period hours of work were never less than forty-eight a week and during the 1914–18 War sometimes rose to seventy-two a week, even for women. But since 1919 shorter working weeks have become established and physical fatigue less evident. There was no reason, in fact, for Elton Mayo and his associates to have been so surprised when a resumption of a mere forty-eight hour week, after experiments in shorter hours, did not lower output. There is no contradiction, between his results obtained in 1928–32 and the earlier long-hours-falling-output findings of 1907–24.

The size of plants does not in itself affect capacity, but has been held as we know to affect *morale* and the will to work. Special stimulants to the will have been introduced by employers—stimulants usually known as incentives. A vast literature has grown up to help boost productivity or to explain or justify labour's often "negative" reactions ranging like a spectrum (57, p. 384) from the yellow of ill-will through the green of envy and unrest to the blue of frustration and the violet and red of fatigue and positive ill-health.

One of the chief questions involved is the relative strength of economic and of psychological or sociological incentives. In the past, no doubt, employers have believed too exclusively in the strength of the incentive provided by the amount of wages and the method of wage payment. Recently, however, the general sophisticated view, influenced largely by Elton Mayo's work, has swung over to the socio-psychological side; and in the literature, as against the practice of incentives, this side now holds the field. This swing away from economic man was justified up to a point and is still needed in explaining management behaviour. But on labour incentives, as on labour groups already considered, that point has been passed and the balance has tipped too far against economic interpretations. The practice of British business men has indeed been somewhat ignorantly criticized by sophisticated *literati*. The following passage appearing in an American University quarterly and written by an "English Research Fellow" is not an unfair example—

> British business men have been far slower to adopt (certain) techniques than their American counterparts. . . . A recent study has shown that British managers are still firmly wedded to incentive payment schemes for workers, although they can give no objective evidence for their commitment and it is now over twenty years since a series of classic studies carried out at the General [sic] Electric Company's Hawthorne Works, in Chicago, first gave evidence of the greater effect of work-group norms on output.

It is true that till the recent publication of *Productivity and Economic Incentives* (45) there was little scientific evidence on the effect of incentive payments upon output. Psychological investigators, no doubt, found the subject dull, and economists just assumed the economic motive without empirical evidence. But though the group norms of Mayo's relay assembly girls rose temporarily under the stimulus of social limelight, his output-restricting bank-wirers hardly support the case for norms as incentives.

The controversy has been bedevilled, as so many controversies have, by sociologist and economist being interested in different aspects—norms, for example, as against efficiency—and trying to answer quite different questions. Thus, J. A. C Brown (24, pp. 188–90) maintains that work is attractive in itself—a retired worker will haunt the gates of the factory where he used to work. Undoubtedly, most people find life boring without *some* productivity. This, however, is not the question economists want answered, but rather how to get people to work *more* productively. Every individual has his own pace of working, for which no special incentive is required: or there may be some conventional group tempo. But the problem in the large factory is to get individuals to work beyond this often jogtrot pace, without cumulative fatigue, and to work in co-ordination. In spite of sociologists' discoveries, it is probably still true that paying so much a piece of work is the most direct way of getting *more* pieces made, and that the more individual the appeal as against *large*-group incentives or profit-sharing, the greater the incentive effect upon output. Amidst the welter of controversy it will be useful steadfastly to narrow the issue to the effect of larger-scale organization, and to keep close to some generally established correlates of size and incentives—

(i) The earnings of workers, we have already shown, are higher in the larger than the smaller factories. This may be the result of greater efficiency of the large plants, but it might also be a means of compensating workers for otherwise less attractive sizes of plant.

(ii) Payment by the piece is more frequent in the large factories. Thus in five successively larger sizes of plant employing from one to twenty-four right up to one thousand or more, the percentage of workers on systems of payment by result was, in April 1961, 13, 24, 39, 49, and 56 per cent (114). This fact is connected, of course, with the earnings difference, since workers usually take home more when on piece-rates than on time-rates.

(iii) In large factories very great increases in output have been obtained by changing from a time- to a piece-rate system (45, p. 267) when other conditions, such as method of work, remained the same, and always provided workers' representatives had previously been consulted. Among the eighty-eight workers with complete records on a number of operations in several factories, fifty increased their output 67 per cent and over, and another twenty-nine over 34 per cent. While no worker's output fell, increased earnings are, as to be expected, correlated with increased output, but their pay did not increase exactly proportionately. Thus the cost of labour in general fell. All the workers were interviewed. Few complained of this lack of proportion or of fatigue and the majority were satisfied, by various tests, economic, psychological, and sociological. No negative association was found between increased output and greater satisfaction, in short, there was little evidence of the more the increase, the less the satisfaction; and those increasing output *and* earnings were positively associated with most satisfaction.

(iv) The piece-rate system is not spreading in industry

generally. In April 1961 the percentage of all workers that was paid by result was 33 and showed little change from 1951, 1953, and 1955, when the percentage remained at 32. For manufacturing only, however, the 1961 percentage was 42.

The main question raised by these four sets of fact, established statistically, is why, if more output is obtained by the economic incentives of piece-rates and if the higher earnings (in the larger plants) are associated with more workers on piece-rate, the piece-rate system has not been extended farther and, particularly, into the smaller plants.

Two logical reasons apply, one at one end of the trend of development, the other at the other end. In the smaller plants, not mass or even "batch" producing, it is often economically not worth while to make the complicated calculations to find the correct piece-rates when so few pieces are to be made on any particular job. At the other end, with mass production, mainly in large plants, piece-rates may be unnecessary. Speed is automatically set as by a conveyor belt, or by automation, or else accurate records are kept and workers dismissed if their record is poor. In short, piece-rates appear to be an intermediate occurrence between the small-scale, low-mechanized and the large-scale, highly mechanized plant on the way to automation.

The expansion of piece-rates is also limited by the difficulty of measuring the exact difference, in effort, skill, responsibility, and working conditions (including safety), required to make a piece in the course of one job as against a piece in the course of another. Unless the time-study and the job analysis are very carefully conducted, some jobs will be found to be "gravy" or loose, others "tight" for earning a given sum of money. On some jobs the day's wage (or earnings) will be thought unfair for the "fair day's" work done. In consequence, workers assigned the "tight" jobs will be envious and liable to accuse the foremen of favouritism to the others. Instead of brimming with high morale, the whole department will be rent with ill-feeling. This besetting difficulty drew my attention early in my inquiries (57, p. 89) to the correlation of little confidence in time study and the type of piece-rate system.

Analysis of the motives actually observed in the real world of

I

large-scale industry (45, table, p. 32) has led me to divide the
varying reactions of labour into three general attitudes, A, B,
and C, of which C was the attitude just mentioned of not wishing
to increase the amount earned whatever the wage-rate. This
is parallel to the Sargant Effect (170, p. 77) of wanting to secure
only a certain fixed future income from interest. In either case,
the higher the rate of interest or wages that is fixed, the less is
the principal, the time worked, or the output required to
produce it; and therefore a high rate of interest or wages tends
to lessen the amount saved or worked. The A attitude, on the
other hand, is largely "transpecuniary," since the workers look
beyond their pay-packet to what they can buy with it, either
for their direct satisfaction or to "keep up with the Joneses."
Occasionally workers may think of saving or (especially
managers) of the prestige of a high gross salary regardless of
the high surtax standing as a status symbol. In any case, the
A attitude leads to more work for more pay. In the B attitude
the pecuniary or transpecuniary A motives exist, but have no
absolute priority. The worker might fear a cut in piece-rates
or might be a complete "Organization Man" keeping "in"
with his foreman; or group solidarity with his mates and fear
of taking work away from them might come first. To this scheme
I have since added (81,) a D attitude, which is not infrequent
in large factories, namely, complete failure of motive owing to
not understanding the system of payment. Plenty of evidence
exists of this situation (57, p. 256) when complicated premium
bonus systems are used, though more effective communication
and consultation could easily alter it. Here I may quote a summary (45, pp. 273–4) of the approach that was almost standard
practice in several large-scale factories—

> The first step was to persuade workers who were to be directly
> affected by proposed changes to consider the proposal. In every
> case the first step had the backing of the official trade union repre-
> sentative, and in some cases the official had been consulted before
> the workers were approached. If opposition was raised, the next
> step was more intensive persuasion and exhortation by both
> management and trade union officials. At some stage there was a
> voting procedure to discover whether there was a majority in
> favour of acceptance. If this failed, a number of solutions were
> possible. But whatever the method of persuasion, if the workers
> concerned are not convinced that they are getting a "fair" deal,

then there will be trouble at some stage. . . . Engineers, business managers and practical economists can certainly hope greatly to increase the national product by economic incentives but only if they take account of the social climate, particularly its liability to storms.

After their intense concentration upon groups and human relations, including communication and consultation, industrial sociologists are now realizing, we saw, the importance of the specific industrial task or job. We must, therefore, refer back to the considerable research done in the occupation field before the somewhat exclusive cult of "sociological man" set in. Two features of special significance to present and future development may be picked out—the monotony of large-plant jobs and the need for human adjustment to machine costs.

Development has included not only large-scale organization but mechanization, and this has, of course, altered and will continue to alter the types of work mainly found in factories. In 1917 I analysed the distribution of all the workers in a large and (then) up-to-date American brassware factory, according (57, p. 64; 70, p. 66) to their relation to their work, and its "physiological and psychological requirements"; 4·1 per cent of the workers were related to the machine "as toolsetters" and about 2 per cent more for machine maintenance, and 35·8 per cent were actually on the machine work—but their relation to the machine differed significantly.

The largest group (13·8 per cent of all workers) were operating semi-automatic machines mainly pulling levers to bring the tools into contact with the material and to engage and release the material. The feeling of monotony and boredom in this highly repetitive semi-skilled work indicated by its falling hourly output curves can usually be relieved by various policies singly or combined. Practicable policies are to select men and women less monotony-prone, to introduce rest pauses or tea-breaks, to allow a variety of jobs during the day and to teach easier-work methods that will allow rhythm and other forms of what Baldamus calls "traction" (45, p. 13), giving a feeling of being pulled or drawn along by the inertia or momentum "inherent in a particular activity, and the opposite of distraction." In "object" traction "the worker . . . feels impelled to reproduce or complete (an object) without interrupting the complete job cycle; in *batch* traction . . . to complete a given batch of work; and in machine and line traction . . . to "keep going" smoothly with a machine and conveyor belt or just a chain of consecutive operations."

The next largest groups were merely "tending" either a chemical treatment (9·0 per cent of all workers) or an automatic machine (6·9 per cent), (usually after filling a hopper with a store of material). This type of work is probably becoming more frequent together with that of maintenance. When automation is introduced into a factory it should certainly increase the fairly skilled and responsible jobs of maintaining and tending machines and reduce the mere operating jobs, and will certainly increase the staff ratio. This conclusion is important, since the monotonous job has so far been the most frequent type in a large plant, and monotonous work is hardly a basis for intelligent enjoyment of life.

As well as changing the structure of factory jobs, mechanization, and automation still more so, introduces an economic need for working *shifts*. Machines are now so expensive an overhead, and they are so likely to become obsolete before they wear out, that they must be used to their fullest capacity—sixteen hours in the day if not twenty-four. This can be achieved without fatigue or other physiological harm to workers by two or three eight-hour shifts or even six four-hour shifts. The main limit to shift work is social and psychological; the natural unwillingness of workers to be at work when their friends are at leisure, thus breaking up their social life. This unwillingness has to be overcome by an economic motive, the chance of earning more per hour at overtime rates on the unpopular unsocial shift.

To sum up, developing industry seems to require economic incentives not only for productivity on a given job which is often monotonous, but for adjustments to new circumstances, particularly to costly mechanization. Economic incentives are not always feasible, but, where feasible, they result in higher production and are worth the "labour trouble" admittedly involved. Only when work is sufficiently automatic that the machine sets the pace can large plants, with their depersonalization, usually afford to abandon some economic individual or group incentive.

CHAPTER V

ECONOMICS AND SOCIOLOGY OF INDUSTRIAL GOVERNMENT

1. The Firm, its Policy and Risks in the Market

The last two chapters have dealt with industrial structure in the strict sense of the site, size, and scope of activities of the plants and firms of an industry. The facts and the trend were observed essentially by snapshots of the situation taken at particular moments, as by a census. The sociology and particularly the economics of industry require, however, for a realistic analysis, continuous "movies" as well as "stills." Men in industry are continuously at work exchanging goods, services, and titles to goods and services in the outside market; and inside certain organizations that engage in this exchange, men are continuously at work giving (and obeying) commands. Economics is primarily interested in demand and supply leading to exchange; industrial sociology in power relations—the command and reply—within a unit of organization. For a grasp of its movement and working as well as structure, the capitalist free-enterprise system may be pictured as a number of unit firms, great and small, floating or tossing "in a sea of troubles."

Outside these firms there is the anarchy of the market. Though firms and industries are linked and interdependent— the input of one, the output of another—yet there is no authority set over them. Instead, there is competition (however imperfect), trade fluctuations, uncertain supplies, and uncertain demands for which firms must produce in advance, investing in specialized capital still more in advance.

For the smaller firms the risk of loss and eventual extinction is high. Death-rates of metal establishments in two zones studied in the West Midland conurbation (12) during 1923–39 were, for instance, 43·8 and 53·4 per thousand annually— about three times the contemporary human death-rate. In

119

larger industrial firms taking the company form, extinction was no more rare. McGregor (134, p. 168) gives annual rates of liquidation between 1885 and 1912 varying from 5·5 to 3·0 per cent of all companies. But the total gains or losses to shareholders of the going concerns by dividend plus changes in the market value of their shares show a wide dispersion. Between 1936 and 1951, for instance (78 pp. 161–8), a sample of 304 large English manufacturing companies ranged from a total gain of 1,535 per cent to a loss of 82 per cent on the original investment. In 16 per cent of the companies shareholders gained in total less than they would have gained had they invested in the safe Post Office Savings bank, i.e. $37\frac{1}{2}$ for the fifteen years at simple interest.

Apart from some peripheral control by the State (73, *passim*) and some auxiliary institutions and services, the main co-ordinating factor in this anarchy is through the price-mechanism. When firms are all small in relation to the size of their industry, price is determined by the whole industry's supply and demand on the competitive market and this situation was, till thirty years ago, the assumption on which economic theory was built. Observation of actual industrial structure has, however, turned economists' attention to the possible power of a few leading firms selling as oligopolists or buying as oligopsonists a high proportion of any product. Prices may not be settled by demand and supply, but as Gardiner Means has it (136, pp. 10–13), may be "administered" by these firms. It becomes important to look further with the help of sociology into the internal organization of large firms and the motives of those found to be their prime managers. The necessary inductive investigations are slow to appear, and only a few economists, such as Hall and Hitch (92), Hague (91) or Andrews (5), have taken the trouble to inquire from business men what is their price policy in relation to their costs and what costs they take into account. Among other discoveries, Hall and Hitch found that the rate of interest, and Andrews that marginal costs, do not loom as large as theory would have it. Where oligopoly prevails, some investigators now consider the main object to be the highest price consistent with not encouraging, by the resultant high profits, the entry of new firms into the industry or the poaching by old firms from other industries. Thus Means (136, pp. 236–48) speaks of a "target price" adopted by the large American steel companies.

The main policy question for most firms is whether, through price policy or otherwise, to expand or not and if so, by how much. This question was taken up in Chapter IV when interpreting the actual facts and trends in the sizes of firms, and stress was then laid on the motives of the different types of prime managers (including entrepreneurs) deciding on policy.

Where the firm wants to expand, by no means always the case (125, p. 7), the central problem when fixed capital is so important in industry is the supply of capital resources, including credit from banks or from linked industries and wholesalers, i.e. bank or trade credit. But the main sources of fixed manufacturing capital in Britain today are the plough-back of a firm's own profit or new issues on the capital market. *Market* is here again used of the relatively unorganized relations outside the firm where the goods, services, and titles are bought and sold or, in the *labour market*, hired and "declared redundant." The original owner-manager entrepreneur (117, pp. 275–80) raised most of his capital by ploughing back profits, and, again, for some years after 1947 industrial companies' boards of directors succeeded in ploughing back 60 per cent of the shareholders' profits (78, p. 144). In America, Berle states (14, pp. 25–6) that only 6 per cent of capital expenditures (including provision for depreciation) by firms between 1946 and 1953 came from issue of shares and 64 per cent from the firms' own savings out of profits. The remainder came (18 per cent) from current borrowing and (12 per cent) from debentures.

In the middle, Victorian, period of capitalism, however, the capital market was, in the view of economists, the normal and assumable main source of capital supply, and the savings of the public still have their effect on industrial capital. Individuals save extensively through voluntary insurance, and the insurance companies buy shares on a large scale (78, pp. 117–18) in industrial companies. Sociological inquiries into the identity and habits of individual savers are thus relevant. Madge (126, p. 100), for instance, found in 1943 the highest savers in Glasgow to be country-born, Presbyterian, right wing politically, and of smart and mentally bright appearance. But buying shares in industrial companies does not extend, in Britain, very far down the income scale. The movement for wider shareholding is sociologically up against the poorer man's desire for security and his suspicion of the Stock Exchange.

The investment of capital involves risk, as we have illustrated, either to the entrepreneur or the shareholder. This measurable risk is due mainly to the capital investment's being specific to certain products and to a certain scale. The expectations of the manufacturer as to the market demand for that product on that scale are most uncertain of fulfilment. Controversy, in which psychologists have joined with economists such as G. L. S. Shackle, has ranged round the questions how the risk-takers or risk-bearers form their expectations of the probabilities of any eventuality and whether there is any basis in past experience for valid expectations. Though, popularly, risk conveys both senses, economists distinguish between risk as a probability that can actuarially be estimated and the kind of "uncertainty" with which business is also faced—probabilities which cannot reliably be estimated. In Table XV seasonal fluctuations measure the more predictable; cyclical slumps the less predictable risks to particular industries. There are in fact three dimensions in the term *probability* and, as I have put it elsewhere (60, p. 91), it is possible to make such a statement as that "this probability is probably improbable," i.e. this particular eventuality is fairly reliably calculable as relatively infrequent! In this three-dimensional complex of probabilities the risk-taking and -bearing entrepreneur may psychologically form some image to simplify his expectation; but the gambling temperament or merely, as Keynes put it, "animal spirits," makes for confidence and favours optimism over pessimism. Adam Smith (173, I, x) also thought that "the chance of loss is . . . by scarce any man who is in tolerable health and spirits, valued more than it is worth." But the shareholder and his advisors certainly have statistical data of past experience, some of which are probably relevant. His investment is not unique, nor all-out, nor once for all.

Even apart from the gambling nexus, the cash nexus or financial incentive to risk is difficult to calculate for the entrepreneur, but it is not so hard to calculate for company shareholders. The entrepreneur's income includes pay for management as well as risk-bearing, but for shareholders who do no managing the risk factor is more isolated. The average compensation in capital gain and dividend received by groups of shareholders in different industries or different sizes of firm do in fact (78, pp. 172–6) seem to vary, as economic theory has assumed, with the risk in those industries and with the increase in size of firms.

Economists have at last concentrated on a "theory of the firm," but they still have to realize that a large modern firm is complex in structure and government, and contains many conflicting interests, particularly between ownership and management. The term that is normally used by economists for all prime decision-makers is entrepreneur. The explicit definition of this term (Sir Hubert Henderson's (94, p. 116)) is a man who manages, owns the capital, and takes risks, but in most large firms, particularly if of company form, no such person is identifiable. To be realistic we must look into the various forms of the firm and their relative prevalence, and the way those various forms may alter economic theory.

2. THE FORM OF GOVERNMENT OF THE FIRM

Differences in the decisions of firms are not unconnected with differences in their form of government. And firms are found to differ significantly in form according to the type of their industry and their size. Of the main legal forms, sole trader and partnerships govern most smaller firms and are found to prevail in building, retailing, agriculture, and the professions sectors; public nationalized corporations of large size prevail in, indeed monopolize, the public utilities and transport sectors; co-operative societies prevail largely in food retailing and manufacturing. Among joint-stock companies, private prevail in the smaller plant, public in the larger plant manufacturing, as well as in banking, insurance, and overseas mining and plantations. The degree of prevalence varies with the particular manufacture, ranging from 65 per cent of producers' taxable income (78, pp. 3–5) in clothing to 100 per cent in most heavy industries. If we define an industrial segment to refer to the prevailing form of government of a firm we can sum up that certain segments are associated with certain sectors— for instance, the company segment with the manufacturing sector, particularly that part using capital intensively. Much

of this association can be interpreted logically enough, since the
main purpose of the joint-stock company is to join stock, that
is to aggregate large capitals; and nationalized industry, with
the taxpayer available, can raise large capitals still more easily
than the company.

As firms become larger they must consider enlarging the
sources of their capital; also of their recruitment of labour and
appointment of staff by the various methods open to them,
separately or combined, old or new: patronage, nepotism,
examination, interview, co-option, even election (as for the full-
time paid co-operative wholesale society directorships). They
must also consider their internal organization, once the staff
is found. Analysis of large-scale industrial organization will
require much the same political science categories and conceptions as are needed for studying state administration and
constitution (124): decentralization and delegation, the span
of control, the chain and unity of command, sanctions, budgeting, arbitration, co-ordination, and the various references
of control—to verify, to compare with a standard, to restrain,
to regulate, and often, to govern, generally. Company law
and the articles of association of particular companies form
the basis of company constitutions, but the board of directors
that is set up will create, or "structure," at least the top positions of the executive hierarchy (and their rate of pay) to which
staff are to be appointed.

The simplest but most inclusive term to cover these problems
in internal organization is rule-sharing and, in the large-scale
industry to which development has led, the problems focus
upon the delegation of power. The size of plants and firms,
which was noted in the last chapter, has been supposed to be
limited by the capacities of the prime manager. If he does not
delegate, nervous breakdown or ulcers are supposed to threaten
him. In some sense he can now delegate to the newer statistical
or econometric techniques, and more reliably and copiously
than to the traditional rule of thumb. Linear programming,
for instance, can help him allocate given resources to the best
advantage, or the theory of stochastic processes allow for chance
events in estimating risks.

But responsibilities which a computer, mechanical or human,
cannot take must also be delegated. Here, span of control and

chain of command both play their interdependent parts. If an administrator can control only four subordinate administrators, and empirical evidence suggests this figure, then mathematically a total administrative staff of eighty-five requires a chain of command of four links (i.e. $1 + 4 + 16 + 64$) involving that much additional communication in the course of the rule-sharing.

Rule-sharing I originally put forward (60, pp. 412–28) as a useful neutral term not referring to any particular doctrine of the separation or the division of power. The more familiar and seemingly synonymous term "the separation of powers" refers to the particular doctrine enunciated by Montesquieu and wrongly attributed to the British, but carried out in the United States constitution, that the processes of legislating, executing, and adjudicating be allocated to different and independent bodies. In the company-form firm these processes, or at least two of them, are discernible. As Haney put it (93, p. 263), the body of shareholders are "roughly comparable to the voters in a democracy, the directors to a parliament, the executive head to a prime minister and the other executive officials to his cabinet." The constitution is usually pictured in the familiar hour-glass diagram (78, p. 19), the large number of shareholders represented by the wide top, the few directors and the fewer chief executive officers at the narrow waist. The policy or laws decided upon at this concentration of power are executed by a hierarchy of managers spreading out down the lower half of the hour-glass into the foremen and the total operating force.

In a book describing his organization one industrialist, at least, frankly uses as chapter headings the executive system, the representative system, the legislative system, and the appeals procedure. Mr. Wilfred Brown claims in fact that his company has a written constitution (25, p. 225) in which shareholders and customers as well as labour are given a part.

Usually, however, firms show little separation of the vertical stages in the process of government and their assignment to independent bodies. The executive is also the legislative organ. Company constitutions follow the British rather than the American political pattern here as well as in restricting to some extent the powers of the chief executive in appointing the Board of Directors. It is for this reason appropriate to speak of the leading individual person, as far as there is one, as the prime manager, suggesting a relation to his board akin to that of the prime minister in the British Cabinet.

A second doctrine in rule-sharing, often called the division of powers, does, however, apply very completely to industry. This separation refers to some balance in the horizontal division of labour between central and local governments; or, in a confederate or federal constitution, between the confederation or federation and the states or provinces. Large industrial firms have to find solutions of a similar problem. Many holding companies own all or a majority of voting shares of subsidiary companies. The existence of holding companies is largely a matter of history, and the way in which the company was originally enlarged. The modern development is the deliberate use of the holding-company device, usually combined with interlocking directors, to create a federal constitution by which responsibility is delegated to subsidiaries for the different regions where the firm operates or, as developed by Imperial Chemicals, for its different groups of products. The holding company has in many books (including my own) been accounted a device for pyramiding control by the ownership of a bare majority of voting shares. But holding companies today seem anxious to hold 100 per cent, not just 51 per cent of the votes of their subsidiaries and to avoid the complication of independent minority shareholders. In short, freedom in organization now seems valued above capital leverage—a logical consequence, perhaps, of the Managerial Revolution.

In this free organization the question of the reserve powers of the central control in the parent holding company looms as large as in political federations and the answers vary as widely. Some industrial firms, notably Tube Investments, like political confederations, reduce these powers to a minimum, which usually includes decisions on capital expenditure above a certain amount, and making the higher appointments.

Once the details of internal organization are known, the industrial sociologist might be able to get away from the legal form and classify the government of firms into the Aristotelian types. Monarchies, oligarchies, and aristocracies will certainly be found in the family business. Democracies will be rare, except perhaps in co-operative societies. But new post-Aristotelian types could be added such as plutocracies, where large shareholders have control; or bureaucracies, where the management reigns, and technocracies, where the reigning managers are, in fact, engineers or chemists.

In attempting this realistic search into the seat of power, we must proceed from the known to the unknown—from the measurable to the hitherto non-measurable. The important measurable elements are—

(i) The degree of divorce of managership from ownership.

(ii) The type of attractives offered managers to come and to stay, and incentives to work effectively.

(iii) The antecedents of prime-managers.

(i) Ownership and management are, by definition, married in the owner-manager entrepreneur. He is usually still in charge of the smaller firms, and many companies, even large companies, are still found where the directors hold between them the majority of shares and often bear the same family name. Even among the 98 very large English industrial companies in 1951, five appeared from the names of the directors and the holders of large shares (78, pp. 136 and 223–65) to be family firms. Among medium and smaller large industrial companies with over £200,000 nominal capital that I analysed (but owing to the cost could not publish) many more family firms appeared. But, on the whole, statistical analysis confirms the development trend, numbered eight at the outset of this book, of the emergence of a governing hierarchy of top managers who, even in a capitalist economy, do not necessarily own the capital.

(ii) When management is divorced from ownership its financial incentive is in the form of a secure salary together with the hope of promotion to a higher one. The American practice of offering managers bonus options to buy shares whose value will vary with profits or dividends is not generally adopted in Britain, so that profits are not in fact a direct payment for management.

In this question of incentives for industrial management sociology and economics are particularly closely integrated. In my *Logic of Industrial Organization*, published in 1933, I devoted a number of pages to the Public School Man as Manager, and subsequent work by sociologists on "motivation"

and "attitudes" gives me no cause to withdraw this integration
of motivation and economics with the study of institutions.
Sociology is now being systematized. March and Simon in
their analysis of organization (128, p. 84), adopt an equilibrium
theory of inducements balanced against contributions presumably affecting measures of attraction or deterrence such as
labour turnover, and thus somewhat similar to my mobility
framework or model (II, § 3). They, too, hope that hypotheses
may be empirically tested.

(iii) The types of top prime-manager I originally distinguished and have subsequently retained (72, pp. 298–315),
based on measurable antecedents, were the self-made entrepreneur, the family head, the financier, the large shareholder,
the part-time director, and finally, the full-time executive
directors, probably owning little of the capital, who might be
ex-employees of the same firm, ex-other business, ex-technicians, or trained administrators.

Many investigators have since tried to find the frequency of
these types, though they usually confined inquiries to company
directors or managers, thus omitting the self-made entrepreneur
and some family heads. Copeman (43, pp. 57, 148 *et seq.*)
found that, with increasing profit plough-back, the financier
was becoming less important and the executive director, often
an engineer or accountant, more so. Most directors were sons
of business men (5 per cent were Etonians) and had begun work
in a large firm; and a bare majority had been employees of
the same firm throughout. Training for executive posts was
closely associated with a father who was a director of the same
firm. Thus, the ex-employee (originally either a clerk, or
accountant, or an engineer) and the family head appear to be
prevailing types.

The Acton Trust (2) found that in large organizations
employing over 10,000 men, nearly half of the near-top
managers aged 45 or more had started from the bottom either
as operatives or clerks, although only a third among similar
ranking younger men. Of such of these managers who held
degrees over half took their first degree in science and technology and were presumably ex-technicians. Summarizing these
English, and comparing them with foreign inquiries, Granick
(211) devotes five chapters to the Technocrat and the Heir,

the first of which contrasts Manager and Entrepreneur. He makes several references to the "parachutist," who, in contrast to the ex-employees or "Organization Man," drops into the top of an organization from elsewhere. These sociologically different types of leader or prime-managers are mainly of interest to an economist as causing differences in policy. Any ex-employee from the same or another business, as Andrews and Brunner (6) point out, would, on his way up the hierarchy, have learned in a hard school to cut costs and thus indirectly to maximize profit. But this conditioning process may not take place with other types, such as the hereditary family head or the ex-technician. Elsewhere, I have assigned marks to each type (72, p. 302) in respect of five sorts of policy and some research has been undertaken that might test my no more than plausible hypotheses. Carter and Williams (34) examined firms they rated as technically progressive or unprogressive to find how far they compared in twenty-nine specific characteristics. Many of these characteristics are akin to the five policies I selected: large-scale innovation, co-operation with other firms, re-investment of profit in fixed plant, large-scale co-ordination, and top appointments. The technically progressive firms rated far higher than the unprogressive in taking trouble to base investment decisions upon quantified data; and rated relatively high "for forward-looking tendency," "anticipating development during a considerable period"; but their position was relatively low in recruitment policy and readiness to co-operate. If the technically progressive firms were led by ex-technicians (and on average they rated high in "status of science" and "top manager a scientist") their result would agree with the high points I gave this type of leader for innovation and reinvestment and with the low points for co-operation, and *no* points for top appointments. On co-ordination this ex-technician, though not rated very efficient by Carter and Williams, proved more so than my hypothetical mark allowed.

3. ECONOMICS AND SOCIOLOGY OF JOINT-STOCK COMPANY GOVERNMENT

The joint-stock company is undoubtedly the most important institution in the British economy, and it has its counterpart in the American corporation, the French *Société Anonyme*, the

German *Aktiengesellschaft*, and, in fact, in all developed capitalist economies. Until recently, however, its study has fallen between the stools of economics and sociology. The economist was concerned with terms of exchange on the market between firms regardless of their form, and the sociologist seemed to scorn the materialist interests involved in firms, whatever their form. Yet there is a somewhat intriguing sociology of the joint-stock company. In political-science terms the company has a constitution, and Lord Salisbury, subsequently Prime Minister, thought (203, p. 211) its particular constitution ideal for the government of the State. As gradually worked out, this constitution has some peculiar features. Ultimate power is supposed to reside in the shareholders, but they vote not by heads but by the amount of shares—normally the ordinary shares—they hold. The directors for whom they are supposed to vote are in fact appointed by co-option; new directors are nominated by the board itself, and thus the board is normally self-perpetuating. There are no invariable rules, however, and realistic sociologists are needed who will proceed by observation of cases and statistical enumeration and summary. Within the company they must look into the number, the appointment, the organization, the status, roles and powers of debenture owners and shareholders of different categories, of directors and of managers with different functions and at different levels. These inquiries should tell us which of these persons forms part of top government.

Outside the company sociologists are needed, too, to examine the workings of the institutional entourage—the financial intermediaries—auxiliary to the company. Economists have since Lavington (117) studied the structure and behaviour of the Capital Market realistically and statistically, notably A. T. K. Grant, R. F. Henderson, or in a more general view of city institutions T. Balogh. Prominent at the launching of the company are the promoter and the houses issuing shares on the market and at its breaking up the Liquidator and Receiver. Throughout the life of the company it is helped by further institutions, particularly the Stock Exchange with its brokers and jobbers, bulls, bears, and stags. Here shareholders can at any moment sell their shares at some price, and get rid of the risks shares carry, thus making their purchase more attractive.

Next (and here sociologists might have a field day) to advise the shareholder on his possible risks and chances of gain come the financial journals, and a host of investment services. These institutions have built up a certain folk-lore, the validity of which does not always stand up (53, 77) to statistical testing. The Stock Exchange is often pictured as a haunt of iniquity, but the fact that, whether folk-lore or "scientific," no system of price-prediction seems very sure, suggests that Stock Exchange values take account of a multiple complex of causes which develop in the long-run and are not accounted for in any simple "system."

To return to the companies at the centre of the "city" entourage, they have at long last been examined socio-economically in America, Australia, and England. Berle and Means' *The Modern Corporation and Private Property* published in 1934 (15) was the American, path-breaking, investigation. Since then Gordon's *Business Leadership in the Large Corporation* (89) has provided a realistic and largely statistical analysis, and in 1959 economists, lawyers, political scientists, and sociologists combined in contributions to *The Corporation in Modern Society* (131). From Australia came Wheelwright's *Ownership and Control of Australian Companies* published in 1957 (200) with a wealth of information. In Britain the National Institute of Economic and Social Research sponsored Tew and Henderson's *Studies in Company Finance* (180) and, in 1960, Evely and Little's (50) *Concentration in British Industry*. My own *Ownership, Control, and Success of Large Companies* published in 1961 (78) was preceded by a pilot study (68) in 1947. My conclusions refer to relatively large industrial, commercial, and brewery companies—registered in London (and thus omitting Scottish companies). They refer to 109 "very large" companies of over £3m. nominal capital in 1951, indirectly by sample to about 258 "medium" down to £1m. and about 1,350 "smaller" large companies down to £200,000 capital.

The conclusions which follow go some way in establishing the eighth trend noted in the first chapter, is "the emergence of a governing hierarchy of top managers in industry who, even in a capitalist economy, do not necessarily own the capital" and are not always responsive to the shareholders—the owners—leading to an "irresponsible" industrial society?

K

(i) Shareholders as a whole cannot be expected to govern their company. They are an extension of the sleeping partner and the prime example of Veblen's "absentee owner-ship." Apart from their qualitative unfitness as too scattered, too busy, or too unbusinesslike, shareholders normally run into thousands for the large companies and are too many to take decisions. Their only effective power comes when a take-over bid is made and every shareholder has the choice of selling shares, and votes, to parties in opposition to the existing directors.

(ii) Shares are held unequally, however, and a small group owning a large proportion of the votes might well be in a position to govern—

> The degree of inequality was beyond that even of the distribution of wealth, let alone income. But some companies were more unequal than others. On average, the twenty largest voteholders in the very large companies (about 0·02 per cent of all voteholders) held about 30 per cent of the votes, but in a substantial proportion they held 50 per cent or more (78, pp. 184–5).

(iii) In 1951 directors and the large shareholders formed in about two-thirds of the companies, distinct groups, and control was divorced from ownership—

> The most surprising fact was the small proportion of ordinary shares owned by the boards as a whole, and the small number of directors found among the largest twenty shareholders. For the companies of all sizes and industries, excluding breweries, the average percentage of the ordinary shares owned by the total board was, in 1951, 2·3 per cent and the number of directors among the largest twenty shareholders only three for every two companies. . . . Combining the test of vote-concentration and gearing, the type of predominant voteholder and the proportion of ordinary shares owned by directors, a certain number of large companies can be identified as probably owner-controlled or marginally so. Thirty very large and forty-nine medium and smaller large industrial and commercial companies, together with six very large and four medium or smaller breweries, were so identified. The proportion of these eighty-nine to the total of 268 companies fully analysed is 33 per cent. Two-thirds of the large companies in 1951 were thus probably not owner-controlled (78, p. 185).

Within most large modern companies quite a conflict of interests may thus arise, not only between directors and owners, and between debenture and preference shareholders and ordinary shareholders bearing risks, but even within the ranks of ordinary shareholders. A shareholder can be held to be the perfect economic man, but a few insiders may be holding large *blocs* of shares for the sake of power besides the long-run attraction, to the supertaxed, of untaxed capital gain. Many outsiders with a small holding and high labour turnover may be looking both to capital gain and to dividends. Their "perfect" economic behaviour will be spoiled, however, by their ignorance, subjection to folk-lore and, occasionally loyalty to the board.

(iv) In this conflict the board of directors is probably gaining in strength. Marshall, in his *Industry and Trade* (130, pp. 316–18), discusses realistically the important question of company policies likely in view of the balance of internal forces at the time he wrote. This type of discussion was not followed up by subsequent economists, an omission particularly unfortunate since the actual balance of forces has been changing radically since Marshall's day. He realized that "the distinctive conditions of joint-stock administration come into view only when the ownership of capital is effectively divorced from its control"; but his conclusion except for the first sentence now reads somewhat doubtfully—

> Those who are in control have not nearly the same pecuniary interest in its economic and efficient working as they would have, if they owned the business themselves. Its higher officials may watch its lower officials, and its directors may watch its higher officials. But its directors can generally keep their positions by faithful, steady work, without showing special initiative; and they often content themselves with that.

Today few directors are content with mere watching; directors are mostly full-time managers and often the initiators of policy.

The growing independent strength of the board of directors is attested by the small size and full-time employment of the board (78, pp. 82–92). In contrast to the boards of banks and insurance companies with possibly several guinea-pig directors, the boards of industrial companies are small. The average board membership even of the very large industrial companies was, in 1951, nine; and the great majority of the members appear to be full-time working executives. The size of boards did not grow out of proportion to the growth in size of companies and here there has been little sign of Parkinson's Law (146) at work.

(v) The recent trend has been toward further divorce of control and ownership. Among the very large companies compared in 1936 and 1951, inequality in ownership was diminishing and fewer had a small group of owners with a high proportion of the votes and thus likely to be in control. In fact, the virtually shareless directors increased—

> In 1936 the average proportion of the total votes held by the largest twenty shareholders was 30 per cent; by 1951 19 per cent. Forty-nine of these very large companies showed a fall in this measure of concentration; only sixteen showed a rise. . . . The proportion of shares held by directors, . . . fell between 1936 and 1951 and also the number of directors among the largest twenty shareholders. There were more directors holding no more than their minimum share qualification (78, p. 186).

(vi) The sharing out of the net profit between dividends and plough-back obeyed no single expected principle, such as a fixed proportion between them, as some authorities (90, pp. 274–5) suppose, a fixed rate of dividend or a fixed rate of reinvestment on assets. In 1948–51 when the share-outs were analysed the fixed dividend was, however, the nearest principle approached.

> Analysis . . . showed that not the assets but the shareholders had priority and that the assets were the residuary legatee. . . . The principle actually adopted by 1948–51 appeared to be for a company to distribute to shareholders just over 1 per cent of assets whatever its profits, and for companies making higher profits to allow their shareholders in addition only about a fifth share of the profits. This policy resulted in a certain stability of dividend but violently fluctuating plough-backs. The amount of the plough-back to reserves and consequent investment thus seems to depend almost wholly on the opportunity offered by the amount of the profit of the preceding period . . . (78, p. 187).

This conclusion, based on the statistical analysis of a large number of large companies, is paralleled by Mackintosh in his recent intensive study of small Birmingham firms (125, p. 108)—

> In the policies of all these firms there is present to some degree an idea for the minimum dividend. .... In the simplest example it can be assumed that there is a minimum satisfactory dividend; if the firm's earnings exceed the amount required to pay this minimum dividend and to meet its requirements of finance for internal use, it will add to the dividend some fraction of the surplus earnings.

(vii) The size of the company had a distinct effect upon its policy and working constitution. The larger the company, the greater the proportion of plough-back and lower the dividend and the wider the divorce of management from control. The average percentage of ordinary shares owned by the board was 2·9 for the smaller, 2·1 for the medium, and 1·5 for the very large companies. The proportion of directors among the twenty largest shareholders was 30 per cent for the smaller, 21 for the medium, and 16 for the very large companies. Analysis of seventeen giant companies with over £8m. nominal capital in 1951 made it appear that control by personal or family ownership compared with institutional ownership, e.g. by insurance companies, was not possible beyond a certain size.

(viii) The effect of the work being done, the "ergological" effect, can be observed even though the question of the top management of a firm might be supposed far removed from materials and markets. For instance (78, p. 189), large engineering and metal companies, compared with very large breweries, had distinctly larger boards, more interlocking directors, more divorce between ownership and control, and higher plough-back of profit. These contrasts may be connected with the types of markets (e.g. linked industries as against consumers), with the growth of the industry and new capital requirements, and with the need for technologically trained leadership.

The realities of the company organization, particularly control by a few inside capital-owners or co-opted shareless directors, thus appear very different to its legalities. Somewhat similarly the implications of the real organization of a company upon its policy are very different from some of the assumptions of orthodox economic theory.

(i) The divorce of ownership of capital and its risks from control and management—risk-bearing from risk-taking—contradicts what Robertson (157, p. 89) considers a proposition so important that it might almost be described as Capitalism's Golden Rule, "where risk lies there lies the control also." Marshall, indeed, laid it down in his own italics (130, p. 645) that "*decisions as to the taking of risks generally and of new departures in particular should remain, for the present at least, in the hands of those who will bear the burden of the risks.*"

(ii) If the managers and owners of the risk-capital are different people and the prime managers, unlike the entrepreneur as usually defined, have no capital, then they cannot maximize "their" profits. They might wish to maximize other people's profits, but this wish would depend on motives different from that assumed in Economic Man—motives such as loyalty to and identification with the company apart from its shareholders, and most fittingly studied perhaps by sociologists and psychologists. This is in fact what I suggested in the last chapter and Table XI when considering the motives for expanding the size of firms.

(iii) Contemporaneously with the increase in management control, the proportion of profits ploughed back (which is the direct responsibility of the directors) has increased considerably. This may be coincidence, but could be interpreted rationally as cause and effect. If managers identify their interests with the company and its growth, not with the shareholders' interests, the way to grow is to restrict dividends and plough back capital, though not necessarily into the same industry. The actual increase in integration in large companies' activities may thus supply a link in interpreting the chain of events. The reserves ploughed back in an industry not expected to grow will be invested elsewhere.

The trend toward plough-back, though noticeable, is not in fact growing very fast or consistently. This is probably due to the risk prime managers run of so depressing the Stock Exchange prices of shares by paying out low dividends that their shareholders might easily accept any take-over bids from other would-be prime ministers. Fisher (53) certainly found that prices depend largely on the last year's dividend.

(iv) Finally, the division of work in the large company should simplify rather than complicate economists' theories of distribution. The question is still asked in some textbooks what are company profits paid for, and the answer is usually somewhat dusty. But in the large company no person is currently paid any profit, and the baffling question of an incentive for what function does not arise. Debenture holders are paid interest, shareholders dividends, managers salaries, and the work that is being paid for is in each case fairly clear: capital, risk-capital, and management respectively. Profits or losses will, of course, accrue to the company as a whole and to any bodies or persons buying and selling at different prices. But a realistic analysis should settle the structural question of payment to precisely *whom*, before speculating on the function of a vaguely conceived profit.

4. The Top Role of the State in Industrial Government; National Planning

National economic planning for long periods was first adopted in relatively underdeveloped countries. The Russian Five-year Plan of 1929 leaps to mind and after that, perhaps, the Indian plan, which will be detailed in the next chapter. In developed countries national planning has been a rallying cry for the Socialist parties, and elements of planning, such as allocation of materials and import quotas, were in fact adopted during the war and its aftermath of shortages in goods necessary for life and efficiency by most of the national governments of the West.

In fear of national stagnation, British interest in national planning has, however, recently been reviving. The contrasting rapid development of the French economy since 1955 has been attributed indeed to planning by a mathematically educated Civil Service (instead of inexpert Classics men moving from job to job) using new econometric techniques based on economic input–output tables. We can quote M. Massé the *Commissaire général au Plan*, himself (214)—

> An economic table is initially a description of material flows moving between the main sectors. But once assured that technological coefficients remain invariable, it becomes an instrument of forecast. If the production of the various sectors and the imports are known, one can directly obtain, by subtracting intermediate

consumptions, the amount of goods and services available for general consumption, investment, and export. Inversely one can take as a starting point consumption, considered as the true end of programming, and by means of reasonable assumptions concerning investments and foreign trade deduce the total production required. Inversely is the right word since mathematical computations consist of "inverting a matrix." This is how a first outline of the Plan is sketched.

This chapter on Industrial Government cannot close without noting the possibility (even where State coercion is deprecated) of overall control by national governments, in the interest of the public as a whole, over the sectional government by industrial firms or associations of firms—or of workers.

Except during wars and their aftermath, planning in the developed Western countries is relatively complicated and controversial, because scarcity of obvious necessities for a bare standard of life and efficiency which we shall find in the underdeveloped countries is not the main problem. In the developed countries, instead, controversy rages among planners on the priorities for private or for public expenditure, for full employment or equality of distribution as against total production or income, on how much welfare or leisure to allow for, or where, if at all, to encourage local development and what weight to give foreign balances. In short, of the four ingredients of planning to be detailed later (VI, § 5), the very first, the acknowledgement of intention, seems missing in a developed economy. However far development has gone, there seems, nevertheless, some intention for further development as measured in an increase in the national production and income and in full, or fuller, employment.

The second ingredient of planning is prearranged tasks or targets. In underdeveloped countries, as we shall see, tasks include, in particular, some specified increase of exports, of investment in capital, research, and education, and of employment.

In the 1961–6 plan for Britain with the same intention to increase production the same targets appear. The National Gross Domestic Product is to increase annually by 4 per cent. In a through-put economy such as Britain's this overall intention involves an annual increase of 5·7 per cent in exports needing 4·5 per cent in imports, as well as 6·2 per cent increase in investment. Unemployment is to be reduced, particularly in those areas where it was relatively high, by the State remitting taxes to industrialists when they invest in new capital equipment. The State's power of taxation is thus indirectly brought to bear in planning the investment of fixed capital. Further tasks are indicated by this first report of the National Economic Development Council (216) to meet shortages for which investment in training and education should be planned. "Skilled manpower shortages have prevailed in this country throughout the post-war period" (p. 24). "A specific obstacle to productivity improvements is the inadequate use of the newer management techniques, especially by small and medium-sized companies" (p. 31). In aiming at higher production a head, planners setting up British targets not unnaturally look to the country with the highest income-a-head. Table I shows this to be the United States, with, in 1957, much the highest figure, almost 50 per cent higher than the runner-up, Canada, and more than twice that of the United Kingdom. My comparisons with the United States (72) show that the differences of the British from the American economy do not lie in the size of plants or firms, which in point of numbers employed are surprisingly similar, or in degree of industrial localization with its external economies, but, lie in capital intensity and, in rigidity and lack of the mobility and incentive studied in Chapters II and IV.

According to most measures of capital intensity, Britain appears to have less than half the American intensity. To use the first measure given in Table XV, the horse-power-a-worker is higher in America than Britain (79 pp. 44–51) in 78 industries out of the 81 where they are comparable and the (median) average horse-power for these industries is 5·9 for America; 2·3 for Britain. This $2\frac{1}{2}$ to 1 relation is confirmed by alternative measures of capital intensity such as capital per worker (47, p. 551).

Rigidity is largely sociological, and observers with experience (47, p. 563) of both countries find a very large mass of British industry which resists rather than welcomes expansion and innovation due to lack of such major components of a highly industrial landscape as costs analysis, search for new products and new processes, and market research. Much of this rigidity could be broken down by education in business analysis at

University level, and here in the low proportion of under-
graduates or graduates taking commerce degrees lies another
measurable difference between the two countries.

Incentives or deterrents are partly sociological, such as the
"status pull and push" against a business career spoken of in
Chapter II; partly economic, such as, possibly, the tax structure. Edwards and Townsend (47, p. 566) consider that, of the
major industrial communities, Britain imposes the highest tax
rates on her senior executives.

By reason of these differences between the British economy
and economies with higher income-a-head, particular attention
must, in setting tasks, be paid to the State budget and targets
for investment in capital and management education.

The third ingredient in planning, one on which the tasks are
based, is knowledge, particularly of the existing supplies of resources. A full survey of possible resources is given in Table XII.
The most immediately important factors are the stock of capital
and capacity to save, skilled labour and its mobility, and the
efficiency of management in factor use. Any plan for Britain
certainly need not suffer for lack of this knowledge of existing
economic conditions, though firms, including public corporations, have proved unwilling to divulge their costs in different
operations—possibly because they have not taken the trouble
to analyse them, even for their own purposes. The Census of
Production and trade returns and the labour statistics on which
this book has constantly drawn lie to hand. These measured
facts are now to be interpreted and put to practical use by the
National Economic Development Council; and this brings us
to the fourth ingredient in planning—some organization to
carry out or control the plan and check up on results. It now
looks as though Britain were going a step further than the pious
aspirations (72, p. 169) of the Economic Survey. Some organ
of the State is apparently to be given a role at the top of industrial government. Instead of leaving it to collective bargaining
and maintaining the *laissez collectives faire* policy, a national
plan may even be worked out for incomes in the teeth of trade-
union opposition.

CHAPTER VI

INDUSTRIALIZATION OF THE
UNDERDEVELOPED COUNTRIES

1. Identification and Contrast of Countries Developed and Underdeveloped

Nine trends in economic development were traced at the outset of this book. Many countries—indeed whole continents—of the world have even today hardly started on this development, and to them the adjective *underdeveloped* is applied. The stage in the trend toward mechanization that was achieved by some underdeveloped countries or continents was given in Table IV; but the only two trends measured by the U.N. for the majority of countries are average income-a-head and percentage of workers in agriculture. These two measures appeared in Table I for the ten least developed, the ten most developed, and the remaining five other important countries.

In any one country the stage reached, whether early, middling, or late, is probably roughly similar for each of the trends. If the data were available most countries could probably be placed as underdeveloped or developed by a regular "syndrome" of tests such as low mechanization and staffing and weak differentiation and small organizations, on the one hand, and high mechanization and staffing and strong differentiation and large organizations, on the other. Certainly, using the two tests almost universally available, there are only marginal difficulties involved in classification. Countries shown in Table I with low income-a-head can be seen to be also countries with a high proportion of agriculturists.

The underdeveloped countries, in the early stages of the various measurable trends of development, form a majority of all countries, and it is not difficult to name the comparatively few developed countries that appear in the *United Nations Year Book*. Though homogeneous in having reached the later stages of the trends, the developed countries are heterogeneous in other respects, particularly in density of population. They fall into three distinct groups: older countries with the high density of populations of over eighty per square kilometre—in order of income-a-head, Switzerland, Britain, Belgium, Denmark, France, West Germany, the Netherlands, and Austria; older countries with the low density of under twenty—Sweden, Norway, and Finland; and the new countries, all with densities of twenty or under—the United States of America, Canada, New Zealand, and Australia. The low-density countries, particularly the new, could certainly all take more development with advantage. It is important to realize that "developed" does not mean *fully* developed. In fact, some *regions* of the developed countries show traits of the underdeveloped such as low income-a-head and are subject to development plans. Well-known instances are the British depressed areas of South Wales and the North-East Coast, actually *called* "development areas," and in America, the Tennessee Valley, the Dust Bowl, and now the West Virginia mining area. Action taken by the developed countries to solve the problem of these underdeveloped or derelict parts and their degree of success will be found to form a useful object lesson for the underdeveloped countries.

We may take an income-a-head in 1957 of $500 as the dividing line (Austria had $543) between underdeveloped and developed countries, and 40 per cent in agriculture. In only two of the twenty-five countries of Table I are these two tests in conflict. Japan and Italy, though not highly agricultural, yet had an income-a-head less than $500: in both countries income-a-head has since 1957, however, been rapidly increasing. Venezuela, not quoted in the table, is another case of conflict, highly agricultural (49·6 per cent) but with income-a-head over $500 due largely to oil production. Four western European countries, Portugal, Spain, Greece, and Ireland, appear as underdeveloped on both counts; all have over 40 per cent in agriculture and income-a-head less than $500. It may at first seem surprising that Canada, New Zealand, Australia, Norway, Denmark, and Finland should pass the "non-agricultural" test, but in fact, owing mainly to labour-saving methods, they all have 20 per cent or less of their occupied population in agriculture, except Norway with 24·6 per cent and Finland with 34·2 per cent.

The developed countries are thus both enumerable and enumerated. In this chapter attention will be devoted to the remaining countries, for the reasons that they have a standard of living near starvation level and that most of them can be helped to increase their standards by industrialization or development of certain services, and that, if trade is likely to be insufficient even in the long run, the question of permanent aid must arise. Accordingly, aid will be considered in the final section of this chapter; but practical policies of industrialization will be considered immediately. First, however, come the questions (A) how low are the standards of living of the underdeveloped countries and how far their people are really on the verge of starvation and likely to remain so; and (B) how far, if at all, industrialization would be able to help raise those standards.

(A) Average income-a-head is, of course, very far from a satisfactory indicator of comparative welfare. An average American though his income be over forty times that of an average Burmese, does not necessarily fare forty times as well. The differences in "welfare" are "over-indicated" by money incomes for certain quite tangible reasons. The more important of these are—

(i) That most of the underdeveloped countries are in the warmer climates where less clothing, housing, and also food are physically required to keep warm.

(ii) That welfare and certainly happiness is obtained in simple social ways without the use of income—ways studied at home by sociologists and in the more primitive countries by anthropologists.

(iii) That the largely urban poverty of the developed countries is more unpleasant than rural poverty at a similar money income.

(iv) That the wants satisfied by a small income will be the more urgent and the average American or Briton with forty or twenty times the income of the average Burmese will not spend it on goods and services of forty or twenty times the urgency. Assuming the Burmese is keeping alive, the average American or Briton will not eat forty or twenty times as much as he. After they have satisfied their hunger they will spend most of their many remaining dollars or pounds on goods and services that are of less urgency. This is an example of the economists' law of diminishing utility which is substantiated statistically by Engel's Law. Food is the most urgent demand and food forms a higher proportion of expenditure, the poorer the consumer. Countries will thus not differ in their food intake-a-head as much as in other forms of consumption. While in America and Britain food forms less than a third of consumer expenditure, in many underdeveloped countries it forms as much as 90 per cent.

Against these four considerations qualifying the apparent differences in standards of living must be set the fact, substantiated later (VII, §3), that the underdeveloped countries have distributions of income more unequal than have the developed countries and that their few rich men push the arithmetic mean average up unduly. On the whole, we may conclude that the average income-a-head forms a useful indication, at least, of the order of magnitude along the affluence to starvation scale.

Two-thirds of the world's population have, according to the warden of the Tombs prison, a standard of living below that of New York State jails. But a fuller comparison has been made with standards of Britons at large (205, pp. 2–3)—

Before the war, the British diet furnished an average of about 3,000 calories per head per day. But on two subsequent occasions, in the critical period of shipping shortage in 1940–1 and in the post-war supply and currency crises of 1946–7, the level fell to slightly below 2,800 calories. . . . In 1946–7 it was possible to secure a completely objective measure of inadequacy, since the results of an extensive survey of the body-weights of adults showed a definite, if small, loss of body-weight during the period when the calorie level was reduced to 2,800 per head per day—a regression paralleled in the loss of weight of children throughout the same period. . . . It appears that the food supplies of countries representing only about 20 per cent of the world's population exceed a calorie level of 2,800. On the other hand, the food supplies of countries representing no less than 60 per cent of the world's population actually fall below 2,200, of which nearly half are below 2,000. . . . Under such conditions there is not only weight loss and reduction in physical activity but also characteristic behaviour symptoms such as lack of mental alertness and coherent and creative thinking, apathy, depression and irritability.

These are the results only of *under*-nutrition. There is besides malnutrition—a shortage of protein and particularly of animal protein, which falls (205, p. 5) from 66 grams per head per day in North America to only 7 in the Far East. And the diets of the less developed countries "also tend to lack adequate quantities of vitamins and essential mineral constituents. This in turn leads to the incidence of specific deficiency diseases." These estimates are developed in detail by Dr. Sukhatme (178, pp. 463–507). His broad conclusion (in italics) is that "should population *grow according to the United Nations medium forecast,*" as early as 1980, "*the world's food supplies would have to be doubled . . . to provide a reasonably adequate level of nutrition* to the peoples of the world."

Are the underdeveloped countries likely to stay thus, relatively and absolutely so very poor? In the answer to this question lies the most vital reason for studying their development. For if the answer points to the danger of a vicious circle of poverty leading to low productivity and thus to further poverty; then the necessity must be faced of somewhere breaking the links in that circle. Once broken, there lies the possibility of a take-off, setting the *virtuous circle* in train where well-fed, well-educated people will have a high productivity and low reproductivity, plough back savings to capital and thus invest in still higher productivity, with high income-a-head and mass-consumption as the final phase.

(B) To break the vicious circle of poverty and possibly condition a take-off, the practical question is the form which development should take.

Broadly, the policy to be discussed is one of increasing the number occupied in manufacturing industries and certain services—the secondary and tertiary industries that have been found increasing in the countries already developed. By concentrating on industrialization, however, I do not wish to imply that it will automatically bring higher standards of living, nor to deny that developing agriculture can ever sufficiently increase income-a-head. My object is rather to point out particular kinds of industry or of services rather than others which should lead to this increase—in short, my object is a suitable, not indiscriminate, industrialization.

Some industrialization will undoubtedly increase the living

standards of most countries at present predominantly agricultural—a prophecy supported, though not necessarily proven,
by the remarkable correlation of high income-a-head and a low
proportion in agriculture. This correlation, already pointed
out when comparing the countries of the world as a whole, also
applies to the 48 States of the continental United States of
America. Of the twelve with the highest proportions occupied
in agriculture, ten were among the poorest twelve, the remaining two among the next poorest twelve. At the other end of the
scale ten of the least agriculturally occupied were among the
twelve richest states and the remaining two among the next
richest twelve.

Sociological reasons for the lower income from agriculture,
are the presence of small-scale subsistence farming and, when
the farmer owns the land, the attraction of independence
compensating, as explained earlier (II, §3), for a lower money
income. Agriculture is a way of life, particularly in underdeveloped countries, and where food is the overwhelming
concern, those fearing to take the risk of full unemployment
in industrial towns may well remain immobile though underemployed on the land.

If agriculture must give place, a policy of industrialization
does not follow as a matter of course. The trend of employment
in the developed countries was in fact found to be toward services rather than manufactures. When indicating activities that
can with advantage be located, and even localized, in particular
countries, certain services will not be neglected, especially not
the tourist trade.

2. Fitting Industry to the Resources of Underdeveloped Countries

Accepting the need for some industrialization, we now tackle
the practical question what particular industries to select for
underdeveloped countries. This selection will rely heavily on
the type of data illustrated in the Appendix and on the experience of the developed countries, in trying to revitalize depressed
industrial areas and, still more to the point, to repopulate rural
areas. Particular industries were specially selected for the
British depressed "development" areas which would employ

the high proportion of unoccupied women and unemployed older men. And in 1947, (68) I suggested measurable criteria in selecting industries for the rural areas. Consideration was given both to *desirable* traits, such as growth and stability, and to traits making a rural location *feasible*, such as linkage with agriculture and small scale of plant to fit populations of low density.

This desirability plus feasibility analysis can be applied to the underdeveloped countries. Desirability points to industries that are growing, or at least not diminishing, and that are not subject to cyclical fluctuations or to great uncertainty and risk. Industries subject to known high seasonal fluctuations (Table XV, VI *B*) are, however, positively desirable if their fluctuation dovetails into and counterbalances the known fluctuation of existing activities.

Besides growing itself, many an industry will lead to growth in other industries which simply follow its leadership. The selection of these desirable leader industries has occasioned considerable controversy, not to say confusion. Confusion has resulted particularly from their being identified with exporting industries and named *basic* and the whole controversy named *the basic/non-basic issue*. If exporting industries really led to more general industrial growth, then Britain, with its "through-putting" economy and high export ratio, should be one of the fastest-growing countries on earth! The practically significant distinction is not between industries exporting from their country, region, or city, but that stressed repeatedly in this book, between industries with a low coefficient of localization tied to serving the local residents, i.e. residentiary industries, and the footloose industries. Instead of importing a product a locality may itself start making it. This import substitution will employ people directly and indirectly increase custom for more residentiary industries, in fact will help development but does not help export.

Feasibility, however, (particularly, the economic possibility of trade eventually being set going without aid), depends not only upon the location pattern of the industry, but upon a country's natural and human resources and upon the size of its internal and external markets.

Location patterns of different industries were discussed in Chapter III, and industries of extremely low or high localization

L

are cited in Table XV. It must be remembered that many industries cannot be located at will, however desirable that location. Mainly by reason of cost of transport (though lack of storability and durability also count), some are restricted to being "rooted" near their materials, others "tied" near the scattered final consumers, and in yet others, plants must swarm together in close localization. On the whole, it is the industries with neither high nor low coefficients of localization that are footloose and "localizable" at will. In selecting industries for location in underdeveloped countries economic restraints are put upon many industries. It is particularly those with a high or a low coefficient of localization that cannot be located at will. Tied industries of a low degree of localization must exist near the consumer, particularly the manufacture of heavy and perishable foodstuffs that are in widespread demand, but of great weight per given value (*see* Table XV, Sections I *C* and v) such as cattle-food or beer. On the other hand, though there is little chance of swarming, the highly localized rooting of early process industries must occur, as we shall note, in those particular regions where heavy materials or produce are mined or grown.

Such resources and all other facilities that are relevant to industrialization that a country may or may not possess are surveyed in Table XII, which is designed as a useful model for a preinvestment inventory or practical check-list. Resources are of four main types: the market position; the economist's four factors of production—land, capital, labour, and management; the economic context of industry; and the legal and sociological context of the whole economy.

The main task of selecting industries is one of fitting together Tables XV and XII, broadly of finding industries with the traits that fit the resources of the country. Putting it negatively, the task is to sieve out the industries with traits that demand resources the country lacks. Industries (as Table XV will always remind us) vary widely in the demand for their products and the resources they require in power, capital, management, manual skill, and materials. Out of this wide choice, each country should select industries demanding the resources in which it has, or might have in the future, a comparative advantage. This task is the same as the vocational selection of

TABLE XII

SURVEY OF NATIONAL RESOURCES

A. MARKET POSITIONS: COMPOSITION OF DEMAND

Size and type of internal market
  Total national income
Foreign markets and sources (their accessibility)
  Types of exports and imports
Linkage
  With source of material and power
  With other industries and agriculture

B. FACTORS OF PRODUCTION

1. *Land*
  (*a*) Natural resources; Acts of God
    Mineral and oil deposits; scatter and accessibility
    Soils; climate; freedom from pest and disease
    Water, rain, springs, rivers, harbours
    Forests; fishing
    Scenery, recreation areas
  (*b*) Quasi-natural: national parks, buildings, and art and antiquities

2. *Capital*
  (*a*) " Infrastructure" (public utilities, industrial aid)
    Power-stations, supply of electricity, gas, and water, transport, and
    communication facilities
  (*b*) Agricultural equipment, irrigation, drainage
  (*c*) Mining and manufacturing equipment
  (*d*) Tourist facilities
  (*e*) Social capital, buildings, and installations
  (*f*) Capacity and willingness to save and *bear* risks

3. *Labour*
  (*a*) Present and future population and "economically active" pro-
    portion
    Mobilization of women; age-structure, migration
  (*b*) Distribution over agriculture and industry, and over occupations,
    skilled and unskilled; mobility
  (*c*) Literacy and numeracy, schools
  (*d*) Trade unionism
  (*e*) Capacity and willingness to work effectively

4. *Management (Enterprise and Expertise)*
  Staff ratio (clerical, technological, research staff)
  Size of plants and firms
  Capacity and willingness to plan, supervise, organize, and *take* risks
  The efficiency of factor use

C. ECONOMIC CONTEXT OF INDUSTRY

Distribution and marketing network, industrial urbanization
Business repair and maintenance services
Financial intermediaries, banks, stock exchange
Facilities for technical and vocational education and apprenticeship

D. LEGAL AND POLITICAL CONTEXT OF THE ECONOMY

Company and commercial law; patents
Land tenure
Administrative efficiency, systems of taxation
State aid for industry, tariffs, tax-remission, risk of confiscation
State controls; planning
Foreign aid

personnel—finding the men to fit into the square and round holes—and is obvious enough. Yet many a country has put forward projects for establishing industries with little thought of their "fit" either for desirability or feasibility.

Since industrial traits and national resources are to be fitted, Tables XII and XV have some similar headings and often use the same measures. Markets appear in both Tables, with the connected questions of total size of industries and national income, of the proportion exported, and of linkage with other economic activities. The factor of management again has affinity with organization (Table XV, vII), particularly the staff-ratio, the size of plants and firms, and also their government.

Some resources are particular to certain undeveloped countries, others are common to all.

3. Resources Particular to Certain Countries

For the practical planning of development the key distinction is between resources that are given by nature, as "Acts of God," and those that have been, or must be, created by man. Economists include under *land* (129, p. 144) all "utilities over the supply of which (man) has no control; they are given as a fixed quantity by nature . . . the term *land* has been extended by economists so as to include the permanent sources of these utilities; whether they are found in land, as the term is commonly used, or in seas and rivers, in sunshine and rain, in winds and waterfalls."

The term may be extended further to include any quasi-natural resources not, like capital, orginally formed deliberately to add to public or private income, but artefacts such as antiquities and historical monuments. Cathedrals were not put up for earthly gain, but have subsequently become a source of national income from tourists. They may fitly rank with resources in land as Acts of God.

Now, land is the factor that includes most of the particular resources of particular countries. Underdeveloped countries differ especially in their mineral wealth such as oil, coal, and metal deposits. Though less well endowed in known mineral resources per head of population than Europe and North America, Asia and Africa have (29, p. 264) considerable resources to build upon. And much exploration is still to be done. Within each underdeveloped continent, however, countries vary from no known mineral resources at all to countries like Kuwait with the highest petroleum resources in the world per head of population. Wide differences between underdeveloped countries are also found in the other natural resources besides minerals, and the quasi-natural resources listed in Table XII. The international Land Survey initiated by Dudley Stamp is classifying soils, and water resources—not only essential to agriculture, but in mountainous country a possible source of power. Climate and scenery are of vital importance to the tourist trade.

Natural resources in minerals, soil, and climate, if they are demanded and accessible, result in mining and agricultural activity, and they often lead to some linked manufacturing, especially if the product mined or grown is costly to transport in its raw state. The earlier processes of metal refining, cotton ginning, bacon-curing, seed crushing, sugar refining, saw-milling, rice milling, and tanning reduce transport costs and are thus economically rooted near their material supplies, as also is the whole process of cement- and brick-making.

Some agricultural demands, for example for fertilizer, may also form a link in the pattern of location. Indeed, next in importance to natural resources are the differences between countries in their market position, particularly the size of their internal and external demand. By definition, income-a-head is low in underdeveloped countries, so that if the population is small and heads few, total income will be particularly low, the home market small and with only rather elementary demands. The foreign market will be large if the underdeveloped country has a particular resource not found elsewhere and if it is naturally accessible and its products not obstructed by artificial barriers such as tariffs and quotas. It is hypocritical of developed countries to advocate trade not aid, and then put up such barriers. A small internal market and little chance of export is, unfortunately, the position of the majority of underdeveloped countries.

Quite recently, in a book entitled *The Economic Consequences of the Size of Nations* (161), the conclusion was reached, on the basis mainly of a study of Belgium, Switzerland and Portugal, that a small size was little handicap to a country's efficiency and did not prevent sufficiently large plants being established in a variety of industries. The book was edited for the International Economic Association and contains contributions from some of the leading world economists. This is all the more unfortunate, as its conclusions are likely to be widely quoted and applied to the really small countries. For, after all, Belgium and Switzerland, if not Portugal, are, relatively to the great majority of underdeveloped countries, far from small. Belgium and Switzerland (Table I), had in 1957 an income-a-head of $920 and $1,223. With populations of about nine and five millions, their total national income was to be precise $8,270 and $6,259 million; that of Portugal without its colonies was $1,755 million. But, to quote only from the countries listed by Andic and Peacock (4), Jamaica had, that year, a total national income of only $410 million, Uganda $321, Honduras $320, Costa Rica $283, Ghana $273, Panama $246, Bolivia $222, and Paraguay $187. And many other countries not so listed (for instance, Liberia, Libya, Mauritania, and the other ex-French colonies of Africa) have equally low, if not lower, national incomes. In fact, of the countries usually counted as underdeveloped, only India, Turkey, Mexico, and Brazil had, in 1957, a larger total national income than either Switzerland or Belgium. Compared to the majority of underdeveloped countries, Switzerland and Belgium, if not Portugal, are not small but large economies.

Few, if any, underdeveloped countries export manufactures to the proportion of Belgium and Switzerland. The remainder, with neither an external market nor a large internal market, have too small a demand to organize plants of economically adequate size, except in those industries where even in developed economies small plants prevail or all sizes of plant are found. Examples of such industries appear under heading VII in Table XV. The selection of some of these industries is not a feasible project in countries where urbanization has not developed sufficiently to yield the external economies of localization. Other small-plant or cottage industries, however, are quite feasible in small-market underdeveloped countries. Some, such as milk-products and grain-milling, may be linked or rooted to the predominating agriculture; others make products in everyday low-income demand like bread. Others, again, like timber, wood containers, furniture, soft drinks make, out of materials in common supply, products costly to transport in relation to their value, and this relatively high transport cost applies to all repairing. Many small countries neglecting selection analysis, either import what they could make or, as with repairs, go without. Industrialization could often include more "import substitution."

It is largely because of the market limitations of small nations that political federations are advocated for many ex-colonies or, failing federation, some common market regions within which separate countries could specialize and produce some goods on a large scale. Unfortunately for standards of living, economic considerations, as the next Chapter will tell, get submerged in the political and sociological excitements of independence.

4. Resource Patterns Common to Underdeveloped Countries

After prescribing the industries fitted to the particular natural and market resources, we are left with certain resources or lack of resources common to almost all underdeveloped countries before development trends have set in. Selection of industries must now be reviewed in relation to these common features, which mostly fall under the headings in Table XII that follow market position and land, namely, capital, labour and management. The absence of capital has received by far the most attention, but the need for capital without distinction of type can be overstressed.

Among capital resources, a certain sector is now distinguished under the curious title of *infrastructure*. This sector comprises public utilities and the basic facilities which *aid* industry, and in distinguishing these industrial aids many years ago (60, pp. 371–5, p. 460), I noted they were often provided by the State, either free, or trading at a loss, at cost, or occasionally for a profit. The items I then listed as in the "industrial aid" class were comprised in transport and communications, provision of markets, supply of electricity, gas and water. No country can develop either industry or tourist services without these infrastructural facilities, and international aid has been channelled into this form of fixed capital as a preliminary "must" which is fairly certain to be relevant to a country's development.

It is when fixed capital for specific lines of manufacture has to be decided upon that selection becomes difficult, and that the careful analysis here being advocated becomes so necessary. The capital that can be supplied from the country itself is limited—mainly for sociological reasons discussed in the next chapter—and the capital that can be given or even lent as aid from abroad is not unlimited. So an agonizing choice has to be made between investment in various uses. Two schools of thought have been in open opposition. One assumes broadly that the return to successive doses of capital for any one use diminishes when other factors remain constant and advocates distribution among many uses so that the extra "marginal" return is equal in all uses. The other school believes with Rostow (168, 169) that take-off is not possible without massive development of some particular use, as textiles were developed in the English Industrial Revolution and railways were, later, in other countries. Apart from these early examples, it cannot be said that any empirical verification of the comparative advantages of these two policies is yet to hand. Meanwhile, practical policy should pay attention to the particular resources of the underdeveloped country being planned for, as well as to resources common to most underdeveloped countries and, once they are surveyed, invest in industries that fit these resources.

The short supply of capital resources in nearly all underdeveloped countries together with abundant labour points to priority for industries with a low intensity of capital compared to their labour content. The extreme examples of low intensity, appearing at least twice in Table XV, among its four indicators, include the clothing trades and leather goods, repair work (including locomotive shops), bread-baking, woodworking, and china-ware. Industries with high capital intensity, however, cannot always be avoided and a conflict of criteria does come up frequently between capital cost and the first-processing of underdeveloped countries' raw material. Heavy capital equipment is normally required to deal with the raw materials in such early process industries, cited in Table XV, as iron and non-ferrous manufacture, oil-refining, cement-making, sugar-refining, coke-ovens, and even grain-milling.

At this point we must meet the argument that the measurements of the characteristic traits obtained from a developed country such as Britain will not hold for the underdeveloped countries. This is undoubtedly true for the absolute measurements. We know already that power-a-worker is much lower *for the same industries* in Britain than in America and lower in certain underdeveloped countries than in Britain. But, relatively to one another, industries probably fall into much the same ranking in respect of capital intensity and other characteristics. We know this is true of Britain and America (69) in respect of power-a-worker. Bohr (20) shows similarity of ranking of twelve industry groups in respect of the ratio of fixed capital to value added in Australia, South Africa, and the United States. Exceptions to similar ranking may occur, however, where two quite different techniques are possible for the same industry, such as cottage hand-loom and mill power-loom weaving of cotton. Yet, even here, a certain uniformity of technique appears to be set when trading is the object. Cottage hand-spinning could not exist in trade competition with power spinning in India unless it was (153, pp. 74 *et seq.*) subsidized and, *a fortiori*, could presumably not exist under world competition. In short, the techniques that result in the measures given for British industries in Table XV are the result of internal and external trading competition over a long period, and the industries probably hold their relative rank fairly similarly in all countries. Observations, statistically recorded, have even shown that in spite of abundant cheap labour, the capital-intensive methods of performing particular industries may yet be economically the more efficient in the underdeveloped countries, as they are in developed countries. Labour-intensive techniques in these industries can then only be justified for reasons other than economic efficiency, such as absorbing labour that would otherwise be unemployed and which, in a welfare state, would be a cost, paid for by the taxpayer.

Proceeding with the survey of resources for the practical selection of industries according to fit, we now reach a country's human resources as factors of production. In fitting industries to the labour situation, policy must consider—

(i) The total of the available labour present and future and, in particular, how far a general economic mobilization would include women.

(ii) The present distribution of labour over agriculture, and industries, and among skilled and unskilled occupations and how far mobility allows change in distribution for the future.

(iii) The extent of literacy and numeracy.

(iv) The incidence of trade unions.

Most underdeveloped countries are short of skilled labour but have a plentiful supply of unskilled, illiterate, and willing though often ineffective men and boys, but (as Chapter II warned) only a limited mobilization of women. The reasons for this limitation and ineffectiveness are mainly sociological (including the low status of even skilled manual labour) and are discussed in the next chapter.

With insufficient resources in capital and skilled labour, management becomes particularly important. What capital exists must be utilized to the full, by standardization, shift-working, staggering hours, and stocking materials, to avoid machines waiting to be fed. Skill, often not fully discovered till after man-power surveys are undertaken, must be husbanded by dilution, work study and work planning, and the scientific management introduced by Frederick Taylor should not be despised. Unfortunately, underdeveloped countries as a whole are as short of persons fit for appointment to the management of large industrial firms as they are of capital. Sharing the English ruling-class disdain for a business career (63, pp. 245–8), particularly as a manufacturer rather than a merchant, the ex-British colonies have too many trained lawyers, too few trained engineers. They are short of potential for the type of manager now (following the trend) making the top decisions in the big industrial firms of the developed countries. Though thereby missing large-scale economies, industries may have to be preferred where high staff ratios or large size of plants or firms do *not* prevail.

Finally, any survey of resources must include the general "context" of industry and of the whole economy. By the economic context of industry as a resource, I refer to auxiliary facilities in which underdeveloped countries are often deficient, facilities leading particularly to external economies. They include organization for the collection or procurement of material and for the distribution of products; the services to advise small businesses (for instance, on the purchase of machinery) or to repair and maintain machines; or financial intermediaries such as banks and the money market, the stock exchange and the financial journals that form, as we have said, the entourage of joint-stock companies.

If industry has an immediate context in the general economic network, this whole network has a still wider political and sociological context in law and government. Most, if not all, underdeveloped countries suffer from a legal and political framework inadequate for economic development, often due to a colonial system where the government confined activity to keeping law and order. Many, for instance, have as yet no company law.

Much of a nation's basic facilities or infrastructure, in particular the roads, and also its education, are provided free, as well as a police and political administration adequate to maintain order and the rights to rewards for work. Facilities provided free require taxation, so that the fiscal system must come into the survey. This fiscal system should be ample and elastic enough for the State to be able to encourage industries to settle, not only by protective tariffs but by tax remissions at least until the infant industries are on their feet and large enough to be capable of trading competitively.

To sum up: industries that are footloose and would fit the *common* features of underdeveloped countries, that is, their shortage of capital, managers, and skilled labour but abundance of unskilled and illiterate male labour and their preoccupation with agriculture, are indicated in Table XV mainly under the headings linkage (especially with agriculture), capital intensity, labour composition, staff ratio, and size of plant. Industries to be selected should, in theory, then, not be capital-, skill- or management-intensive, and not dependent on employing women. They should be linked with agriculture, have a low staff ratio and small need of skilled labour and make goods to meet the more elementary needs of food, clothing, housing, and furniture.

Do the industries that are now actually present or absent in underdeveloped countries bear out these hypotheses and prescriptions?

(i) Industries first-processing agricultural products, either industrial products or food products, are usually present in all underdeveloped countries.

(ii) Labour- not capital-intensive industries are found in the presence of hand-loom weaving of textiles, in the extent of the clothing industries and in the absence, in all but the largest underdeveloped countries of such capital-intensive industries (unless subsidized) as aircraft, electrical engineering, iron and steel, and motor-car manufacturing.

(iii) The industries that appear to flourish, at least relatively, in underdeveloped countries can be found fairly exactly and comprehensively by comparing the "activity structures" of underdeveloped and developed countries. Classifications of industries are usually too different for different countries, but a chance of an exact comparison is presented in Puerto Rico, which answers the same census questions as the United States. Like other underdeveloped countries, the bulk of its workers is in agriculture. Yet of the twenty industry groups, Puerto Rico has a higher proportion of all manufacturing workers than the United States in four groups—tobacco manufactures (largely exported), food, leather and clothing—and has more than half of the United States' proportion in clay and stone products, and furniture. In none of the other fourteen groups does the Puerto Rico proportion rise above a quarter of that of the United States.

(iv) Industries apparently requiring a high staff ratio though not a particularly high capital intensity, such as the chemical group, are also absent or only found in a very rudimentary form in underdeveloped countries.

(v) Preliminary investigation of a number of countries suggests that some industries, like most food, clothing, and woodworking, fit all sizes of market and stages of development, that others, in particular textiles, pottery and glass, late-stage chemicals (such as soap, paints, or starch), and simple engineering, fit the middle stages and market sizes, others again, like the large-plant and intensely capitalized industries, fit only the later stages or larger market sizes. Much more research (and ergological interpretation) is required into the industries that are in fact flourishing at various stages of development and sizes of market, if the underdeveloped countries are to be wisely advised in their plans for industrialization.

5. THE CASE OF THE TOURIST TRADE

Few, if any, of the smaller underdeveloped countries export manufactures, and exportable commodities are hard to suggest. Yet one commodity capable of employing many persons in some underdeveloped countries, small or large, is very acceptable to a certain category of foreigner—the tourist. For some underdeveloped countries with an unfavourable visible balance of trade, the tourist trade is capable of reversing the balance; though invisible, tourism acts as an export. The countries where tourists go sell their attractions to the foreigner for his nation's currency, just as they sell the exported visible products of their industries. The characteristic of the exportability of products thus arises again. This time it is free of the fear of adverse tariffs (though not of a limit to the foreign exchange allowed to tourists). But there remains the possible drawback of an "import-content." If tourists have to be fed entirely with imported food and served by imported chefs, *garçons* and couriers, tourism will hardly contribute much to a country's national income.

Eire can be cited as a country benefiting greatly from the tourist trade. Its gross receipts in respect of tourism travel, etc., were in 1958, for instance, £34·6m. or as much as 28 per cent of its visible merchandise exports and re-exports. As relatively few Irish became tourists abroad, the net receipts were not far below the gross, and as Ireland is not a great food importer, the import-content of the food provided for the tourist was low.

Export markets require careful research to find what merchandise the foreigner demands, what limits his country's tariffs or quotas impose, and what competing exporters can supply cheaper. Similarly to any industry, the demands of the tourist market and its hazards must be carefully analysed by the country planning to develop tourism, with a view to discovering the demands of the type of tourist being attracted and likely to be attracted and, in competition with other tourist centres, the kind of attractions and facilities to supply and to encourage by tax concessions or direct subsidy. Tourists may (if on a cruise or motor tour) be one-day trippers, may plan to stay a week or a month, or may be retiring for life in foreign parts, as they do in Cheltenham or the Channel Islands. The day trippers and the poorer hiker or pilgrim are less important economically to most underdeveloped countries. Among week-long or month-long tourists, who are growing rapidly in number, great diversity is found. The elderly will want rest and shopping facilities and possibly lectures on what they are seeing; the young, recreation. Moreover, the demands of all types of tourist often seem strange, if not primitive, to the inhabitants. The study of their habits and wants is anthropology in reverse. The native must analyse the "white man."

Often I have found the actual and potential demands of the tourist uncatered for, because unknown. A questionnaire issued in winter to local guests in Jamaican hotels (44), who mostly turned out to be elderly couples, elicited their disappointment with the shops available. In particular, the American habit of bringing back gifts to friends and relatives and, particularly, children (for the elderly couples had plenty of grandchildren) was not understood, and thousands of dollars were thus lost to the island economy and taken back to the American continent. Moreover, the hotels—dotted at intervals along the north coast, east of Montego Bay—were isolated, and residents of the different hotels could not easily mix. In the winter season the few young people who could afford the trip were "lost" among the many elderly couples and soon left. In a Jamaican broadcast in 1958, I suggested accordingly that a New Town should be planned, with cafés, recreation facilities, and public beaches where the young from different hotels could mix, and with large-scale shops where the older tourists could find the wares they missed in the small hotel gift-shops. Again, in Jordan's Jerusalem it was not realized that the tourist would be keen but probably elderly and would be tired after the long visit to the Temple area. No suitable cafés existed where he could sit and rest, and no taxis were possible within the Walls to take him back to his hotel—and no hotel suitable for tourists was nearer than half a mile outside those walls!

These failures to meet tourist demands should not be smiled at as part of the simple minds of underdeveloped people. Let

us not forget the iron fixity of English meal (and drink) times
—also the procrastination of English waiters in bringing the
American his ice-water. Some rationalize this by contending
that ice is bad for the stomach, but this is hardly the point. The
customer, particularly the tourist customer, is always right.

The demand of the tourist is primarily for the particular
scenery, climate, history, and art or recreation which he cannot
find at home—demands which directly involve the services
of travel agents, attendants at museums, guides, transport
workers, maintenance men, and diggers at the sites. If he is at
some distance from his home and the tour takes longer than a
few hours he will demand, secondarily, refreshment during the
day and accommodation for the night. And there are tertiary
demands, such as obtaining souvenirs in shops.

Climate and scenery indeed are quite free. In Jamaica (44),
where 95 per cent of tourist expenditure could be assigned, only
6 per cent went to transport and 4 per cent to entertainment,
tourists paid roughly 50 per cent to hotels, 29 to shops, and
another 6 to food and drink outside hotels. Once inside the
country, the tourists' secondary or tertiary demands for accommodation and food or for shopping are thus the chief income
raisers, but the real leverage *under* tourist spending are the primary net attractions of travel and entertainment. The word *net*
points to certain drawbacks of travelling: the distance to be
covered (and paid for) from home or from other countries
likely to be visited, and certain worries of life abroad, including
possible language barriers and the risk of being cheated. Table
XIII lists the main considerations in eight columns. The main
types of the original positive attractions, the resources for tourism, can be summed up as five: climate, scenery, recreation (e.g
ski-ing, swimming, fishing), local colour, and the various cultural
interests which, avoiding sophistication, we shall call "art and
history." All but local colour have appeared in Table XII
under Natural and Quasi-natural Resources. Three columns
rate the drawbacks; those of distance may be measured in
money or, for the rich, in mere time. To tourists able to afford
it, air travel has brought islands, particularly, much "nearer" in
time and convenience.

To test the rating of resources, a few countries, most now
admitted tourist successes, are, in Table XIII, given marks

under these heads based partly on measurable fact, partly on subjective valuation. Recreation has higher marks in the under-developed countries because beaches are not already over-crowded by the local inhabitants. Equal weight is assigned to

TABLE XIII

ASSESSMENT BY RATING SCALE OF NATIONAL RESOURCES FOR TOURISTS*

Country	Climate	Scenery	Recreation	Art and History	Local Colour§	No Language and other snags†	Small Distance from Market		Total Rating out of 9 (Minimum 4)
							Original e.g. U.S.A.‡	As By-product	
Switzerland	0	1	1	0	0	½	1	1	4½
France: Paris	½	0	0	1	1	½	1	1	5
France: Riviera	1	½	1	0	0	½	1	1	5
Italy	½	½	½	1	½	0	1	1	5
Britain (parts of)	0	½	½	1	½	1	1	1	5½
Canada (parts of)	0	1	1	0	0	1	2	0	5
Mexico	1	½	0	½	1	0	2	0	5
Jordan	1	1	0	1	½	1	0	½	5
Jamaica	1	1	1	0	½	1	1	0	5½
Israel	1	0	1	0	½	1	0	½	4
Ceylon	1	1	½	½	½	1	0	0	4½
Puerto Rico	1	½	1	0	½	0	1	0	4
Greece	1	1	1	1	½	0	0	½	5

* Particularly as attractive to American tourists

† e.g. Dishonesty, spitting on pavement, etc. High cost of living should also be taken into account but varies from year to year. If stay is long it may become as important as cost of travel, i.e. distance from market

‡ Maximum 2 points

§ e.g. Calypsos, trooping, folk-dancing, bazaars, festivals

each of the headings except distance from original market, i.e. home (e.g. the home of the largest tourist purchasing power, the United States of America), which is weighted double. To the average tourist, the distance away is no doubt more important than any other single consideration. Nearly 50 per cent more United States' citizens visited Canada, Mexico, Central America, and the Caribbean than visited Europe and the Mediterranean. Less important, perhaps, and certainly less easily measured than distance, are the snags of language and behaviour such as spitting or wolf whistling. Honesty and con-

sideration for tourists, even by customs officials, is important.
If a country once gets a reputation, "has an image," of cheating
taxi-drivers or shopkeepers or fierce officials, many tourists may
well keep away.

Once market research establishes the type of potential
tourist and the rating of tourist attractions, publicity can function more effectively. Advertisement can be concentrated on
the organs read by the likely tourist—for instance, church
periodicals for visitors to Jordan's Holy Places. Statements and
pictures must tally with the real facts and developments. Some
countries publicize what they have not got, others miss out
telling points for the tourist. For instance, Jordan records its
temperatures, humidity, and rainfall, but omits hours of sunshine, and officials were surprised to learn that northern Euro-
peans were interested in such a humdrum statistic.

So much for the demand side of the tourist trade and its
stimulation. If, on the supply side, we measure the characteristics of the tourist trade according to the headings of
Table XV the primary distinguishing traits will be found under
headings I, V, and VI—connected with the market, with
localization in places where tourists' primary demands are
satisfied, and with seasonality.

Unlike most other services, such as retailing and transport,
the tourist trade is localized and is not dispersed wherever the
consumer-population is found. In fact, by very definition, it
must be plied away from the consumers' home. Planning for
the tourist trade, therefore, follows the same principles as
planning for any manufacturing industry which is rooted and
material-oriented, and must localize in the relatively few places
in the world that possess tourist attractions. In wide regions—
the Middle West and Great Plains of North America, the
Steppes of Russia, the Midland and Northern coal-fields of
England—there are few tourist attractions whatever. It happens,
however, that many countries which suffer economically from
being a small market (for instance, the Caribbean islands,
Jordan, Greece, or Ceylon) possess the very resources that prove
attractive to tourists throughout their entire area.

While extreme localization of the tourist trade favours certain areas and the trade is growing, it exhibits a concentrated
time as well as *place* incidence of demand—in short, considerable

M

seasonality. The extreme of seasonality is found in Jordan, with its rush of pilgrims and sightseers to Jerusalem and Bethlehem at Christmas and Easter. Seasonality is normally due, however, not to particular feasts in the toured country but to the annual work-cycle of the tourists. It must always be the object of a country's tourist trade to fill in the off-season and get the maximum yearly occupancy of hotels and the other overhead facilities. Switzerland succeeded, thanks to the importation of ski-ing from Norway, and Jordan should succeed with its variety of climate, from Jericho, almost a thousand feet below sea-level, to Jerusalem, nearly four thousand feet above.

Besides its seasonal fluctuations, the tourist trade is uncertain and risky—in the economist's useful phrase, it is highly "income-elastic." For the working-class, holiday (150, p. 107), expenditure rates a higher elasticity than any product listed in Table XV, 1 F. With rising incomes, people take avidly to tourism; with falling incomes, tourism is often the first form of expenditure to be cut out. And, in addition to depending on the prosperity of the tourists' own country, the trade is highly sensitive to possible crises and revolutions in the country to be toured.

Apart from extreme localization and seasonality, the characteristics of the tourist trade's complex of natural attractions, services, and facilities present generally a more favourable fit to the resources of underdeveloped countries than do most manufactures. The trade is labour- rather than capital-intensive, can employ women, older men, and boys, and does not always have to be large-scale! The *bistro* can flourish side by side with Savoy grills. Though feasible in many countries, the trade cannot, however, be captured without effort. It requires basic transport facilities, a modicum of literacy, including foreign languages, skill in cooking, waiting, and guiding, and is management-intensive with high staff ratios.

A particular advantage to underdeveloped countries is the tourist trade's linkages with manufacturing industries, such as the craft work that can fashion souvenirs, always provided they are not imported from, say, Birmingham. These are the *by-demands* of tourism. Other industries, such as furniture-making and pottery, are helped by the adding of hotel to home demands. Thus this linkage brings us to the repercussions and percolation of the tourist trade over the whole economy and to the workings of two forces to which economists have for long drawn attention: external economies and the multiplier.

Internal economies, it will be remembered, arise with the growth in size of the plant or firm; external economies with the growth of a whole industry regardless of the size of its constituent units. Wherever the tourist trade grows many units may flourish, either in the same line of business or in co-operating lines, to meet the primary, secondary, and tertiary demands of the tourist. After disporting himself or being shown the sights and sites, he must be fed and rested, and in the afternoons and evenings sold souvenirs and entertained. All these lines of business co-operate to keep the tourist interested and happy, and, if possible, never bored. His pleasure should be unalloyed, and the external diseconomies of the sight and smell of gas-works or factory chimneys (reminding, perhaps, of toil back home) kept away, together with unsightly posters, and hoardings and beggars. The Welfare State has its uses even here!

Making a civic survey for the planning of Worcester (85), my colleagues and I recommended this town, suffering from the loss of industry, as said earlier, for a tourist centre. Its resources were its own attractions as a cathedral city on a fine river and proximity to Stratford on Avon and the Malvern hills. But this selection involved the removal from the riverside of certain workshops and the zoning of noxious factories to leeward of the winds found to be prevailing over a ten-year period. The mere size of the resort is important. The external economies of the tourist trade will be greater the larger the resort up to a point, but after a certain size, scenery and recreational facilities will suffer from the diseconomies of urbanization. It is probably significant that no town founded on its tourist attraction, even if it has attracted "life" residents as well, contains more than 300,000 inhabitants. Miami is probably the largest, and numbered 292,000 in 1960. The largest British tourist resorts are Brighton, with Hove, and Bournemouth, with Poole, each just short of 250,000 inhabitants. Blackpool has about 150,000, but no other British resort has more than 90,000.

The multiplier was first used to estimate how investment in

public works would give employment to the unemployed, indirectly, round by round, as well as directly; it can be applied to underdeveloped countries so long as they, too, have resources unemployed. Investment in *construction* of hotels and other capital facilities for tourists gives immediate employment to building workers. In this, the first round, greater advantage usually accrues to an underdeveloped country than in factory-building, because stone or brick and the skilled builders for hotels are usually found locally, whereas the machines, steel structure, and the construction workers for factories have usually to be imported. In the second round the workers building hotels and other facilities spend most of their earnings in retail shops on consumer goods. Similarly, in the third round shop-assistants and shopkeepers and the wholesalers and producers of the goods earn and spend most of their earnings on further goods and services. At each round there is, however, some money spent on materials which may be imported, and out of wages some saving, and spendings at home get less.

The conception of the multiplier arises in the original investment in hotels and other tourist facilities. A process of multiplication also occurs with a number of rounds in their operation. In selecting the hotel trade for investment, the relevant question is how far its operation compares in generation of income and employment with operations after investment in manufacturing or agriculture. Each round involves one of three patterns: a three-element pattern, as in selling souvenirs, where materials, wages, and profits are involved; a two-element pattern, where services such as transport and entertainment involve only payments to wages and profits; or a plain one-element pattern like tipping. Wages (including salaries) are mainly paid over, like tips, to retailers. Materials are mainly bought by payments to wholesalers or direct to producers. Home retailers, wholesalers, and producers then all repeat in the next round the threefold pattern of profits–wages–materials. Gross profits go in taxes, in plough-back, and depreciation, or else in dividends, and it is relevant to know how far dividends are distributed to citizens or to foreigners.

The advantages to national income and employment of the operations of tourism and hotel-keeping over most manufacturing lie—

(i) In the greater labour content of the services involved. Little material is used in transport and entertainment and much labour, often skilled, in waiting, guiding, and cooking.

(ii) In the high food content of the materials, much of which could be raised in underdeveloped countries with their high agricultural occupation.

(iii) In the by-demand of the hotel guests for mementos and souvenirs, many of which could be made locally, in small craft shops.

Multiplier effects work so long as resources are unemployed; but, especially in a small country, importation of goods and services from foreign sources may soon have to occur and the multiplier stops. Resources for growing high-quality food will, if they do not exist, have to be built up if tourists are not to involve high food imports. The tourist trade should, indeed, stimulate agriculture.

If we are to go beyond mere theory, its empty boxes must be filled with the actual proportions of the income and the workers employed. A realistic investigation of this sort was undertaken in Jamaica starting from a hotel-by-hotel, item-by-item analysis of the provenance of hotel purchases, whether from home or from foreign sources. The conclusion (44, p. 299) was that, even excluding tips, 60·7 per cent of tourists' expenditure remained in Jamaica. The import-content roughly of two-fifths is, for a small economy, low compared to the machinery and raw-material imports required for all but first-stage manufactures rooted to local resources.

6. Aid, Trade, and Planning

However ideologically repugnant to the capitalist outlook, accustomed till recently only to annual budgets for *government* expenditure, most underdeveloped countries have been advised for practical reasons to adopt *national* plans extending over a period of years. National planning can be defined (72, pp. 267–8) by—

> pointing to its opposite, the market mechanism whereby, to quote Adam Smith (173, IV–2), "every individual . . . neither intends to promote the public interest, nor knows how much he is promoting it. . . . He intends only his own gain; and he is in this . . .

led by an invisible hand to promote an end which was no part of his intention."

In contrast, national planning is an intention to promote the public interest by the more or less visible hand of the State. Fully fledged it is (72, pp. 267–8) "an acknowledgement of intentions embodied in prearranged tasks based on knowledge of existing conditions and controlled or carried out by an organized structure which should include a review of the progress of the plan." The tasks must be logically co-ordinated and the *organized structure* state-controlled, either by nationalization or by offering private-enterprise incentives (tax remission, tariffs, cheap facilities) for the carrying out of the national plans. Applied to the underdeveloped countries *intention* is essentially to increase standards of living (as consciously stated in the Indian plan) by setting "targets" for national income and the proportion to be invested, in hopes of a "take-off"; embodiment in prearranged *tasks* (the programme) includes industrialization and tourist facilities which have just been discussed on the basis of *knowledge* of existing resources. Facilities, both for industry and tourists, such as machines for factories, or plumbing equipment for hotels, can, in most underdeveloped countries, be obtained at present only from abroad, either by "trading" exports or by aid in loans or grants from state-governments or the United Nations, or else by loans from private capitalists.

The facts of international trade are tolerably well recorded; the total visible and invisible items of merchandise and service and the balance of payment are measured and these statistics available for many countries. The classical "colonial" pattern for underdeveloped countries is for their visible exports and imports to balance or even for their exports to exceed imports in a "favourable" balance. Their exports are normally raw materials, food or fuel of a few categories, such as coffee, tea, citrus fruits, rubber, copper, tin, iron ore or oil produced under the control of capitalist firms in the developed countries, and paying them dividends—hence the frequent "favourable" balance. The imports are manufactured goods, particularly metal capital goods. This type of trading is the opposite, but, since world exports and imports must be equal in value, it is the necessary counterpart of the highly developed British, Dutch, or Belgian through-put economy measured in the first chapter, and may indeed be part-cause of the colonial empires of those countries. Materials are extracted—pulled out—from the land for manufacture abroad and for feeding the manufacturers, and manufactures, normally capital goods, such as machinery and vehicles, or parts of them and tools of industry generally, are taken back in exchange for the products of the extractive industries. In contrast to the "through-put" it is a "pull-out take-back" economy, equally measurable statistically in its export and import structure. This "colonial" *economic* trading structure is likely to persist yet awhile, whatever *political* changes may occur.

In some underdeveloped, as in developed countries, there is an unfavourable international balance of payments on account of the visible items, due to the invisible items, including foreign grants, loans, and credits. Malta, for instance, imports many times the value of merchandise that she exports; but makes up some of the difference by the invisible items of service in ship repairing and maintenance, tourism, and remittances home of emigrants.

Other underdeveloped countries, Jordan for instance, have an unfavourable total balance of trade, visible and invisible, a gap that can be made up for only by aid in gifts or loans. Such aid cannot be indefinitely multiplied. The number of possible aiding countries is limited and the calls are heavy upon their resources for social welfare at home and for their own development. Underdeveloped countries must, therefore, increase their exports or substitute home production for imports. Though a high proportion of their workers are found in agriculture, many underdeveloped countries actually import more food than they export, and often there is an economic case worth research for increasing food production as import-substitution, rather than industrializing. Certainly, in underdeveloped countries, as Myrdal says (143, p. 227) "however rapidly industralization proceeds, the great masses of their working populations will for decades and, perhaps, generations, be employed in agriculture, and the levels of living of the rural masses will mainly be determined by their productivity there."

To get back to the overall plan, targets, which must include trade and agriculture as well as mining, are measured statistically in money or heads and must be internally consistent. These measurements, not simply for government budgets, but for the nation as a whole, mark great progress in the application of statistics to economic and social affairs—mark in fact a new discipline of social accounting, not yet, unfortunately, appreciated or understood in some civil services. Often included in these targets are the proposed government expenditure or budget, and income ceilings for salaries, wages, and dividends, and some estimate by projection of the increase in population and the labour force. But the framework essential for development consists in planned changes in four statistical task or target aggregates which should combine satisfaction of intentions or goals with a realistic appreciation of what is feasible.

(i) *The Gross National Product*

When income from abroad is added and the excess of indirect taxation over subsidies subtracted, total domestic expenditure becomes this G.N.P. It is the national income used for calculating the average income a head.

(ii) *The Total of Employment*

This aggregate, partly dependent, partly independent of gross national product, is particularly important for underdeveloped countries because of their high unemployment and underemployment, and the liability of both to rise still higher with the fast increase in population. In some plans the employment target only reckons, in fact, to mop up the addition to unemployment due to population added.

The employment target is independent of gross product, particularly where investment saves labour and more is produced with less labour; or where fuller use of existing capital is planned, for instance, by working shifts. And sometimes the total employment is kept up, uneconomically, with no greater product by "feather-bedding" labour. The employment target will, of course, favour the selection of labour-intensive industries and thus often exclude the capital-intensive heavy industries which might eventually have greatly increased the national product.

(iii) *Exports*

The amount to be exported is not always stated in plans; indeed, for underdeveloped countries relying on agricultural or mining products, export values are extremely fluctuating and unpredictable. Recently, in fact, the prices of such raw commodities have fallen considerably and the "terms of trade" (export in relation to import prices) have, for the underdeveloped countries, worsened. This implies that, to import the necessary machines and capital equipment, underdeveloped countries must export more of their produce in volume.

(iv) *Capital Investment*

Total (gross including, net excluding, depreciation and maintenance) of capital and services for sectors, e.g.—

For *agriculture*.

For *industry* making capital or consumer goods.

For *infrastructure*, i.e. basic aids for industry and agriculture (such as transport facilities, power generation, water supplies, communication, irrigation schemes).

For *education*, especially technical.

For *research* and exploration.

The second Indian plan (1956–61) had, for instance, the following key figures for its framework of target increases over the previous period.

	Percentage
Total national product	+25
Total employment 10–12 millions	+12
Capital investment increased from 7 per cent to 11 per cent of national product distributed as follows—	
To agriculture and community development . . .	11·8
To industry which may be divided into subsectors (e.g. capital or consumer goods) or into control segments (e.g. public, small crafts, companies)	18·5
To transport, shipping, roads, etc.	28·9
To irrigation and power	19·0
To social services, including education	19·7
To miscellaneous	2·1

India is more developed than most underdeveloped countries. Typical of planned investment programmes in countries relying more on plantations is that for Malaya, 1956–60. Here, agriculture, especially rubber growing, was to increase 23·4 per cent, but industry and mining only 1·9 per cent. The same high proportion, however, goes to infrastructure: for India it was, as just shown, 28·9 + 19·0 = 47·9 per cent, for Malay 41·5 per cent. Econometrics is now applied in planning. A useful example in a fast-developing country is that of Chenery and

Bruno (37) applied to Israel. The investment ratio and the national product targets are quantitatively related and must be consistent. If capital investment is increased it will subsequently increase national product, the precise extent depending upon the capital/output coefficient and the "multiplier," which may vary from time to time. Most underdeveloped countries have capital investment ratios considerably below that of developed countries, and if education is included as an investment the distance between the two, as Kuznets suggests (118), becomes still wider.

The knowledge of a country's resources (as surveyed in Table XII) which is part of national planning often shows up the practical *economic* limits on plans, let alone the *sociological* limits to be discussed later.

To the factors important in plans for *all* countries mentioned in the last chapter, Chenery and Bruno add, apart from the inflow of foreign resources, two that are particularly important for the countries as yet underdeveloped: the present and future composition of demand; and ability to plan and carry out development activities.

As for demand, when the total invested is subtracted from the gross national product, together with direct taxation, then privately spendable income-a-head will not, if population is increasing fast, grow much, if at all. This, alas, has been the experience of many a planner. If a country is ultimately to be viable it will certainly not do to expect too rapid an increase in present private standards of living. Nehru put it bluntly (143, p. 354) "self-help and self-reliance is the thing, and austerity is at present the prerequisite for future prosperity." Social contacts with the affluent world make austerity hard. Nurkse (145, p. 62) notes the "demonstration effect": "It is much easier to adopt superior consumption habits than improved production methods. . . . The temptation to copy American consumption patterns tends to limit the supply of investible funds by inhibiting the willingness to save." Other economists have pointed, however, to the incentive to production presented by the desire to "keep up" with the Americans. In fact, total productivity is likely to go up; and the *proportion* "saved" as already said is not a useful concept where consumption is inadequate for efficiency.

In view of the increase in population and the sociological obstacles to production, saving and taxation set forth in the next chapter, ability to plan and carry out development activities, in order to raise standards of living by trade and home investments alone, is probably not possible for the bulk of underdeveloped countries in the immediate future. Only a few, such as Japan certainly, and Israel or Puerto Rico probably, have achieved or are approaching a "take-off" when they can rely on their own resources. The practical question is thus at what points the necessary aid should now be applied with the prospect of building up trade in the long run. Part of the answer already given is selecting the specific industries and services to fit the specific markets and resources, material and human, of a country, bearing in mind the balance of payments. Priority in aid must be given to these particular "fit" industries and services, and to the particular bottleneck factors of production in short supply, whether it be capital, management, working skill, or research.

Our survey of markets and resources threw up, in particular, the need to develop large-scale management, at least in manufacturing for export or import substitution and in the tourist trade. Rostow (168, p. 50) has pointed to the need in any "take-off" of a group within any underdeveloped country which is prepared to accept innovations. But there is a scarcity too, of routine managers and of research specialists and in fact, as our third trend of development indicated, of all persons educated enough to form an industrial staff. Whether in agriculture, manufacturing industry, tourism, or infrastructure, investment involving postponement of immediate consumption may be in material capital, or in services such as education and research, or both; and it would be useful always to set forth in plans a percentage of national product to be invested in education and training for management and also applied research, similar to the percentage usually given for capital investment. The type of investment is not independent of the industry invested in, since, as the Appendix shows, some industries are capital-intensive, others management-, research-, or labour-intensive. But, in general, the supply of management, as of all staff and skilled workers, is short in the underdeveloped countries.

In the countries now developed the art of management was,

in the early years of their industrial revolutions, mainly picked up by experience in small-scale entrepreneurship. This system had its inefficiencies, notably nepotism, which, in the wide kinship sociology of underdeveloped countries, might be carried to even greater breadths. If development is not to take the whole century it did in most of the developed countries, education for management must play a large part. Wherever markets and the location of materials permit, large plants have already been set up (and are likely to be set up faster)—many of them nationalized. Successful large-scale managers are thus less likely to be of the ex-entrepreneur and more of the trained administrator type.

Sociological obstacles are probably less formidable, as we shall see, in education and research than in the necessary local saving and capital investment. If aid is eventually to promote trade, investment in education may well in the long run, lead to more net export or import substitution per unit of aid expenditure than investment in capital. Whatever education and research is invested in, may take place either at home in the aided, or abroad in the aiding country; and in either location education may be either in school or else in learning on the job. When at home, in fact, nationals are quite often attached as apprentices or "fellows" in a United Nations technical assistance project.

Much less has been written about investment in human capital, in education and research, than in material capital, and we cannot finish this chapter without some pointers to the needs and practical directions of such investment—

(i) The scarcity of management and skill is mainly the result of past restriction of the higher appointments and even of skilled workmanship to the colonizers. A local *élite* of skilled technicians, experts, and managers must be educated and trained to fill the more responsible posts now at last open to the ex-colonials. Many authorities have asserted that this training must, if funds are limited, be instituted at all costs, even that of postponing universal elementary education and risking a mandarin class of superior intellectuals.

(ii) In higher education a practical turn must be encouraged and nationals sent abroad to read for University degrees in engineering and management or, probably better value for money, similar courses established at home. Models are to hand in the courses for the B.Com. degree, introduced into modern British Universities beginning with Birmingham in 1900, and in the first and higher degrees in Business Administration found in American Universities and Institutes of Technology.

(iii) Industrial Management and tourist catering follow certain principles common to all branches of business, and all students in commerce or administration can be taught certain tool-subjects, such as accounting, commercial law, statistics, and econometrics, and the use of English, as well as market research and economics. Sir William Ashley, first dean of the Faculty of Commerce at Birmingham, considered these subjects capable of forming a liberal education provided that the *rationale* or (as I should say) the *logic* of their procedures was made clear.

Other, more specialized subjects could be added to the curriculum according to the special career envisaged. For manufacturing, elementary engineering; for hotel management, foreign languages and some sociology to explain and cope with foreign behaviour, also, perhaps, elementary plumbing!

(iv) Training its citizens abroad, either in Technological Colleges and Universities or in the field, or both, will be necessary till a country has sufficient training facilities and staff at home. This points to the high priority of training students abroad who will be willing to return home as teachers, eventually to train industrial staff or further teachers at home.

(v) Many of the natural conditions and resources of underdeveloped countries in climate, soil, oil, minerals, and, above all, water are not yet known and require geological and meteorological survey and research. Until experts can complete surveys, only a temporary plan can be laid down as to which of the "rooted" industrial, agricultural, mining, and tourist activities depending immediately on these resources should be developed, and to what extent. In the course of the surveys nationals can be trained as experts.

(vi) Before costly investment is undertaken in industry,

staff, foreign and national, is required for "preinvestment" "feasibility" studies. To attract tourists, preinvestment surveys are also required of possible sites for national parks and recreation facilities and for archaeological excavations. A further research might well examine what monuments and scenery are worth protection from hoardings, bill-boards, and other tourist deterrents.

CHAPTER VII

SOCIOLOGICAL LIMITS TO ECONOMIC DEVELOPMENT

1. Conditions for Economic Success: the Tripod for Higher Living Standards

PLANS were outlined in the last chapter to develop industries and some services in hitherto underdeveloped countries so that the higher standards of living which these countries desired could be attained. These plans looked toward trade rather than aid for the long-run solution and were mainly economic in selecting as likely to be successful industries and services with characteristics fitting the characteristic resources of the country.

Man is not a purely economic creature, and the question must now be raised how far his total nature and circumstances will allow these plans to come to fruition. The question is particularly pertinent when, returning to Table I, we realize that in many underdeveloped countries average income is rising less fast than in developed countries and that, instead of narrowing, the gap between the two groups is widening.

As stated by Andic and Peacock (4), "the *relative* position of the less developed countries has worsened considerably." While the 40 per cent poorest people had, in 1949, 6·5 per cent of the aggregate world income, in 1957 they had only 5·0 per cent.

Owing to the fall in the value of money, it is difficult to reckon the absolute change in the real income-a-head of individual countries between 1949 and 1957. But Table I measured, as explained, the relative changes since 1949 compared to total world change. Only three of the ten richest countries in 1949 (they were the same as in 1957) fell relatively in income-a-head: Britain, Denmark, and New Zealand. But among the poorest countries in 1949, though a few rose fast, a higher proportion fell relatively, among which Burma, Pakistan, India, and Bolivia are conspicuous. Why, in spite of aid, did the gap between the underdeveloped and developed countries widen instead of narrowing?

The most obvious check to the success of aid and other plans for raising standards of living is the standard of living itself. A high proportion of people in underdeveloped lands are physically on the verge of starvation and thus incapacitated from working full out. Even though sufficiently fed, once they obtain employment, semi-starvation in childhood may leave its mark. To quote a Colonial Office survey (144, p. 119.), "the listless, apathetic and ineffective Africans of farm and field, of shamba and street corners, bear upon them the brand of malignant malnutrition."

This conclusion is important for practical policy of aid or trade. If underdeveloped countries increase exports by turning from subsistence farming to specialized agricultural produce their own nutrition may suffer. In any case the productivity of labour might often be raised and trade helped in its competition with other countries by aid for feeding workers quite as much as by equipping them with machines or other capital. Thus, if investment is defined not just as a possible result of saving out of consumption but as any spending, including consumption of food, for the sake of greater capacity to produce in the future, then, paradoxically, such consumption would count as investment, just as would technical education. Certainly investment in capital and education may have little effect on the worker's productivity, if, however well educated and equipped, he is going hungry.

Another physical circumstance possibly limiting productive capacity is climate. Some underdeveloped countries are certainly enervating, particularly in their low-lying tropical areas. Other underdeveloped regions, however, such as the fertile Middle East and Northern Africa, set in the midst of desert, are stimulating. Climate may explain the low income-a-head of some underdeveloped countries but not of all of them. And with the gradual elimination of tropical diseases, physical geography is likely to play a less important role in limiting development. The main causes for limitation must then be sought *behind* incapacitation by semi-starvation and enervation.

Why should men be starving? Colin Clark tells us (41, pp. 503–4) that the Dutch return in product per square mile is six times the Indian, and if all the cultivable land in the world were farmed at Dutch standards of skill and hard work the world could support at least four times its present population. This, obviously, is a big *if*, but calls for an answer to the question why Indians and other underdeveloped peoples do not in fact exhibit the hard work and skill which developed people do. The basic obstacles in the path are neither natural, physical, technological, nor economic, but sociological. This point was put clearly by many physical scientists at the special Plenary Session on Food and Population of the British Association for the Advancement of Science at Cardiff in 1960.

H. D. Kay, an Emeritus Professor of Biochemistry, may be quoted (104, pp. 58–9)—

> Sociology and social psychology have for some time been accepted as sciences, and it is perhaps in these growing regions of knowledge that scientific research and the application of existing techniques and of future findings is going to be most fruitful in solving some of the more stubborn, long-term problems of many of the hungry countries. There is as much need, in my view, to lessen the psychological and social handicaps which harass these countries as there is to remedy shortage of capital and the almost complete absence of modern agricultural technique. . . . It is *not* shortage of basic scientific knowledge nor of sound and practical methods for applying it to agriculture or dietetics that is the major obstacle to fairly speedy improvement of nutrition in most of the hungry countries. . . . It is rather the extreme slowness of implementation of that knowledge, a slowness caused by political, sociological and psychological obstacles, to overcome which effective techniques have still to be found.

In the content of this present book, political and social psychological are included in the title *sociological*; and in the last chapter greater integration will be urged for these social sciences with economics and with natural sciences. In the present context of the underdeveloped countries the need will become particularly obvious of integrating social anthropology, human geography, demography, social psychology, and even political science.

Before setting forth sociological factors, as an explanation of *continued* low standards of living, we must, however, call to mind what exactly has to be explained. The standard of living refers to a *minimum stable income per head below which no one* (or at most

N

only a small fraction of the population) *will fall*. The standard of living is thus a tripod standing upon three legs: the total national income; the number of heads; and the form of distribution of income among those heads. Standards of living may fail of achievement because the total national production and income is too small, heads too many, or forces making for more equal distribution too weak. Each of these three legs of the tripod will, in the following sections, be examined in turn for sociological causes of failure.

2. SOCIOLOGICAL OBSTACLES TO GROWTH OF PRODUCTION

The first leg on which a high standard of living rests is high national production analysed (in Chapter II) into the elements of productivity, proportion occupied among the population, and structure of occupations or industries. Plans for raising national production were discussed in the previous chapter, but in spite of aid from abroad, only slow progress was noted in most underdeveloped countries. They were in fact so far behind the developed countries in their production that it seems too optimistic to assert that they are in the stage just previous to the Industrial Revolution—that of England, for instance, in the early eighteenth century. Judging from the standards of living of the bulk of their population, their economy is more like that of England in the Middle Ages, if not the Dark Ages. What hope exists, then, of any substantial raising of productivity in the course of, say, a century instead of a millennium?

The main hope held out in the previous chapter was the experience and knowledge already acquired by the developed countries which can be handed on immediately through the direct advice and action by citizens of the developed countries, and, in the longer run, through the education of the local inhabitants. Lack of knowledge appears at first sight the easiest obstacle to overcome, since knowledge can be taught and teaching is labour- not capital-intensive. Most underdeveloped people are eager for education and for training as teachers, and do in fact readily learn and teach. The only obstacle appears to be insufficient financial aid to education.

But, looking below the surface, obstacles to education often have a deeper sociological foundation than the purely financial. Even when funds are available, it is often not the most suitable candidates who are trained as teachers. In many a country, particularly where the Mohammedan religion prevails, women, the most suitable teachers for younger children, are likely to be barred, whether educated or not, from leaving the shelter of their home after attaining marriageable age. Furthermore, if finance and teachers are available, the teaching curriculum is often unsuitable. In Mohammedan countries much of the time in elementary school is spent reciting the Koran, a mere feat of verbal memory. At later stages the prestige value of universities teaching law and "cultural" subjects (particularly where Oxbridge influence is still strong) takes precedence over faculties of commerce, technology, and, of course, over the secondary schools that would prepare candidates for universities, whatever they teach. In consequence, universities are handicapped by the poorly prepared material they receive and do not make the contribution they might to economic development.

Let us, however, suppose the obstacles to have been surmounted which check the education in technology and management of at least some inhabitants of underdeveloped countries. Can these "key" men, or *élite*, rapidly change the economy of their countries and lead them toward a take-off?

Underdeveloped economies are not all, of course, at the same sociological stage, particularly in their organization of agriculture. Two types of general economy are usually distinguished, that of a price system centred on a market and that of State authority. Much of the economy of the underdeveloped economies follow, however, neither system, but is ordered by social tradition and custom in broadly speaking one of three subsystems: the feudal estate with landlord (often an absentee) and serfs or peons as still prevalent in Latin America; the independent peasant; and the primitive community. In the last two there is little differentiation of employer and employed in production, and all three subsystems subsist on their own. Whole communities, or single peasant families or feudal estates, produce wholly or mainly for their own consumption. There is little cash crop and exchange of goods or services is exceptional.

Compared to that for sociology, particularly social anthropology, there is little scope for economic theory. Obstacles to

production can usefully be considered under the standard four
"factors of production" only if the effects are noted of different
sociological stages, particularly, in contrast to the market economy, the traditional tribal and communal organization. In
virtually all underdeveloped countries sociological obstacles
check (A) labour productivity, (B) land productivity; and also
(C) capital, and (D) management formation as well as productivity.

A. Obstacles to labour productivity take at least five forms—

(i) In the primitive communal organization the product of
the individual worker is submerged in the group. The labour
situation is indeed the prototype of that which Mayo found in
the Hawthorne factory. Lewis (121, p. 59) puts forward two
definite limits to what can be achieved by communal organization. There must be *local* benefit, "the villagers will build
a minor road connecting their village to a main road, but
they will not build a main road for all and sundry, without
payment"; and *general* benefit, the work "must not be
obviously of much greater advantage to some than the rest."
Communal action, he considers also is limited to "stable
economic situations where routine action is all that is required and no industrial initiative." Emerging from the
primitive community to be employed in industry is far from
an easy transition. Clark Kerr (105) distinguishes the early
stages as that of the uncommitted worker who earns money
in industry for a single specific purpose, such as the price of a
bride, and then returns to his community; and that of the
semi-committed worker whose wife and family remain on the
tribal land and to whom the worker returns periodically to
help in cultivation. In terms of "labour cohesion" used
earlier (IV, §8) for developed countries, the uncommitted will
have a high labour turnover, the semi-committed a high
absence rate. Both such relapses increase industrial cost and,
moreover, make any long training of workers not worth while.

(ii) Under all social forms of organization the most
obvious example of an obstacle to the contribution of labour
is its deliberate *in*capacitation during the periods of fasting,
often followed by all-out feasting, as commanded by certain
religions. During Ramadan, which lasts over a month, for

instance, true Mohammedans do not eat during daylight and all have to wake long before dawn to partake of breakfast. They do not eat again till sunset. The loss of food and sleep and the irregularity of meal-times combine to lower physical productivity and increase irritability. Nor do the days of feasting that follow help to make up the output lost.

(iii) Not only may the work of the given labour force be restricted but industrial work may, for certain classes of people, absolutely be taboo. The outstanding case is that of women, not only in Mohammedan but other cultures, and the proportion of women to men occupied in industry has been shown as far lower in most underdeveloped than in developed countries. Economists would expect logically that poverty would stimulate more women to work in industry and thus help with the family income in the poorer than in the richer countries. But where so many men are unemployed or underemployed, this is sociologically "unthinkable."

(iv) Loss of industrial labour and a lower mobilization also occurs where idleness has respectability if not positive prestige, and fit persons must be carried by the economy as passengers. The beggars of India come to mind and those monks of many lands who do not engage in production, directly or indirectly.

(v) Finally, obstacles to labour mobility such as caste-systems tend to restrict output since the worker potentially best able to tackle a particular job may be tied to another for which he is not fitted and demand for workers unsatisfied in one job cannot be supplied from another. Immobility affects equality of incomes still more than total income and will be further considered later.

(B) The productivity of land affects agriculture rather than industry, but agriculture occupies the majority of the workers in underdeveloped countries, and we cannot, when discussing the general standard of living of any country, omit consideration of its major economic activity. Moreover, industrialization and tourism may fail to bring a higher net standard of living, if agriculture is not developed and any addition to gross income from industry and tourism has to be spent on importing raw materials and food.

Now, it is precisely in agricultural development and the productivity of land that sociological obstacles are strongest. The traditional communal system of holding and working the land Lewis (121 p. 121) considers to be now far from allowing the land to yield its potential product. "Communal tenures worked passably in Africa so long as populations were very small in relation to land, but population pressure everywhere causes such tenures to . . . handicap innovation. Livestock cannot be bred selectively unless they are segregated and their mating controlled; neither is it convenient to experiment with new agricultural methods."

Under less primitive organization, where individual peasant subsistence-farming prevails, the legal system of land tenures often fails to give an incentive to work the land or to invest in improvements; and usually results in relatively unproductive sizes of holding.

Religious practices play a part here also; notable are the sacred cows that graze the land of India, so lacking in water anyhow, without giving return to man in food value or even leather.

In Indonesia too much of the land is said to be ideal for pig-raising. Unfortunately, the prevailing Mohammedanism forbids the eating of pork.

(C) Unlike labour and land, the existence of industrial *capital* cannot be taken for granted and obstacles occur to its very formation.

Apart from the economic difficulty of poor people saving any part of their income, there is the psychology of those who are rich enough to save, but who do not invest their savings in productive capital and instead buy jewellery, build temples or their own palaces, or just hoard money. Here the under-developed countries are behaving very much as the older countries now developed did in their middle age. The medieval cathedrals are a lasting (and, aesthetically, a happy) example of a high proportion of savings that did *not* go into helping further production.

In answer, however, to the poorer countries' own desire for higher standards of living we are discussing not aesthetics, but economics. Investment (i.e. capital formation) is insufficient and when formed is often not as productive as it might be.

Discussing companies, we found three distinct steps in capital formation—

(a) saving;

(b) entrusting savings to certain financial institutions such as industrial companies;

(c) those institutions in turn equipping industries.

The original source of capital in most of the underdeveloped countries and most of which were then colonies, involved entrusting savings to private capitalist bodies, mostly companies, in the developed colonizing countries. Our thrifty Victorian predecessors, placed their savings into companies which equipped tea and rubber plantations or copper, tin, diamond or gold mines, or public utilities. In fact, companies were at first far more frequent in the colonial than in the home industrial field. This capitalist company method of providing capital for the underdeveloped countries got a bad name because of gunboat diplomacy, and more important today, because profits were often not reinvested in the underdeveloped country and much of the salaries paid to the staff from the colonizing country were spent on imported goods or saved and sent back home. In short, the economic multiplier was low.

Whether their image of colonization really applies today or not, the ex-colonies and the present independent underdeveloped countries have taken an almost immovable dislike to foreign "capitalist exploitation." Many of them have lately nationalized the equipment capitalists provided for them, for instance in refineries. This hardly encourages the others. The original, "capitalist" source of capital must, in some countries perhaps, be left out of account for the future. The first obstacle to capital formation is thus often political.

If foreign capitalism is not acceptable, and finance by foreign governmental loan or gift is insufficient, as it may well be for long-run development, underdeveloped countries are thrown back on their own resources for capital. Can they save, invest (i.e. entrust) and equip for industry on a sufficient scale? The obstacles are formidable at each of these three stages. Saving is checked by poverty, and a changing age-structure with more children to feed will increase poverty and in particular hold down savings, and, anyway, incomes are so low that saving would only be at the cost of working capacity. Entrustment is checked by the lack of intermediaries operating in the country itself. Savings in underdeveloped countries are, indeed, sometimes entrusted through intermediaries in developed, often neutral countries, such as Switzerland; but though this helps individuals in underdeveloped countries, it does not necessarily help the country as a whole. The final, capital equipment, stage of investment is handicapped by investors' excessive fear of taking risks in particular ventures, and by the high interest that can be got by lending for some purpose other than equipping industry or development generally.

Once formed, the equipment must be fully utilized and maintained. The tendency has been noticed to equip underdeveloped countries with the latest capital-intensive, automatic machinery, as a psychological matter of prestige, rather than economic calculation. But often there is no adequately trained maintenance and repair staff and the expensive equipment remains idle for long periods.

(D) Management, like capital, does not exist in sufficient quantities in the underdeveloped countries, and we must look at the obstacles to its very formation as well as to its productivity. Since this formation must be by education rather than "picking it up" through experience, the most obvious obstacles will be economic—the financing of schools and universities. But economic policy will not by itself overcome the sociological obstacles to education already indicated in unsuitable curriculum; dearth of women teachers; low prestige of an industrial career; or class immobility—any more than it can overcome the lack of will to innovation and to take risks.

3. INEQUALITY AND LIMITS TO THE STABILITY AND MORE EQUAL DISTRIBUTION OF INCOME

The standard of living toward which underdeveloped countries strive includes, with a certain average income-a-head, the notion of less inequality, particularly of no one below a certain minimum of poverty. A further aim is usually included in the notion of a standard, that of stability or security, which may first be examined. How do the underdeveloped countries fare, compared with the developed countries, in the economic security of their nationals and of the nation as a whole?

In the more primitive societies the sociological set-up (prevalence of caste and extended family or kinship and sense of community) makes for the greater security or, at least, the greater feeling of security of the individual. On the other hand, dependence upon primitive agricultural technique makes the economy vulnerable to periodic natural catastrophes, such as droughts or floods. On entering the world market, a developing nation is at a further comparative disadvantage. Exports of the primary agricultural or mineral commodities in which it normally specializes are subject to violent price changes, largely due to fluctuation in supply and inelastic supply and demand. Even the tourist trade, we have seen, suffers both when political upheavals in the country to be visited engender fears and when, in the visitors' own country, there is a business slump and few can afford the luxury of holiday travel. Thus, conditions natural and sociological as well as economic limit and upset the stability of underdeveloped economies. The stability and security of labour in *developed* countries since 1945 form a telling contrast; and even before that, in spite of industrial slumps, unemployment insurance smoothed out incomes. In the depression of 1929–35, for instance, the real total income of the working-class in Britain did not, measurably (65), fall.

We now turn from the distribution of incomes through time to their distribution at any one time among persons and classes. A simple measure of the inequality of incomes within any country is the percentage of the total income accruing to the richest 10 per cent of income-receivers. After subtraction of income tax, Morgan found this index of inequality (141, pp. 821–33) was, around 1947–50, 40·8 per cent in Puerto Rico but in the United States of America 27·0 per cent. In Ceylon 9·7 per cent of families received as much as 32·5 per cent of income, but in the United Kingdom 13·1 per cent of incomes received 30·2 per cent and, in 1952, Lydall and Lansing (124) give the top 10 per cent 26 per cent. Pareto has attempted to establish a general law (149, pp. 693–700) of the form of distribution of incomes within a nation. Whether it is universal or not, his formula can be used as a yardstick to measure which countries have a greater, which a less degree of equality in incomes. Colin Clark (39, p. 538) thus found that while the older developed countries varied within the middle degrees—the newly developed countries had the least degree of inequality, the underdeveloped the most—

> The greatest degree of equalization of incomes is found in Australia and New Zealand and the Prairie Provinces of Canada. These are developing communities where access to economic opportunity seems to be open to many. On the other hand, Argentine, Brazil, and India appear to be developing a very high degree of income concentration.

The United States had a highly unequal income distribution in the 1870s and again round about 1929. In recent years this inequality has been much reduced. France for the last fifty years has had a more equal income distribution than Britain.

Extreme poverty has been the lot of sections of the population of developed countries in the past, and their statistically recorded experience in overcoming primary poverty may prove useful in estimating the breaking point of obstacles in the underdeveloped countries. Primary poverty was defined in 1899 as income insufficient for the bare physical subsistence of a family even when the utmost economy is exercised by husband and wife. At that date Seebohm Rowntree found in York 15·5 per cent of families in primary poverty. Subsequent events point the lesson (73, p. 185)—

> Between 1899 and 1936 when wages boards, national insurance and pensions were being introduced, the percentage of all families whose income was below that necessary for bare subsistence had dropped from 15·5 to 6·8 per cent. This insufficiency was due to low wages for 8 per cent of all families in 1899, but only for 0·6 per cent in 1936. Between 1936 and 1950 Rowntree used as his poverty line a higher standard than bare subsistence. Individuals whose income was below this standard fell from 14·2 to 0·37 per cent of all individuals surveyed, a change due mainly to a composite of full employment, family allowances and food subsidies.

Previous to their development, the countries at present developed suffered the consequence of poverty, not excluding premature death. Even as late as 1900 (57, p. 309), general labourers, the poorest paid of all occupations, suffered over twice the average occupational mortality rate. Extremes of poverty amidst plenty were due to very low incomes of persons even when fully employed; no income from the chief breadwinner when unemployed; and no income from other (often numerous) unoccupied members of the family. All of these immediate causes of extreme poverty are to be found in the underdeveloped countries, though not easily distinguished owing (154) to a further cause looming larger—the situation of *under*employment, when (as often in family subsistence farming) productivity is so low that when a "worker" leaves, the total output is much the same as before.

Some of the roots of inequality—low wages, unemployment, unoccupation and underemployment—are *economic* and have already been mentioned as early stages in the trend of development—

(i) The high proportion of persons engaged in primitive agriculture and thus with a very low income. In a plantation economy the disparity between the wealth of planters and labourers is particularly obvious but it is not so extreme as between landlord and peasant.

(ii) The absence of mechanization and, therefore, the low productivity of the bulk even of *industrial* labour doing the heavy mechanical labouring that is performed by machines in the developed countries.

(iii) The low staff ratio in industry and the absence of any large middle-class.

But the main roots of inequality are *sociological* in the wide sense of sociology, including demography and political science.

(iv) A differential birth-rate. Fifty years ago (58, p. 36) the birth-rate of English working-class families was almost twice that of the upper or middle class, and evidence of a similar differential today has been found (212, pp. 136, 280) in underdeveloped countries such as Lebanon and Chile.

(v) The social immobility imposed by custom, often with a religious sanction. The extreme case is the untouchables caste of India—a segregation difficult, apparently, to change.

(vi) The mass of illiterates. This situation is not deeply sociological and is easier to change, given financial resources for education.

(vii) Political power in the hands of the educated *élite*—small in numbers because of the restriction in education, and becoming almost a mandarin class. Here, probably, lies the main cause of failure in several underdeveloped countries to use and enforce "progressive" income taxes as a means of redressing inequality.

(viii) Weak state and trade-union action.

Trade unions' main objective and one of the State's has been to increase labour's wages and particularly to institute minimum wages and measures for economic security. This action has been followed by diminishing inequality and often, too, by increasing productivity via, as I have put it (73, p. 65), six routes: the physiological and psychological conditioning of workers, more inter-industry and inter-firm mobility, and the spread of mechanization, directly or indirectly.

In many underdeveloped countries trade unions apparently have a large membership though not always paid-up. But they are often political machines rather than organizations giving thought primarily to the possibility of permanent economic advancement and security of their members. The danger lies in overdoing claims and raising wages too high in relation to labour productivity. Economists have held that wages equal marginal productivity, but we need not stress the finer points. It is enough to assert that wages cannot in the long run exceed labour productivity, i.e. the average output-a-worker minus raw materials, fuel and depreciation of capital equipment and the cost of management and risk-bearing. The productivity of labour is lower in underdeveloped than developed countries, and wages cannot be on the same level. Efforts to make them so, with no prospect of raising productivity, would simply drive the country out of trade in the competitive export market owing to its higher labour cost per unit of production. Unfortunately, this truism (however platitudinous it appears to economists) is not always accepted by labour in underdeveloped countries— indeed, a certain proportion of labour in developed countries does not appear to accept it either.

In all developed countries individual *laissez faire* has been modified and the state has intervened in industry for the purpose of making distribution more equal and providing security in a number of ways which I have distinguished (73, *passim*) by appropriate prepositions. The State has defended labour FROM exploitation, overfatigue, and ill-health by Maximum Hours and Minimum Wage Acts or acts to set up machinery for

that purpose, and by participation WITH employers and trade
unions in wage negotiations; it has provided services FOR industry, such as employment exchanges, or technical colleges to
further mobility, and has provided direct palliatives and security
AGAINST the hazards of life and work from the womb to the
tomb by providing benefits for childbirth, children, sickness,
injury by accidents, unemployment, and old age and death of
bread-winners through national insurance schemes. Finally,
in its direct operation OF nationalized industries and in its
planning, taxation, or control OVER private industry, the
State itself has often set a certain standard of fair shares between
wages and other forms of income.

Attempts have been made to carry these various roles of the
State in developed countries over to the underdeveloped by the
agency of the International Labour Organization. Allowing
enough time for full consideration (and omitting Communist
and recently created states), we find that conventions drawn up
before 1939 had by 1962 been signed by a fair proportion of
underdeveloped countries on accident compensation and minimum wage fixing machinery, by a small proportion on insurance against sickness, by a very few on old age pensions,
and on invalidity and survivors (e.g. widows and orphans of
bread-winner) insurance. Only one underdeveloped country
had agreed to perhaps the most direct "equalizer and stabilizer,"
provision for unemployment, partly, no doubt, because of the
difficulty in distinguishing full unemployment from chronic
underemployment. On the whole, the governments of the
underdeveloped countries do not seem to have gone far in trying to equalize or to stabilize the incomes of their citizens.

Will industrialization of these countries or developments of
the tourist trade increase inequality still further? To judge
from the more recent development of the countries already industrialized, development should tend to equalize incomes, and
living and working conditions, if the stubborn sociological and
antagonistic political forces can be overcome. The older developed countries of Europe had, after all, to overcome medieval
feudalism, and then the aristocratic set-up of the eighteenth
century. A revolution did this in France, but in Britain almost
feudal sociological forces were recently still potent, as Tawney
has pointed out (179, pp. 74–5).

England is peculiar in being marked to a greater degree than most other communities, not by a single set of class relations, but by two, of which one is the product of the last century of economic development, and the other, though transformed by that development and softened by the social policy of the democratic era, contains, nevertheless, a large infusion of elements, which descend from the quite different type of society that existed before the rise of the great industry. It is the combination of both—the blend of a crude plutocratic reality with the sentimental aroma of an aristocratic legend—which gives the English class-system its peculiar toughness and cohesion.

In short, sociological forces may check equality and security for the poorer classes, as they check production, if industrialization keeps, or increases, power and the wealth created in the hands of a few, without effective opposition from labour or the State. Indeed, the State itself, in the hands of the rich and the traditionalists, may not be particularly enamoured of a more equal distribution.

4. THE POPULATION EXPLOSION

The third leg of the tripod upon which rests the future standard of living is the number of "heads." Population is now said to be "exploding," and the expression is well taken. Coale has calculated (42) that world population doubled in the two centuries between 1650 and 1850. It increased on average 50 per cent a century. But instead of a similar 50 per cent rise between 1850 and 1950 the rise was 100 per cent, and population is now increasing at a rate of 500 per cent a century and shows little sign of abating. Population, moreover, is particularly "explosive" in those very countries, identified as underdeveloped, which can least sustain this explosion. A projection for the half-century from 1950 to 2000 is given by Glass (87, p. 17)—

Population Projection for A.D. *2000; 1950 being 100*

Developed Regions	170	
Africa	250	
Asia	280	
Latin America	350	(Doubling in 28 years)
All Regions	244	(Doubling in 41 years or fivefold a century)

Though all the nine trends outlined in the first chapter should take place except the last, that particular trend—increase in the standard of living—may not, as a result of population increase, ever take place. If the principal object of industrial development is higher standards of living, this population explosion which offsets the effects of industrial development must certainly be examined particularly to discover the reason why increased supplies of labour cannot increase production proportionately. At the present low world level of income-a-head the immediate production needed is mainly food raised by agriculture, and beyond a certain point agriculture cannot, in the long run, increase production at the decreasing or constant cost that manufacturing can. Together with labour, capital, and management, agriculture requires, unlike manufactures, an extent of more-or-less fertile land, and such land is, in fact, scarce.

Diminishing returns are, of course, delayed when new capital in irrigation schemes or fertilizers or more capable and knowledgeable management and labour are applied to the land. But these new factors do not have the same open horizons that they have in manufacture. Natural resources—the land factor —still present a limit and, unless new fertile lands can extensively be opened up (as the Middle-West of America was in the nineteenth century), the new input of labour, capital or management has to be piled on intensively to more or less fixed land.

The law of diminishing return is that with successive "doses" of expenditure or "inputs," the additions to the total output diminish; not necessarily that the absolute *total* return diminishes. But more and more frequently in countries where labour is plentiful, doses of labour are applied to a fixed supply of land in such intensity that output eventually does diminish absolutely. If, as in India, cow-dung has to be used for fuel to cook with, the cattle will not be fertilizing the land, and if there is over-grazing and wholesale tree-felling erosion of the soil will diminish the productivity of the land, absolutely. And the more the number of workers who need to cook with dung and the cattle who need to graze, the less, absolutely, will be the return. In Africa agriculturists cannot, after exhausting resources, move on to fresh pastures as they used to do, since all possible pastures are getting settled. There is not just a diminishing but a devastating return. The result is often that population moves off to the cities, though industry offers no increase in productive jobs. Indeed, of all the trends mentioned in the first chapter, urbanization is being realized the fastest in some underdeveloped countries, particularly in Latin America.

Minerals are included by the economist in "land," and they are obviously wasting assets. Prophets have recently been inclined to optimism about the length of life of the resources at present in demand. But if a population increase of $1\frac{1}{2}$ per cent annually is combined with a standard of living and similar demands, say, only two-thirds that of Americans today, then Villard shows (194, pp. 189–95) that by the year 2100 total demand will increase eightyfold, and not many years supply of coal, petroleum, steel, or copper will be available—in fact, of the last three commodities, only between one and ten, thirteen, and one year's supply.

The immediate cause of the population explosion is not an increase in the birth-rate, but the maintenance of birth-rates in the underdeveloped countries, with a spectacular decrease in their death-rates. India, with Pakistan, had in 1910–14 an annual crude death-rate of 31 per thousand population. In 1951 the rates were 14·4 for India and just above 11·9 for Pakistan, and they have been falling since. This decrease can be reasonably imputed to biological and medical knowledge applied in controlling (often to the point of eradication) the killer diseases, such as malaria, smallpox, sleeping sickness, and yellow fever. In any realistic model of the balance of forces affecting changes of population, such as I have presented (58, p. 19) for Malthus's argument, this factor (then summed up as Public Hygiene) must be brought into account. The point of practical importance is that this *death control*, whether by immunization of persons or destruction of disease-carriers, can be, and has been, effected by a few expert *elite*; but effective birth control depends on acceptance by large numbers—a much more difficult operation. Two significant diagrams in the United Nations *Demographic Yearbook* for 1955 (183) compare changes in birth- and in death-rates for some seventy nations. Between 1945–9 and 1950–4 all nations but one show a fall in death-rates, but in their birth-rates the nations are evenly split between those rising and those falling.

Many underdeveloped countries have now a crude death-rate as low as the developed countries. This rate is due, however, to the age-structure of their population. With their birth-rates maintained, underdeveloped countries contain a much higher proportion of young people. A more exact and comparable indicator of health is the expectation of life at birth given in Table I. The men of *all* the ten countries of highest income-a-head, except Belgium with 62·0, show an average expectation of over 66 years. None of the seven most underdeveloped countries where data was available, except Ceylon (with 60·3 years), have an average expectation over 50. But life expectation is rapidly rising. Linton (122) has drawn maps showing the rise between 1920 (when average expectations of less than 40 years occurred in almost all South and Central America, Africa, and Asia) and 1950 when life expectations shorter than 40 occurred only in Central Africa, India, and China.

We do not want, presumably, to put death-rates back up again. So if production cannot be exploded faster than population—quintupling a century—the only way to increase production-*a-head* is to reduce the birth-rate. Recent birth-rates are given for all the twenty-five countries listed in Table I wherever they are available. At a glance, it can be seen that all the ten countries with the lowest average income-a-head have birth-rates clearly above the rates in any of the ten most developed countries. They range from 34·2 to 50·0 compared with 16·5 to 28·3. What are the factors accounting for this maintenance of high birth-rates?

For practical purposes I have referred to the "human factor," as analysable, broadly speaking, into human ability and human willingness. In the maintenance of high birth-rates the double reference, as also the distinction, proves again of practical importance.

Most writers seem to have plumped for unwillingness to control births as the determining element. Economists say much about the willingness—nay, the positive desire—to have children for work in agriculture at an early age, and for props to the old age of the parents. Sociologists stress religious beliefs about the importance of multiplying, the ritual of ancestor worship, and the lack of any will to maintain or acquire a standard of living. To interpret the difference in birth-rates between countries, *more* weight than at present should, in view of the evidence, be placed on people's knowledge of methods

o

and ability in controlling births; *less* on motives and will. After all, unless couples know that there are means of preventing births, they may not think contraception possible and may not will it because they don't think about it. As Himes says in his *Medical History of Contraception* (95, p. 392)—

> It is bad sociology to overlook the means or mechanism by which the Vital Revolution has been and is being achieved. Economics has been guilty of this error in emphasizing almost exclusively the rising standard of living to account for small families.

But sociology need not fall into the same trap. Unwillingness to have more than a certain number is probably not such a new phenomenon, confined to developed countries, as all that. It may have been present, at least among the wives, in the countries now developed long before their birth-rates fell; it was latent because the capacity to prevent births was not known. This may be the situation at this very moment in the still underdeveloped countries. Queen Victoria's plaint is well known of the "great inconvenience a large family would be" yet she had nine children. In a Puerto Rican inquiry (177, p. 159) 63 per cent of women mentioned less than four children and 91 per cent four or less as their ideal number. This number is corroborated in the United States, where women have high status and where knowledge of birth control is almost universal.

Where, through lack of knowledge or facilities, couples are unable to practice birth control, the course of events has followed the three propositions of Malthus (127), particularly the bald second. The first was that "population is necessarily limited by the means of subsistence"; the second that "population invariably increases where the means of subsistence increase, unless prevented by some very powerful and obvious check."

Just after Malthus died, means of subsistence increased dramatically owing to the effects of the Industrial Revolution, England becoming the sole "workshop of the world," and the opening up of the American Middle-West. The population of the areas affected, before birth control took effect, increased rapidly, but not as rapidly as the means of subsistence and standards of living rose. Malthus's third principle was that "the checks which repress the superior power of population and keep its effect on a level with the means of subsistence are all resolved into moral restraint, vice and misery." Malthus was a clergyman and would undoubtedly have classed birth-control methods, as abortion, under "vice." Elsewhere he classed checks to population more neutrally as positive (e.g. death) and preventive. Subsequently the latter proved powerful. The differential effect of birth control as a *preventive check* on population is evident in the fall of English birth-rates since 1880, when wide publicity followed the Bradlaugh–Besant trials of 1877–9. It is also evident when comparing Catholic and Protestant regions in the same period and in the same country, for instance (58, pp. 38–9, 36, pp. 67–77) in Holland and Canada. In Asia, Africa, and Central and South America, containing the bulk of the world's population, the standard of living remains, with little or no birth control and fast-increasing population, at a subsistence level. Though he is critical of some of Malthus's wording, Flew (55) best sums up the practical applicability of his central argument—

> For the rough and practically vital understanding of the populations explosions now occurring in so many of the underdeveloped countries, Malthus's simple model of an enormous power of increase opposed by various counteracting forces is perhaps both necessary and sufficient. For it can bring out that, in these countries, the application of modern medical knowledge is weakening the positive check, while nothing is occurring to produce a proportionate strengthening of the preventive check.

Indeed, in his combination of probable economic and sociological (58, pp. 23–5) hypotheses with attempts to verify by statistical induction, Malthus's methods form a model, unfortunately not followed by subsequent generations of economists.

The practical importance of weighing ability no less than willingness as factors in the birth-rate is that so many authorities believe that willingness to control births will arise automatically as standards of living rise and families "aspire" to yet higher standards. Till then they see no point in worrying about spreading knowledge of birth control and studying its acceptability. Unfortunately in many underdeveloped and all too slowly developing countries standards of living may never rise and few have shown, up to the present, much evidence of any spread in "aspiration" effect. Though no precedent existed in developed, in a few underdeveloped countries efforts have been made and encouraged by the state-government to set up family-planning clinics, or otherwise to teach "know-how," to sterilize, or even, as in Japan, to allow abortion. Elsewhere few signs have appeared currently of lowered country-wide birth-rates. Other factors besides higher incomes were probably necessary in the past experience of countries now developed. Allocating points to different occupations for likely degrees of ignorance, low "informability," and women's status, as well as lower income, it became evident to me that, in the England of the early twentieth century, access to and acceptability of knowledge strongly influenced the size of families. Doctors, teachers, cotton operatives, and other urban factory workers had families much smaller (58, Table C) than miners or farmers living in relative isolation.

Other surveys have found other limits to know-how. Extreme poverty and grinding toil induce ignorance and fecklessness, and even moderate poverty will keep up the birth-rate because of the expense of appliances and chemicals, and the lack of privacy in inadequate housing. Lella Florence (56, p. 199) has shown the extent of the distaste of wives, rich or poor, for pre-pill birth-control methods. Know-how, not in itself technically difficult to master, must thus in practice be supported by enabling facilities and acceptability.

High production, but low reproduction, is the main formula for raising standards of living. Research is continuing, looking for the most suitable appliances, technologically, for high yet economic *production* in underdeveloped countries where capital is scarce and labour plentiful. So also, research and laboratory and clinical testing, are beginning (212, *passim*) for a reliable yet accessible and acceptable method of lowering *reproduction*. The contraceptive pill received in 1960 its first European clinical testing in Birmingham, but with developments in plastic apparatus, more and even simpler and cheaper foolproof methods may yet be invented. However, the birth-control leg of the tripod, so necessary if industry is to lead to higher standards of living, is not likely to be firmly and widely established if the censorship continues which is now imposed on discussion at the United Nations. As it is, the return likely to be obtained from the international aid involved in development is just more and more people at the old level of bare subsistence.

5. SUMMARY OF FEARS AND HOPES FOR STANDARDS OF LIVING

To sum up the practical possibilities and sociological limits to rising standards of living in the underdeveloped countries, the grounds for optimism may first be stated. They apply either to some particular countries or fairly generally.

Several underdeveloped countries have particular resources —comparative advantages—as the basis of trade: minerals such as oil or iron ore; scenery, a winter climate or artefacts to attract the tourists; or harbours to facilitate trading. Several are large enough to form a market sufficient for mass-production. All, or nearly all, underdeveloped countries have a tropical or sub-tropical climate where products, such as coffee, tea, cocoa, and cotton, can be grown, which are far more costly or even impossible to grow in developed countries, and have a plentiful labour supply that can be trained. Moreover, the know-how for higher production, if not for more equal distribution and lower birth-rates, which has only gradually been acquired by developed countries, could, it is thought, be rapidly transferred. Know-how for equalizing wealth is specially important where particular resources exist, since, like oil, they may at present be in only a few hands.

Grounds for pessimism are also particular and general. Several underdeveloped countries form only a small market, and have few minerals or convenient harbours, or little natural scenery or few artefacts to attract the tourist. And all, or nearly all, suffer from the violent price fluctuations of primary products and find export earnings growing slower than the necessary import demand for capital goods. Sociological obstacles too (including political and administrative) block the effective adoption of productive, equalizing, and reproductive know-how. And even if productivity rises this is likely to be achieved by a lower level of employment. Though the bulk of the effort must come from within, without some external aid to pump-prime their trade, grounds for pessimism seem to me to prevail for most of the underdeveloped countries.

A summary of the practical feasibility of and yet sociological limits to rising standards of living must stress the present abject poverty of underdeveloped countries and the vicious circle from poverty to poverty. It can be represented graphically—

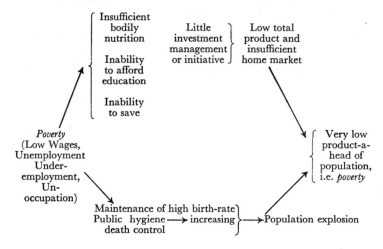

The practical question is where to break the chain of events in the circle. If certain sociological traditions are broken, as they are being broken by contacts with the developed world, some writers believe that saving and initiative may eventually appear automatically, indeed, that they are already appearing and raising productivity; and that with rising productivity and standards of living birth control, too, will appear automatically. But this process, if it occurs at all, will be slow and probably only sporadic; and meanwhile the highly successful death control will most likely overwhelm any possibility of a rise in product-a-head of total population.

The most hopeful solution is an attack on several fronts. Productivity must be raised by better nutrition and by education, saving increased by checking any consumption which is unnecessary to higher productivity, and at the same time a check put on birth-rates. One of the unfortunate features of the birth-control controversy is the claim that raising productivity is to be preferred to checking population. The two are, however, not alternatives, but, if a high standard of living is to be achieved, are both essential in coping with the otherwise desperate situation, together with the third leg of the tripod—equalization of incomes. This is the point of my tripod metaphor. Each leg is required if the tripod is not to topple over.

The several fronts to be attacked are not, however, equally vulnerable. The most tractable front is education, since mainly finance and the planning of a useful type of education of a *limited number* of people are required. This, of course, may seem a tall enough order. But the barriers against education are weak compared to those checking payments high enough to assure nutrition for all and yet checking unnecessary consumption. Since the co-operation of all couples is involved, the strongest barriers of all are those which stop birth control matching the existing death control. In only a few countries, probably, can this all-front attack be successful with the finite means at the disposal of the countries able and willing to provide aid. As Ritchie Calder has said (31), the growth of population makes planning aid "like running up the down escalator." He substantiates his simile—

> In the decade which followed President Truman's call for a bold new policy, some $30,000,000,000 went into the 100 countries and territories we call "underdeveloped"; that is, from all sources —multilateral, and bilateral and private investment. The overall effect was to raise the per capita income from $90 to $100— an average increase of a dollar a year during the decade. The annual income grew at the rate of 3 per cent but their population grew at the rate of 2 per cent per year.

A real take-off into trade does not, at this rate of progress, appear likely in many underdeveloped countries. The prime-pumping example of Marshall Aid supplied to the developed countries of Europe in 1947 is not being followed. A practical example—a real object lesson—is the most effective persuader. Economic aid on any large enough scale to be effective may have to be confined to a few key countries that show some hope of co-operating—for their own benefit—in the attack *on all fronts*.

Underdeveloped countries differ widely in their chances of effective development. Unfortunately, many of the countries which have the particular economic advantages of climate and mineral resources are countries where the sociological obstacles to education, saving, income equalization, and birth control are strong. Since the obstacles to birth control and legal abortion appear the strongest, the underdeveloped countries likely to prove the most effective object lesson in raising standards of living by an all-front attack are those whose birth-rates are already falling. Among these are Japan, with a fall in crude birth-rates per thousand from 28·2 in 1950 to 16·8 in 1961 and in the same period, Israel, with a fall from 34·7 to 24·9, and Puerto Rico, with a fall from 39·0 to 31·0.

Obviously more research is called for, if the balance of economic and sociological forces is to be correctly assessed that will raise standards of living. My final chapter sets out practical policies for development and the methods and fields of research that have proved, and are likely to prove, fruitful.

CHAPTER VIII

SOCIAL RESEARCH FOR INDUSTRIAL DEVELOPMENT

1. The Need for Sociology in Development

The social sciences are, by definition, sciences about society, that is, about groups of persons, or relations between them, not about single isolated individuals. Social psychologists and social anthropologists certainly draw this distinction in segregating themselves from *individual* psychologists and anthropologists; and a committee of the British Association for the Advancement of Science (22), basing its conclusions on the practice of the Royal Society, met no demarcation dispute. The recognized *natural* sciences were found to investigate "those attributes of man which are common to other species. . . . They do not deal with . . . facts arising from the contact of man with man."

The sciences that do deal with the "contact of man with man" are, like the natural sciences, many in number; though for brevity but not to imply restrictions this book only bears the two titles: economics and sociology.

Of all the social sciences, economics has in the twentieth century attained the greatest systematization. This does not mean that economists are agreed on the definition of their science. Between those who focus on exchange and those who, like Lord Robbins, focus on scarcity, Cairncross (30, p. 8) offers a "compromise" definition—

> Economics is a social science studying how people attempt to accommodate scarcity to their wants and how these attempts interact through exchange.

He brings in the scarcity that Lord Robbins has favoured because it "is more fundamental than exchange." But it is too fundamental. Lord Robbins considered economics "the study of human behaviour as a relationship between ends and scarce means which have alternative uses." This definition could include the study of almost all rational action by human beings—in politics, the arts, games, or military strategy and tactics. Scarcity is certainly one very critical problem in economics, as we have learned when observing the less-affluent countries with natural resources insufficient for their population. But scarcity, as R. L. Smyth has pointed out (174), is not the only economic problem, and in an affluent society not a very obvious one.

When the classical textbooks of economics are examined they will in fact be found to centre upon terms of exchange in a market, that is, upon the quantities exchanged of goods, services, money, titles to money, and factors of production, and upon the prices and costs at which these quantities change hands, thus forming people's incomes.

These terms may appear (59, pp. 90–4) on any one of three levels, monetary, physical, or as Marshall's "real costs" psychological. The monetary terms are the easiest to measure, and *economic* is frequently defined, for instance by Pigou in *The Economics of Welfare* (149, p. 11), as the part "that can be brought directly or indirectly into relation with the measuring-rod of money."

The national income is the point from which most modern textbooks start out—a macro- rather than a micro-economic approach—thus reviving Adam Smith's concern with the *Wealth of Nations*. This national income from which the calculation of standards of living derives, is the sum of all money values exchanged. It excludes goods and services not exchanged and hence all gifts.

Cairncross (30, pp. 7–8) is clear that in societies where there is no exchange there is no economics. Primitive communities, before any development has taken place, are such societies, and it is significant that all their activities—industrial, family, religious—are studied by the social anthropologist. These communities do not, in fact, differentiate their economic from any other part of their social life. In Table XIV social anthropology is thus placed above and across the social sciences such as economics and politics, studying later and more differentiated societies.

In developed societies exchanging, though a very distinct part of life, is not the whole of social life or even the whole of industry, and the coupling of sociology with economics in the title of this book is meant to indicate the co-existence of many other socially important factors in the world of industry. Sociology, as said already, is used broadly to refer to all the social sciences, excluding only economics. The exclusion is not a matter of principle, and certainly there should be a supersociology covering all the social sciences. But it is a matter of convenience to distinguish economics and sociology, both because economics is a fairly well-defined discipline and because the sociology of industry has hitherto been sadly neglected.

Industrial development has been accepted mainly as an economic phenomenon, and the nine measurable trends in development which were traced in the first chapter leading to higher incomes-a-head are mostly economic. Yet, in analysing the cause and limits of industrial development, we have repeatedly come up against social relationships, "contacts of man with man" that are not economic. It will be useful to bring together and review chapter by chapter the sorts of contacts they proved to be.

Many of the economic trends adumbrated in the first chapter had prominent sociological aspects, particularly urbanization, the emergence of a management staff, large organizations, and their government by the management. And few trends ran in a straight line. Economic systems have to face up in fact to twists and changes in the conditions of supply and demand— conditions that are partly technological, but partly psychological or sociological and are rooted in the changing patterns of consumption.

The second chapter, dealing with the mobilization and mobility required for adaptation to the trends in development, was shot through with necessary references to sociology. Full mobilization of economies was found checked by the family roles and conventions restricting women's industrial occupation, not to mention the facts of life—in short, biology. Social biology, though from 1930 to 1937 recognized by the chair at the London School of Economics held by Professor Lancelot Hogben, is now merged in demography dealing with the population of individuals grouped by sex, age, locality, marital status, social class, and so on, all of them factors that affect the economics of labour in industry. Social class was found a particularly strong obstacle to the fulfilment of the economist's hypothesis of mobility by differential net advantage—an obstacle recognized in his "non-competing groups." And his conception of net advantages itself recognized many psychological motives other than differential wages, security and prospects, for instance, status, independence, respectability, and sociability. Sociological traditions and attitudes were found opposing adjustment to economic trends strongly enough, to be recognized by economists as "friction" or a "lag."

Chapter III, on industrial location, brought in the geography of human and natural resources and was largely concerned with measuring the extent and causes—the social ecology—of urbanization. The modern conurbations are mainly economic in origin, but the problems of the town and country pattern which they raise has greatly exercised sociologists, notably Lewis Mumford. Chapter IV dealt directly with the size of organized associations such as the industrial plant and firm and with the motives, if any, of an entrepreneur or a salaried manager for expansion. Indirectly, psychological problems of morale and motivation arise when labour is employed in large numbers within one organization and the relative strength of economic and other incentives to productivity comes into question. Here, again, though factories and firms are economic in origin, famous contributions to the understanding of their functioning have been made by industrial psychologists, sociologists, and anthropologists, like Elton Mayo.

The title of Chapter V was the economics and sociology of industrial government. Appeal to sociology, particularly the political science branch, was shown to be necessary when the unit of organization was large, required a division of labour in financing and ruling it, and, so often, exhibited conflicting interests among its rulers.

Chapters VI and VII dealt with the underdeveloped countries, and in their investigation the distinctive approach and mutual help of economics and sociology was made explicit. Chapter VI concentrated on the economic aspect; the fitting of industries and the tourist trade to natural and human resources so as to produce, by trading, maximum national income. Chapter VII concentrated on the sociological limits to this economic development. Limits were set, not only on the aggregate of income, but on its stability and equal distribution, and on the average per head of population. The limits include traditional attitudes and values, and also customs and taboos affecting the will and ability to work, save, think, or plan. They have been laid bare by social anthropologists and have emphatically to be taken into account when predicting future development. Limits were also found to be set by forms of political government and by the small size of many states, affecting the size of the market.

2. Types of Social Sciences Required

Reference to social relationships beyond economics have been found necessary in the course of this book for elucidating the events of industrial development. Their study will be seen, when analysed, to fall into two main categories. In the one are studies of groupings of persons in families, cities, factories, firms, companies, trade unions, and states, in the other are studies of the behaviour, activities, performance, attitudes, beliefs, motives, and scales of values of these groups. Using Talcott Parsons' words (147, *passim*) one may, for short, distinguish the study of actors and that of their acts.

Since the focus of economics is the act of exchanging and the ensuing values, and performance in production, consumption, and distribution of exchangeable goods and services, the second category—social behaviour—is its main field of interest. Most textbooks in fact deal even less than Marshall's *Principles of Economics*, where five chapters (129, Chapters VIII–XII) are devoted to Industrial Organization, with the nature of the actual groups engaged in exchange activities.

An objective test of the main interest of any science is to look at the index of its standard textbooks and to rank the number of references of the different words. If, for economics, we pick Cairncross's *Introduction to Economics* (30), the fourteen words in the index with the greatest number (eight or more) of references under subheads are: Money, 18; Costs, Margin (and Marginal), 17; Wages, 16; Unemployment, Capital, 15; Profit, 12; Firm, Banks, Monopoly, Trade, 11; Rent, Market, 9; Price, 8. If, for sociology, we pick McIver and Page's *Society* (135), the fourteen words in the index with the greatest number (again eight or more) of references under subheads are: Class, 28; Culture (and Cultural), 26; the State, 20; the Family, 18; Society, 17; Association, Environment, 16; Community, 15; Technology, 14; City (or Town), 12; Heredity, 11; Attitudes, Customs, 10; Authority, 8.

It is clear that the interests of the two main social sciences are very different. Economics is interested chiefly in money and money payments in exchange for things: costs, wages, profit, rent; and in the relation of man to his paid work or its absence—unemployment. And if we concentrate on *industrial* economics we find the same types of interest. Taking a period of years, articles in the *Journal of Industrial Economics* concerned with costs and prices outnumbered those concerned with structure three to one. Sociology, on the other hand, is interested in groups of persons: class, the state, the family, society, associations, communities, the city.

Nevertheless, when all the social sciences are surveyed certain interests emerge that are common to them all, or to most of them. Among the most frequent references in economics, for instance, were those to *firms*, *banks*, and *markets*. These are all groups of persons, the main interest of sociology. And among the most frequent references in sociology several were not groups so much as the system of acts, thoughts, powers, or behaviour of groups; *technology, attitudes, authority, customs*. This overlapping of interests is an important point in the argument for the greater integration to be urged later.

The social science most clearly defined, next to economics, is political science when it is separated from the ethics of political philosophy. It has the same concern as economics with behaviour, but is also concerned with the behaving groups, and the emphasis is not concentrated on behaviour. Instead of exchange, the behaviour studied by Machiavelli and Hobbes was the exercise of control, of influence, and, more formally, of power: "all politics," writes Catlin (35, p. 79), "is, by its nature, power politics." But the emphasis, particularly if the work of Stubbs and Maitland and other constitutional lawyers be included, is as much on the groups exercising power, particularly the State, as on the terms of power—on actors, as on acts. Catlin devotes two main chapters to the "Power Hypothesis" and "Freedom and Authority"; and two to the "Forms of Government; Democracy and Tyranny" and "Aristocracy and

Oligarchy." Laski, in his *Grammar of Politics* (1925), has two parts; one dealing with sovereignty, rights, liberty and equality, property, and authority; the other with institutions, the judicial process, and international organization. Henry Sidgwick, wrote in the first chapter of his *Elements of Politics* (1891) the inquiry "has two main divisions (1) one relating to the Work or Functions of Government, and (2) the other to its Structure or Constitution."

This equal emphasis on structure, actors, forms and institutions of government, as on functions, acts, and behaviour is understandable, since the procedure and organization of groups armed with compulsory power are more important than those of small economic groups voluntarily exchanging goods and services and usually in competition. Where competition is displaced by oligopoly or monopoly of large firms, however, economists should certainly pay more attention to the nature of the groups exercising this economic power.

Economics and political science thus both study, though with different emphasis, behaviour and the behaving groups and there emerges a fourfold division of inquiry into (1) political behaviour, (2) economic behaviour, (3) political groups, and (4) economic groups. These cross-divisions are shown as four areas numbered 1 to 4 at the core of Table XIV. Their position indicates, vertically, the established conventional connexion between the two parts, structural and functional, of political science and between economic behaviour and economic organization. The position in the table also indicates, horizontally, the less conventional affinity between political and economic behaviour and between political and economic structure. Catlin (35, pp. 144 and 148) has stressed in at least two of his propositions the analogy between the two types of behaviour. "Democracy conforms, in theory, to the type of a consumers' market, with freedom maximised"; the "law of the (political) market . . . that all security involves an exchange of some general freedom in return for some security which we value more as assuring a particular liberty to realize what we wish."

The affinity with political structure and the use of terms and conceptions of political science has already (V §3) been noted in studying large-scale industrial organizations' delegation of power (amounting often to a federal constitution), their use of

TABLE XIV

AREAS OF THE SOCIAL SCIENCES

UNDER-DEVELOPED AND UNDIFFERENTIATED COUNTRIES	Archaeology; Social Anthropology; General History; Human Geography; Ecology		
Differentiation:	Power Sanction (Political Science Column)	Exchange Sanction (Economics Column)	Tradition and Other Sanctions (Sociological Column)
DEVELOPED AND DIFFERENTIATED COUNTRIES A: Values and behaviour	(1) Relation of state government and the individual Authority and liberty Bargaining power "Command and reply" analysis	(2) Terms of exchange of goods, services and factors of production (value and distribution) (2x) Incentives to work, move, save, risk "Demand and supply" analysis	(7) Traditions Social codes Crime Religious practices (7x) Attitudes, motivation
B: Group structure and government 1. *Associations* (a) Close	(3) Legislature, and other "bodies" The state constitution	(4) Factories	(8) Church congregations Clubs
(b) Scattered	Political parties The electorate	Trade unions Companies or other firms	Church organization
2. *Communities* (a) Close	(5) Pressure groups	(6) Industrial conurbations and localizations Informal small factory groups	(9) The family Small groups
(b) Scattered		(10) Industrial and occupational activity-structure Markets	Social Classes (11) Population, vital statistics and age grouping

Sciences for separate Areas in Developing and Developed Countries
(1), (3), (4)?, and (5) Political Science
(2), (4)?, (6)?, and (10) Economics; Sub-area 2x, Industrial Psychology
(6) Industrial Sociology
(7), (8), and (9) Sociology
Sub-area 7x, Social Psychology
(11) Demography or Social Biology

cabinets and committees such as the Board of Directors, and their methods of appointment and dismissal, of promotion and demotion, and of pecuniary and other incentives to work and to stay within the organization. In both areas the question arises of the degree of member "commitment," including the cohesion of an organization, measured by the turnover of its members and of the degree of apathy measured in politics by the percentage of constituents polling, in industry by absenteeism. It is significant of their lack of interest in power that company shareholders have a high turnover and that absenteeism at their general meeting is usually well over 99 per cent.

Political science is, in fact, often extended to include, in an L-shaped area, box (4) in Table XIV as well as boxes (1) and (3). Catlin, for instance (35, p. 43), considers "the study of trade-union structure and of personnel management essentially political in character." The area (2) which economics analyses is thus quite restricted and even so, part of it, 2x, is studied by industrial psychology. Realistic economics, however, often extends to areas (4), (6) and (10). These quasi-political and psychological questions are becoming more and more important as economic organizations grow. What goes on inside the large organization overshadows the unorganized market forces acting within the industry. The outstanding question is *who*, within the firm, makes the top decisions as to what to make and in what amounts, at what price and by what investment, and why. Political science, which has dealt with similar problems of who? by what acts? and why? in connexion with state government, is perhaps a more appropriate discipline than economics to elucidate the relationships and development within large industrial organization.

Even when the organization and exercise of power and control are added to exchanging, they do not constitute the whole of man's industrial life and cannot wholly explain or foretell the course of development. Table XIV allows room, therefore, at its foot and in a third column for groupings (and their types of behaviour) other than political and economic—for unorganized groups which must be studied in forecasting the industrial future, and in planning realistically.

Before development and differentiation start it is hard, as already said, to distinguish economic, political, or other human activities, and social anthropology has evolved, to study primitive man's undifferentiated social life as a whole. Here the sanction for acts is often neither power nor exchange but tradition and social duty. As Firth (51, pp. 142–3) puts it, "powerful incentives to work lie in the individual's membership of a social group." Though "in the long run contributions and rewards may be assumed to even out," . . . "in the short run it is the impact of the social obligation that is most marked, the frequent rendering of the service with no apparent equivalent return."

Development is a dynamic process and its study extends

P

from the primitive to the present. One task of history is to connect the primitive with the developed society and to follow development through from the past in each or in all of the activities involved. While anthropology and archaeology are put at the head of Table XIV as studying the past, general history and ecology are placed with geography in the next row as studying past and present, near and far.

For the later stages of development, sociologists, though they differ widely about the scope of their science, agree in distinguishing two types of group, the *association* expressly organized for the pursuit of an interest or group of interests in common and the *community*, like a family or a town, whose members (135, pp. 8–15) "live together in such a way that they share not this or that particular interest but the basic conditions of a common life." Members of these communities may live close together, as in cities, or to widen the concept may be more or less scattered, as a market. Political science, like economics, is clearly more interested in organized association than in communities. But other social sciences have grown up (such as industrial psychology and industrial sociology) to explore the unorganized *communities*.

A few economists and sociologists have joined with geographers and demographers to inquire, as related in Chapter III, into the large-scale communities resulting from industrial urbanization, known in America as metropolitan areas, and more expressively in Britain as conurbations. No recognized name has yet been conferred upon this study of the (external) relation of industry to place, though a widely conceived "human ecology" might fit. On the other hand, the terms *industrial psychology* and *industrial sociology* have been coined to identify studies exploring the internal functioning of industrial production. At present this field of exploration has largely been confined to one factor of production—labour.

Industrial psychology sprang to life and flourished during and after the First World War and dealt with the selection of workers for jobs and the reactions of individual workers to the long hours that then prevailed and to various physical working conditions and incentives. It was quite as much industrial physiology as psychology. The switch to industrial sociology came when factory hours were reduced to a normal forty-eight-hour week and when Elton Mayo (133) drew attention to the importance of studying informal face-to-face *groups* rather than a rabble of unrelated individual workers. Some of these groups had a scale of values, described earlier (IV, §8), in ludicrous contrast to the management values. Industrial sociology, like psychology, still concentrated on the obstacles presented by *labour* to efficient production.

It is now time that psychological and sociological inquiries turned to the obstacles checking the factors of production, other than labour, in their co-operation to supply the individual and the corporate consumers' demands; obstacles checking effective organization, management, investment and saving, risk-taking and risk-bearing. Psychology must also be brought in to analyse the present demands of the consumer and his change in demands that makes labour mobility so necessary, and to forecast future demands. Economists stimulated by Keynes have been constructing their own models of "consumption-functions" assuming (118, pp. 343–8) an automatic, purely economic, relation between the proportion consumed or saved and total income. This certainly requires modification by sociologists. Veblen (191) with his conception of conspicuous consumption had already stressed the importance of emulation of families with higher by families with lower incomes, and "keeping up with the Jones's" in affluent, highly developed, countries has its counterpart in the peoples of the underdeveloped wanting to keep up with people in the developed countries—in the "demonstration effect" stressed by Nurkse (145, pp. 62–5).

Moving down the table from values and behaviour to structure and government, the groups and societies involved in industry present a bewildering variety; but they have analogues already being studied in other than economic walks of life. At one end of the scale are those "associations" which may be distinguished as *bodies* where people are together in close proximity, for instance a factory, and under more or less ordered discipline with rules of procedure and a drill. At the other end of the scale are loose, imperfect, communities such as the market, varying in membership from day to day according to variations in prices and consumers' tastes and such, too, as an industry itself, containing factories varying in their integration or specialization and with different degrees of localization.

The plants that are members of the same industry may have no formal relations unless there are trade associations or agreements for restrictive (or other) practices. Between these extremes of coherence and incoherence comes the firm, often owning several plants, sometimes in different industries, and also trade unions, both of them in scattered locations but both with organized government. Both have close affinities in structure with the State government, on which political science concentrates. The Webbs' classic study of trade unions, *Industrial Democracy*, is divided, in fact, into the two parts that are standard in political science: structure and function.

The distinction drawn between behaviour and structure, whether political or economic, is of considerable practical importance because the tools of research used upon each facet are very different, and workers using different tools are inclined to draw apart instead of combining to see industry and industrial development whole. In thinking out probable behaviour, the economist uses cost and demand curves to show how the cost of production and the demand-price might vary with amounts produced or demanded. On the other hand, social *structure* is probably understood most easily by starting out with organization charts or with some kind of formal pattern or matrix. These forms can show graphically, by spacing of area and mutual position, how persons or groups of persons (communities, boards, general meetings) are subordinate, co-ordinate, or superordinate to one another inside a hierarchy or may overlap, or may act outside the hierarchy.

In my *Logic of British and American Industry* (72, pp. 56–7) I found it useful to picture the interrelations of lines of product or processes with plants and with the firms owning those plants by patterns of structures showing squares for plants, circles for the firms, and letters for the lines. To represent the government of a firm that is a company, we found (Chapter V) the hour-glass a more realistic pattern than just a circle. The whole hour-glass may further be pictured with many other hour-glasses of various sizes as forming industries each placed in a market. This anatomical model of structures within structures should then make clear one of the main complications in the use of sociological terms such as *function*. The function of a company in the external market may be to make shoes, but inside the company the function of the annual shareholders' meeting is to elect directors, and the function of the directors, besides appointing managers, includes making a profit and declaring a dividend for the shareholders. In short, the function of a company is very different if it is a relation between the company and its consumers in the market *outside* the company, or between the shareholders and directors or the manager and workers *inside* the company, or between the directors and the managers of its separate factories. Economists contrast the external economies of a large-scale industry with the internal economies of a large firm *or* a large plant (*above* p. 90). But practical decision-makers wanting to enlarge their business would dearly like to know whether it is in enlarging existing plants or in building more of the same size that the economies will arise.

The external functions of subgroups like plants are many of them the internal functions or functioning of a superordinate, such as a multi-plant form. Functions cannot in fact be usefully discussed without a realization of the complex structure often involved, and I have consistently urged (72, pp. 1–4) the importance to economists of some structural approach—putting the question *who* as well as how and why. Economists are too prone to discuss scale, demand, supply, savings investment, without specifying whose scale; or who are the demanders, suppliers, and investors and savers, and even whether they are organizations (possibly with conflicting interests within them) or, as so often assumed, unorganized individuals. This abstraction becomes ridiculous when incentives or mobility are discussed without reference to whom incentives are addressed or who is supposed to be moving, or even whether it is everybody or just a sufficient few. And when economists do make a reference to the actual persons involved, quoting perhaps Lord Keynes's view that "the decisions which determine savings and investment respectively are made by different people" (108, p. 175), they do not always take account of all the facts. In every year from 1950 to 1960, though not in 1961–2, British company savings considerably exceeded personal savings (in five of the years they were over double), and as we saw (V, §3) company directors decide *both* how much to save by ploughing back profit and also how much capital to invest. Here in inquiring what structures or organs perform what functions the anatomical chart is particularly apt. An example is the hierarchy of cities presented on page 66 to answer the question in what functions if any do cities of various sizes specialize.

3. INDUCTION, ISOLATION, AND INDICATION

The last two sections have stressed the need for sociology in observing "in the round" industrial development and have described the parts which economics and each of the other social sciences, such as political science and social psychology, can most effectively play. In this and the next sections we shall sum up briefly the methods by which economics and sociology in its various branches have reached conclusions as exact as possible, particularly conclusions of practical value.

In primitive societies where taboo and custom prevail no one does what is "not done." But in developing or developed societies, in order to be exact in summing up so variable an element as human behaviour and organization, methods must, wherever possible, be statistical. Thanks to a spate of manuals, I need no longer explain, as I had to do in 1929 (60, Chapters V–IX), the elementary measures whereby statistics tries to sum up frequency distributions by averages and deviations, and to find correlations and measures of their reliability or uncertainty. On the contrary, the danger is of too slick a use of statistical measures such as (79, pp. 29–31) striking an average size of plants of any industry when there is in fact no representative typical size.

To avoid thus riding "smooth-shod" over the facts and riding, too, into pitfalls, certain rules of procedure are needed for pursuing industrial development (to practical purposes) and not just describing the facts. Following the distinction in the Cambridge Economics Tripos, when first set up, between Analytical and Realistic papers, these procedures might be referred to by three Rs, as rubrics for realistic research. The definition in basic English of realistic as "thinking in a way which takes the facts into account" is certainly the type of research required. But we will be more specific as applied to Industry and help the reader memorize the procedures as the five Is: induction, isolation, indication, integration, and interpretation. The last two procedures are closely related, and the first three (now to be discussed under A, B, and C) are part of the normal method of research used by the Natural Sciences.

(A) Induction refers to the attempt "empirically" to discover probable general regularities or laws from the observation of the available facts, not from presumptions. I prefer using "inductive" to using empirical because, to quote the *Oxford Concise Dictionary*, empirical carries the sense of "relying solely on experiment; quack." Facts are observed and recorded not usually at random but to test some working hypothesis. Russell contrasts an hypothesis (169, p. 194) with a theory. "The investigator believes the theory, whereas he only thinks the hypothesis sufficiently plausible to be worth testing." *Some* studies claim to be realistic merely if their propositions can be illustrated from a few actual cases, but a true test must take account comprehensively of *all* cases covered by the hypothesis or else a truly representative sample of them.

Most so-called economic laws are theories and were not discovered by observation of facts, but by deduction from empirically untested and usually untestable, "unfalsifiable" assumptions. As Hutchison puts it (99, pp. 63–4)—

> The prevailing tendency to call propositions of pure theory "laws" is misleading and inappropriate, and appears to be a survival from eighteenth-century rationalist philosophy and theology. . . . We suggest that the term law should be reserved only for those empirical generalizations such as Pareto's or Gresham's law or the law of diminishing returns or diminishing marginal utility. It is such laws as these that it is the central object of science to discover.

To the empirical generalizations cited by Hutchison should perhaps be added, as of interest to industrial development, the classical Law of Increasing Return in manufactures (but emphatically not the short-run U-shaped "law" of diminishing return). Since, to quote Dr. J. N. Keynes (107, p. 206), Malthus, in the second and later editions of his *Essay*, pursues an inductive method of inquiry and his reasoning is directly based on historical and statistical data, we can add Malthus's law of population. Engel's Law, confirmed repeatedly, affecting the market for food products, may also be added, and Zipf's Law (III, §3) particularly affecting urbanization and the relative size of transport, marketing, and industrial centres.

Though needing further confirmation besides the British experience of 1930–5 and 1951 and the American of 1929 and 1941–5 (69 and 79) and the Italian of 1951 (26), laws might emerge out of the frequent identity, described in Chapters III and IV, of industries with larger sizes of plant and industries with (*a*) the more intensive capitalization and (*b*) the higher localization of industries. Modern econometrics may well be on the eve of inducing *wide* generalizations on industrial economics, and certainly H. L. Moore in his *Laws of Wages* and *Synthetic Economics* and (Senator) Paul Douglas of Cobb–Douglas formula fame may be counted as pioneers. Empirically discovered laws are formed from the less general to the more general and can, therefore, only be expected slowly to emerge.

In addition to laws that state more or less uniform "relationships," sequences can be empirically discovered and measured as the trends listed in our first chapter. The less general relationships called *effects* could also be empirically tested. They are special cases, and often special exceptions to a general proposition whether it is an empirical law or not. The best known is the *Ricardo Effect* that (155, Chapter XXXI) "every rise of wages will have a tendency to determine the saved capital in a greater proportion than before to the employment of machinery. Machinery and labour are in constant competition, and the former can frequently not be employed until labour rises." This special application of the "principle of substitution" has recently been empirically tested and verified by Seymour Melman (138).

Again, the "effect" attributed by Marshall (129, III, vi, 4) to Sir R. Giffen, that a rise in the price of bread may result in more bread being consumed by the poor because they are forced by the rise "to curtail their consumption of meat and the more expensive farinaceous foods" is definitely an *exception* to the general proposition that a rise in price diminishes the demand. The Sargant Effect (129, IV, vii, 9) is an exception to the general proposition that a rise in the price of anything increases its supply. When only a fixed amount of interest is wanted, then if the rate of interest is raised, not more, but less is saved. When applied to labour the Sargant Effect has often been demonstrated. Where labourers want only a fixed income, then the "effect" is that the greater the rate of wages per piece or per hour, the less the pieces made or the hours worked—the higher in fact, as shown, among others, by Vernon (70, p. 99), the absenteeism. Again, the Florence Effect described earlier is an empirically discovered exception to the general empirical law that the more concentrated the location of an industry, the larger its plants. The special circumstance associated with this effect is the existence of a large town or conurbation in which medium or small plants of an industry are often found highly localized.

Few empirical laws or effects have been worked out, largely, perhaps, because of the prestige attached within the economics establishment to the propositions of pure theory. As Hutchison writes (99, p. 60), "empirical laws are obviously regarded as inferior and unsatisfactory and even denied the dignity of the term law altogether."

In his Valedictory Address to the London School of Economics (17, p. 464–5) Lord Beveridge drew attention to the strange reactions of leading economists to Lord Keynes's "General Theory" when (109) it appeared in 1936—

> It is the duty of the propounder of every new theory, if he has not himself the equipment for observation, to indicate where verification of his theory is to be sought in facts—what may be expected to happen or to have happened if his theory is true, what will not happen if it is false.
>
> That is the demand that would be made of the propounder of a new theory in every natural science. It is not the demand that has been made of Mr. Keynes by his fellow economists. I have read with some care ... the reviews of Mr. Keynes' book in the three leading organs of economics in the English speaking world—the *Economic Journal*, *Economica*, and the *Quarterly Journal of Economics*. Each review is written by an acknowledged leader among professional economists. None of them takes the point that the truth or falsehood of Mr. Keynes' theory cannot be established except by appeal to facts; none of them tests it by facts himself. (The only reference (in all three reviews) to observation of facts as having any bearing on the subject under discussion appears to be a single sentence ending Part I of Mr. Knight's review.) The distinguishing mark of economic science, as illustrated by this debate, is that it is a science in which verification of generalizations by reference to facts is neglected as irrelevant.

The very assumptions from which pure theory deduces its propositions (instead of inducing them from facts) are coming more and more into question. As Kuznets puts it (112), "much of the work of economists in the field of economic growth suffers from excessive timidity in attempting empirical coverage, with an almost insufferable boldness in drawing unlimited generalizations from a mere handful of facts." Marshall himself thought (129, Appendix B) economists argued as though all mankind had the same habits of mind as city men, and since his day psychologists and sociologists, not to mention political scientists like Graham Wallas (197), have shown most of mankind most of the time to be acting irrationally. Even top industrial managers, according to Katona (103), we may recall (IV, §7), cannot be assumed to aim at maximum profit. Yet, following the synthesis I put forward in Chapter II, man is not completely irrational and it is up to realistic economics and sociology to find his degree of rationality—the amount of Economic Man within him.

(B) With observation and hypothesis, Russell (169, p. 194) joins experiment, and he describes experiment as differing from observation by deliberate control of conditions or isolation of factors. Like natural scientists, social scientists are confronted by multiple causation, but disclaim experiment on the effects of one isolated factor at a time as in a laboratory. In the design of their research they can, however, select times, places, or persons where the factors they are studying are isolated from other disturbing factors, or they can study the effect of changing one isolated condition at a time, as, for instance, methods (IV, §9) of wage-payment on the same group of persons, at the same job. This is often feasible in a factory, where conditions generally are standardized.

Many fallacies or pitfalls have to be avoided that are due to neglect of isolation, and in my *Statistical Method* (60, pp. 205, 209) I gave an example each of fallacies of "mal-selection" and of "mal-control," one rather obvious, the other less so, but often committed—

> Some health resorts have higher death-rates than industrial districts. The moribund tend to go to health resorts and before condemning these health resorts as fraudulent, one should *select* invalids, if possible of similar degree of invalidity, and find whether they do not die off at a more rapid rate in industrial purlieus.

If persons know they are being experimented with they may, according to circumstances, be inordinately enthusiastic, sullen or self-conscious, and may thus render generalization and application to conditions of ordinary life impossible. Though it sounds the right and noble thing to do and is generally advocated, it is for this reason unscientific to "enlist the workers co-operation" when carrying out any new industrial policy.

Though this caution about the isolation of factors and policies was written before the publication of Elton Mayo's observations of the relay assembly girls at the Hawthorne Works (164, p. 181), it is very relevant to any practical policy arising therefrom. The practical question is whether the self-consciousness and keenness (resulting in higher output) engendered among the operatives by the investigators consulting and "questioning (them) sympathetically about their reactions" was likely to last when the policies were applied in the ordinary routine of the factory.

The purpose of isolating two, or a few, characteristics or events is to find whether coincidences of certain of the events, but not others, are repeated in a pattern relatively frequently enough to be significant of some causal relation. The fallacy of "coincidence" lies in insufficient recurrences being observed and also in insufficiently exact coincidence in time or place, and here I took even Dr. Freud to task (60, pp. 196–7) for interpreting losses of gifts from relatives critical of the recipient as a wish to forget them, before the frequency, incidence, and closeness of timing of criticisms and loss were established exactly.

This test by the isolation of certain events in recurrent coincidence when all other events vary has been applied notably (28) in the statistical analysis of industrial fluctuations. Here Wesley Mitchell's *Business Cycles*, published in 1913, discovered certain uniformities occurring during major cycles lasting throughout the nineteenth and early twentieth century. As Mitchell summed up (140, p. 5) his own discoveries—

Longer experience, wider knowledge of business in other countries and better statistical data have gradually discredited the view that crises are abnormal events, each due to a special cause. The modern view is that crises are but one feature of recurrent "business cycles." Instead of a "normal" state of business interrupted by occasional crises, men look for a continually changing state of businesss—continually changing in a fairly regular way.

Lord Beveridge (18, p. 286) found, in fact, four uniformities repeated in the cycle of the British economy, so dependent, as we have seen, on international trade: "the parallel movement of prices and production; the greater range of fluctuation in certain industries either as making durable goods or producers goods; the greater range of fluctuation in British export industries; and the earlier incidence of fluctuation in British export industries."

(C) The procedure of indication has not been given as much attention as induction or isolation. But it is quite as important now that so many more statistical data relevant to the social sciences are being presented officially or otherwise. The question is how far available statistics can be found to measure or "indicate" the real issue under discussion, including ultimate aims. Economics and sociology are presented with certain practical problems, but the really relevant facts required to solve these problems may not tally with the available measured data. To meet this sort of dilemma between relevancy and availability I have distinguished (71) the real but often not directly measurable issue from the measurable index, or several alternative indices which are available in the statistics, or which can be derived from them, and which are more or less nearly related to the real issue. Thus the issue of capital intensity, so important for development, is measured in Table XV by several indices or as they are now coming to be named "indicators," and the size of plants is indicated by number of persons employed, though this takes no account of the difference in material equipment. Critical articles such as Winsten and Margaret Hall's "Measurement of Economies of Scale" (202) should be appearing side by side with the growth in statistical data, not only to design indicators for hitherto unmeasured characteristics, for instance, the degree of vertical or other integration, but to set forth the pros and cons of the various indicators already available. Recently, for instance, the market value of their shares and debentures were used as an index of the size of companies, and it seemed to me a duty to my fellow researchers to warn them off this index (75) because it might, and often did, measure the opposite of what was intended. Market values of ordinary shares would *rise* if, out of a given profit, more were paid in dividends, but this would result in less being ploughed back— that is, in a lower total of assets, which is the usual index of the size of firm. Again, an indicator which this book has repeatedly used is the national income, and it has proved of the greatest value for the internal control of a nation's economy. However, if national income-a-head is used externally as an index of welfare compared to that of other countries more thought should certainly be given to its limitations, the different sociological circumstances, and the available statistics of the countries being compared. Unfortunately, most economists, and sociologists too, are engaged in higher and more abstract things than scrutinizing and evaluating the mundane produce of official statistical departments. Thus data often promising enough for realistic research go unused, or misused. Yet this critique of statistical indices, for instance, our questioning in Chapter II of the comparability of the definition of "occupied" in the statistics of different countries, should be quite respect-able. It is similar to the critical scholarship exercised by the historian and the editor of literary texts to establish the cre-dentials of their data.

Finally it should be said that the process of indication some-times serves a still higher purpose than finding measures for important concepts; no less than defining more clearly and con-cretely the concepts themselves. Sir John Clapham's simile of the empty boxes (38) of economic theory in which no phenomena can be filed, is valid, not only because the econo-mist provides no measurable indicator of qualifications for ad-mission to boxes but sometimes because the very thing to be measured is not specified. Scale of production (72, p. 4), may refer to the size of the output of a particular product or process, the size of the plant, or the size of the firm, and this ambiguity may not be noticed till the data have to be measured and classified according to some indicator. Ambiguity also haunts such concepts as capital-intensity, which few economists (T. Barna, with his use of fire-insurance valuations (9, pp. 1–36) is an honourable exception) have tried to measure or compare for particular industries by any accurate indicator.

4. INTEGRATION AND INTERPRETATION

To integrate is, basically, to "complete by addition of parts; combine (parts) into a whole." Research for industrial development calls for adding together and combining the different social sciences, and sometimes the natural sciences, too. These sciences are at present cultivated and taught as special disciplines, largely with their own special tools of research.

The social sciences have already been surveyed, so here discussion can be confined to instances of three useful lines of integration, two of which involve interpretation too: (i) the same terms, conceptions, and tools of research could, with advantage to clarity and understanding, be used in discussing the interests the several social sciences have in common; (ii) reference is useful for interpretation from one social science to another, and so also is (iii) some cross-reference from social sciences generally to the natural sciences.

(i) A *common interest* for most social sciences is that of the structure (including the government) of the societies involved. Economic behaviour is different from political or social behaviour, but the associations involved all have some sort of constitution, rules of procedure, methods of appointment, sanctions, and so on. The government of large industrial firms and companies, analysed in Chapter V, now has devoted to it a vast bibliography. Outstanding authors (some of whose books I quote and number in my bibliography) include J. C. Baker, Chester Barnard, Wilfred Brown (25), Henri Fayol, Mary Follett, David Granick (211), E. Jaques (102), Herbert Simon (128), and L. Urwick. Many have their own individual terminology, but, in describing his own firms' organization, and management, Wilfred Brown found terms of political science, such as the Representative, Legislative, and Executive Systems, and the Appeals Procedure, quite natural as chapter headings. *Executive* has, in fact, long ago been taken over by big American business from political science. Under the editorship of Milward (139) large-scale organizations in central and local government, in nationalized undertakings, in banks, insurance, and manufacturing companies are all discussed, using similar concepts, such as centralization, delegation, co-ordination, executive committees, functional management, and speed of decision. The details of organization depended upon the work performed, but, and this is the point, their details though different could be described in similar terms, compared as to similar needs of organization and analysed with the same tools. It is high time that, at least on the structural level, political scientists of the State broadened their outlook to integrate what is essentially a political science of large-scale industrial firms. They would then have many more cases from which to generalize.

For practical purposes the study of industry is no more confined than political science to questions of structure, but reaches for the interrelation of structure and activity. It is interested, for instance, in the effect of a single-firm industry—a monopoly —upon price or output behaviour; in managerial rather than capitalist control of a large company upon investment and dividend policy; or in the effect of nationalization or consumer co-operation upon costs, quality of production, and the use of resources. The structure and government of industrial organization must be analysed more systematically, and along political lines. I put three "categories" to the Aristotelian Society (64)—

> State government and the government of large firms have many characters in common and the same three vital political processes: the process of sharing work among the persons and groups in a society, the process of selecting persons to do each work-share and, most essential of all, the process of ruling (including training and incentives). Every organized society has some (alternative) variety of structure and also some (alternative) variety of selection of work-sharing and of ruling process as between the persons or sub-societies composing it.

Integration of political science and economics should thus test what particular combination or syndrome of varieties of selection, work-sharing, and ruling process are "viable" and are associated with success in development.

(ii) Interpretation is, indeed, joined to integration in the heading of this section because a fact or trend observed purely in one special discipline can often be explained (but usually is not) by *cross-reference to another social discipline*. Weber and Tawney's attribution of capitalism and the Industrial Revolution to Protestant forms of Christianity is the classic case, though

its validity is still under discussion. And most classical economists, particularly Adam Smith and Malthus, were by no
means "purists." Malthus (127, Vol. II, Chapter VIII) discusses at some length how decisions are reached about postponement of marriage by men (women are omitted) in the
different English social classes: gentlemen; tradesmen and
farmers; labourers and servants. Recently, to interpret wage-
rates, Lady Wootton (204, pp. 100–6) has drawn in sociology
and "dealing in ethical currency." Collective bargaining between trade unions and employers' associations is in fact based
upon tradition and precedent on the reasonable relation between rates for various grades, occupations, and industries. In
this realm of *laissez collectives faire*, as I have suggested, the
"reasonable" wage-rates settled for are often the opposite of
economically rational.

Other instances were cited earlier where the facts normally
studied in sociology strongly affect those studied in economics.
The reader may be reminded of the effect of the institution of
the English public schools and the ancient universities, and
their scale of values, upon the management efficiency of their
alumni in industry; and of the institution of the family upon
women's wages and employment. In general, economics and,
as Graham Wallas brought out in *Human Nature in Politics*
(197), political science, too, assume too readily man's rationality. Both should make more room for such anthro-
pological notions as sentiment, snobbery, taboo, myth, fetish,
ritual, herd-instinct, or the "gentleman-ideal." They must
accept man's irrationality, but study irrational behaviour
rationally. Conversely, in predicting a fall in Britain's population by 1950, demographers underrated economic motivation
and, basing their prediction on the slump year of 1933, failed
to integrate the economists' knowledge of business cycles and
man's rationality in having fewer children when he has
suddenly become poorer.

(iii) Economists limited their possible cross-reference to the
physical sciences when they assumed, for purposes of argument,
the state of the industrial arts to be stationary, and confined
their studies to long or short "normal" periods, not secular
movements (129, p. 379). Thus they missed the Marxian, or
any other interpretation, of development based on the progress

of science. Apart from growth, integration with the natural sciences has proved most useful in interpreting many another statistically observed economic phenomenon. Obvious instances are the observed correlations of a fall in output and a rise in accidents with longer hours interpreted by reference to the physiology of fatigue, or disparities in economic reward and the size of firms interpreted by reference to the wide distribution of innate psychological ability as between individuals in a population. Again the connexion of biology (16) with the food resources to meet the population explosion strengthens Malthus's theory, and reference to physical traits is implicit in the quasi-Marxian social relations of science such as my ergological interpretation of different industries' structure and government, including their possible nationalization.

For useful research, in short, too little cross-reference has so far occurred. Economists, still under the spell of the invisible hand, have not, as we have noticed, looked sufficiently into the structure and government of the visible hands, bodies, and organizations, the results of whose behaviour they study; and this behaviour is too often described impersonally in the passive voice. A structure of larger firms governed by managers may, for instance, make quite a difference to prices and output in any industry, as compared with a structure of many small-scale entrepreneurs.

Interpretation through integration of the social and natural sciences has been advocated, particularly by economists, over and over again, but the difficulty is to get anyone to practise what he preaches, or to practise integration without preaching. Historians and to some extent regional and human geographers are, however, natural integrators. They bring together for their particular period and their particular regions all types of relevant knowledge. In fact, integration has been achieved for past historical epochs and for the more distant regions more extensively than for events here and now.

The word interpretation rather than explanation has been used because, defined basically as "to make clear the sense of words, writing, etc." (presumably including statistics), it suggests a closer follow-up, as practised by the natural sciences, of the duly established statistical trends and correlations, and not just speculation from fancy assumptions. Examples of this close

Q

follow-up occur in my comparison (II, §4) of women's with men's wages and in my interpretation (IV, §1) of an increase, but a slow increase, in the size of factories. Here, interpretation is a matter of filling up the gaps in the statistical correlation by various non-statistical lines of argument.

This brings up the second use of interpret as "take (behaviour, etc.) as having a certain purpose, cause." Statistical correlation, however high, of two traits does not tell us which is cause, which effect. They may both be the effect of a common cause or, as I have illustrated by genealogical trees (60, pp. 178–83), hold some other relationship. Interpretation non-statistically, or by further statistics, must make a "canvass" of possible causal relations. In my *Statistical Method* (60, Chapter XIV), from which I have quoted, the frequent applicability of the Laws of Evidence was pointed out, and (in addition to arguments derived from allied sciences, already discussed) three further lines of interpretation: mathematical deduction, step-by-step reasoning on certain general presumptions, and the common-sense purpose and introspection, on which economists rely so much. In this reliance a grave risk of error lies in the economists being intellectual and relatively affluent while many they write about are neither. Yet purpose certainly enters among other causes, into human affairs. Useful, too, is the Aristotelian distinction between this "final" type of cause and three others: the "material," the formal, and the efficient cause. To natural (material) causes there is added in human affairs the deliberate (formal) implementation by an (efficient) body of persons of some (final) purpose.

5. PRACTICAL DEVELOPMENT POLICY, VIRTUOUS AND VICIOUS CIRCLES

For the practical application of our economic and sociological diagnosis the first consideration is whether any supposed ills disclosed are part of a vicious circle and not likely to be prevented or cured without "breaking" action; or whether these ills are part of a self-rectifying process and simply one phase of an eventually virtuous circle.

The economists' conception of a stable equilibrium is the classic example of a supposedly virtuous circle. The pendulum that deviates out of the perpendicular to left or to right is bound to swing back again to normal. Thus if supply falls short of demand, prices will, under competition, rise and thus provide an incentive to suppliers; if demand fails to take off supplies, prices will, under competition, fall and thus provide a deterrent to suppliers. Many virtuous circles, not so universal as the classical economists assumed, exist as admitted of the "take-off" only to some degree. This view repeats our early conclusion (II, §6) that industrial development cannot be expressed in monolithic, perfect, thesis or antithesis, but in syntheses only measurable, statistically if possible, as matters of degree. Competition or monopoly is seldom perfect, and there are various degrees of imperfection in markets and sources of supply.

A thesis of virtuous economic circles was the philosophy underlying the *laissez-faire* policy of the nineteenth century; and an antithesis, of vicious circles to be planned against, forms part of much present-day philosophy. But we must still continually discover and rediscover what to let alone and what not to. Contrary to present "enlightened" opinion, but much to the benefit of freeing resources for planning elsewhere, there are directions in which *laissez faire* could be (and often, unobserved, has been) reintroduced because, in Galbraith's phrase (84), of some "countervailing power." Railways, as my colleague Gilbert Walker pointed out in 1933 (196) (though his view has only gradually been officially recognized and acted upon) no longer held a monopoly of inland transport. The competition between rail and road, if recognized earlier, might have left the railways much more free of government regulation in its rate structure, without risk of exploiting their customers. Again, the growth in the extent and strength of trade unions which the higher subscriptions due to higher wages permit, and the possibility of collective bargaining based on equal bargaining power, has made state protection of the worker against lower wages less necessary. To use my phrase, *laissez collectives faire* (73, pp. 89, 163) has in several industries taken the place of the state-enforced minimum wages of the wages councils.

With virtuous circles may be classed behaviour that is necessary to the economy and which the community can obtain cheaply because psychologically and sociologically it runs harmoniously "with the grain" of natural human proclivities. One example is the love of the peasant owner-farmer for his land and for the independence it gives him. Other examples are the taste for certain types of work, such as fishing, which, as Adam Smith remarked (173, I, Chapter 10), "natural taste . . . makes more people follow than can live comfortably by them." Marriage of risks is relevant here and, generally, people's taste for gambling, so that a small chance of a large profit may induce the often necessary risk to the community to be taken at, *on average*, a lower cost than otherwise.

Released from paying out heavily where natural proclivities can be harnessed to the economy, or from interfering where competition or non-government collective bargaining will do, the state can concentrate on attacking by its various powers the permanently vicious circles. Some of these powers, distinguished by prepositions, were cited (VII, §3) as breaking circles making for greater economic inequality both in the developed and the underdeveloped countries. Equality is generally accepted as a virtue; what other circles are considered vicious or virtuous must, of course, depend on the general ethical orientation.

Economics, sociology or any social science, as I maintain elsewhere (61, *passim*, 73, pp. 11–16), work in the indicative not the ethical, optative mood. As sciences, they cannot lay down the ultimate aims or ends of society, however measurable these aims may be. Joan Robinson (163, p. 147) quotes Popper urging economists "to combat, not foster the ideology which pretends that values which can be measured in terms of money are the only ones that ought to count."

To be practical, the social sciences, though they cannot as sciences determine what is welfare, must take account of the public opinion which, in a democratic country, will be needed to implement their conclusions. They must recognize, if not the aims, at least the aversions of the people with whom they are concerned and if possible find their measurable indicator or indicators—for instance, rates of unemployment, or (accepting the Barlow Commission Report of 1940) city congestion, or low living or working standards. In short, the vicious circles which are most usefully and scientifically tackled by the social sciences, in the manner of operational research, are those where public opinion admits a specific ill such as unemployment, inequality, instability, ill-health, or illiteracy and where that illfare can be measurably indicated.

In the present poverty-stricken condition of underdeveloped countries the world's "number-one" vicious circle, recognized by most economists, for example Nurkse (145, pp. 4–5) and put in diagram form at the end of the last chapter, is that starvation begets starvation, ill-health ill-health, poverty poverty.

Economists and sociologists do not agree among themselves, however, whether this vicious circle will be broken more or less automatically or not. Some maintain that if, somehow or other, standards rise among part of the population, this *élite* will then, to maintain their standards, learn to control their birth-rate and thus cumulatively raise standards further. A precedent is to be found in English nineteenth-century history. Unfortunately, the new accessibility of food resources in the American Middle West and the then unique position of England as the workshop of the world, is not likely to be repeated elsewhere. My own view, shared by many others, is that this quasi-automatic reduction of the birth-rate cannot be relied upon to act, or at least to act quickly enough; and that a vicious circle, continuing a low income for many heads, must be broken by positive action. This action must take the "tripod" form of controlling the number of heads, distributing aggregate incomes more equally among the heads, and increasing that income from any given resources. The attempt to increase the ratio or surplus of output and income in exchange for a given cost of all "inputs"—the striving for efficiency as usually defined—is peculiarly the economic means of achieving higher living standards. It involves not just more investment but increasing the productivity of each of the separate factors of production, labour, capital, management, and land, while giving full consideration to their sociological setting. Chapters IV and V were largely concerned with industrial efficiency in developed, Chapters VI and VII with industrial efficiency in underdeveloped countries.

The starvation-begets-inefficiency-begets-starvation circle apparently endemic in underdeveloped countries was, till recently, epidemic in the countries now developed, occurring during the slump of their trade cycle, and the slump areas of their location pattern. Lack of employment in these phases and areas led to increasing incapacity of the worker, increasing incapacity to greater unemployability. Accordingly, the State organized insurance as a palliative against the hazard of unemployment. But as the fully developed countries learn to smooth out temporary and local slumps, and as preventives are added to palliatives these countries approach general affluence. Other aims are then put forward that can be attended to beside higher standards of living and security, and more equality— aims that are less easily indicated by statistical measures.

Equality (as among consumers) is now extended to cover among producers the aims of Jeffersonian democracy and the diffusion of ownership advocated by Belloc and Chesterton in opposition to highly centralized decision-making. A circular trend has developed in which large plants and firms with measurably more concentrated management have increased mechanization and the application of science (an application that will certainly continue, unless the final application occurs in an atom bomb), whereupon mechanization tends to result in turn in larger plants and larger plants facilitate the further use of more machines. This circle is considered vicious by many people because concentration centralizes authority, reduces the number of small, independent industrialists and increases that of organization man. Here, a clash may well occur between efficiency and democracy similar to the dilemma in underdeveloped countries between large federations and many small independent states with small markets.

Trying to find a balance of net advantages between industrial democracy and efficiency certainly involves integration of sociological and economic research and will probably result in a compromise degree of democracy and of efficiency. Democratic aims in industry seem to have gone too far for purposes of efficiency, for instance, in the constitution of the Co-operative Wholesale Society, where twenty-eight full-time paid directors are appointed by election, and in the practice of most Co-operative Societies of not appointing university graduates for management posts (32, pp. 312–16). On the other hand, most big capitalist businesses will, for the sake of democracy as well as amenity, have to allow considerable negotiation and consultation at an early stage about making changes in the working conditions of their employees, either at plant, at firm, or (as in development councils) industry level. Workers and management must, in particular, agree on adjustments as a consequence of technological development in the workers' social life—on the working of shifts, for instance, or mobility between industries. A circle (considered vicious by many) in which conurbation breeds larger conurbation arises by two processes. People migrating to large cities to man expanding industries, form, with their resultant income, a market for the city's services, which in turn attracts more people as workers. And once land outside the conurbation is occupied by a smoky factory, a dump, or ribbon development, the amenity value of neighbouring land falls, and it can be bought for further industrial development.

This circling or spiralling from big to bigger business and big to bigger urbanization does not occur in all circumstances, and it is part of the task of practical research to find where it does or needs to, and where it does not or need not occur. Large-scale linked industries may be needed for industries where firms are specialized and small. In trades, such as house-building, retailing, and agriculture, owing to ergological factors, few plants farms or shops are big, but bigness may, perhaps, be necessary, as already said (IV, §5) somewhere in the whole productive process of which they are a part. Nor do most building or retailing operations require bigger cities. But in the activities where ergological processes (technology and sources of supply and market) foster large size, as particularly in manufacturing, the trend will probably be cumulatively toward larger urbanization, unless deliberate policy intervenes (80, pp. 22–4), say to discourage footloose industries not linked to the main industries of the locality.

In the policy for breaking cumulative circles, of big breeding bigger (and analogous circles if thought vicious), the State has relations with industry similar to those, distinguished by different prepositions (VII, §3), for dealing with poverty, inequality, and insecurity. The differences in relationship indicated by different prepositions (73, pp. 47–50) are of practical importance, since very different attitudes and forms of administration are required in the government departments or agencies concerned, according as they form the third, second, or primary party. Political structure, in short, will differ with the kind of relationship required. It is as a third party that the State defends the small trader, as well as the consumer, *from* monopolistic agreements between big businesses by means of the Restrictive Practices Act administered semi-legally; and participates *with* industry informally to establish democratic negotiation and some joint consultation within industrial plants, such as occur when piece-rates were introduced (IV, §9), so that the stronger party will not accumulate further strength. As a primary party the State publishes information compulsorily collected *about* industry and provides services *for* industry such as economic, technical, and management education. This can be seen as an attempt to make the democracy more knowledgeable and not cumulatively weakened by ignorance as against the privately educated, and also as an attempt to introduce more mobility and to stop certain highly respectable but not necessarily (marginally) useful professions attracting the most intelligent supplies of young people and thus becoming cumulatively still more respectable. The State, as a primary party, also undertakes through nationalization the operation *of* monopolies largely in order to check cumulative exploitation.

This primary operation calls for initiative and enterprise and requires a structure of government quite different to the requirements for a legislating and mediating third-party relationship. And as a second party directly facing industry the state requires yet a different organization, including a technically expert civil service, and a different procedure. As a second party the State exercises various controls (including tax and subsidy policies) *over* industry not only to develop it but to avoid spirals in stability (e.g. against inflation). In zoning industrial areas and town-and-country planning generally (including the building of new industrial towns), to defend living conditions and amenities *against* industrial and housing sprawl, the State must employ economists competent in industrial location because families must live where (80, Annex B) the chief *male* income-earner works.

In the practical procedure for breaking up vicious circles reliance must be placed either on compulsion or inducements to voluntary action or in some degree to both. In Western civilization the stress is on voluntary inducement; but it is often forgotten that it is easier to induce persons to act in a particular way if they are provided with the proper capacity and facilities for doing so. Recent sociology has in its diagnosis laid, in my view, too much stress on psychological willingness and motivation, too little on "capacitation" and on the facilities for greater capacity, including information, education, and "enlightenment." This conclusion was reached in such diverse directions as the stimulus to wider economic mobilization and mobility between industries, and to the checking of the birthrate.

The practical policy indicated by this conclusion is that more effort should be devoted to providing the required capacities and facilities, such as workers' housing and the means of moving, or access to birth-control appliances, medicaments, and clinics, and more effort in making people accept the facilities provided by breaking down traditions through education or "object lessons."

Furthermore, where willingness and motivation was not overstressed compared with capacity and facilities, as in the stimulus to labour productivity, my conclusion was that *economic* incentives had, in the modern literature, been overmuch despised, if not forgotten. Men in underdeveloped as in developed countries appear up to a point to react strongly to rates of pay, and more should be discovered by integration between economists and psychologists as to the critical points involved.

As part of the policy of making people more capable of industrial development in the underdeveloped countries and also among the working- and voting-masses of the developed countries must come the realistic teaching of the economics and sociology of their industrial systems. A realistic treatment, down to earth but up to date, must begin with the trends and the trains of causation in each country and follow through to the latest developments. It should stress the anthropology of the less-developed countries, and not stop short of the sociology of company development and managerial revolution in the developed countries. But, more than that, communication must be widespread, intelligible, persuasive, and acceptable. Economic development based on knowledge in the natural sciences has been lop-sided, not so much because knowledge has advanced unevenly, but because sometimes, as in death control, its social application depends on only a few experts operating on nature or on a population that need be only passive, while in other fields, as birth control or agricultural productivity, implementation depends on the widespread active co-operation of the population—a co-operation seldom achieved. Industrial and agricultural technical development halts, as we know, not because of lack of scientific knowledge in the world, but because the people who have to co-operate do not accept and apply to their particular business the sufficient science that already exists. Similarly, considerable economic and political knowledge exists of financing and management of the State and of industrial organization. But this knowledge has not been successfully communicated and has not been accepted.

An important factor in accepting a new technique is the vehicle of communication being used, and here a common world language, a lingua franca, and visual aids are almost essential. An obvious lingua franca for the world generally is English, which, in the form of Basic English, is easily learned and easily adapted for the natural and the social sciences (82). Indeed, both Basic English and visual aids may, by avoiding the ambiguities that beset the language of the social sciences, make existing knowledge clearer both in developed, as well as underdeveloped societies, and I have made a point in this book of defining many of my terms according to the *Basic Dictionary*.

A last word. I was careful, just above, to write not that "sufficient" knowledge existed in the social as perhaps in the natural sciences, but merely "considerable" knowledge. The laws and effects enumerated in this chapter, even if accepted as fairly scientifically established, admittedly do not cover much ground. It is in the hope of pushing from existing to further conclusions based on the realistic analysis of the facts of industry that this book has been written.

MEASURES OF THE RANGE OF CHARACTERISTICS AMONG DIFFERENT BRANCHES OF MANUFACTURE

REFERENCES have been made throughout the text to the wide range of characteristics or "traits" shown by different industries, even by different *manufacturing* industries. These differences are of direct practical importance in framing a policy for the location of industries in depressed areas or in underdeveloped countries. In fact, industrialization as a policy is somewhat meaningless and likely to be hit or miss unless the particular traits are known of the industries that are proposed to be introduced. Most of these traits are measurable, and with progress in census-taking some have been measured and correlated. All the summary measurement for all industries cannot, however, be found in any one document, and though such a document would certainly help practical research into industries, there is no space here for a comprehensive tabulation. While waiting for such perfection, this appendix attempts to give as many of the significant traits as possible with their range, illustrated from the half-dozen or so manufacturing industries at the two extremes of the range. The number of illustrative industries varies with the total number of subdivisions of manufacture made in the original data. Some surveys deal only in a few "orders" or "groups" of manufacturing industries, and the extreme cases I give are proportionately fewer.

Besides the immediate practical importance of the measurement of industrial traits, a more fundamental importance lies in tracing the association between traits and suggesting trains of causation. This tracing of trains, already attempted (69, 79) for localization, size of plant, and power-a-worker, could certainly be extended. How far, for instance, is there a "logic" connecting the particular material and market traits of industry (including its linkage with other industries) with its capital intensity, labour composition, and space and time incidence; how far does this ergology and technology affect the industry's organization and government?

The ergological theory of a "work" basis for the economic and sociological differences between industries has determined the order of the Sections in Table XV that follows—starting from work done and technology via economics to sociology and, possibly, political science. Indices measuring the materials, markets, and the work linkage of different industries appear as Sections I and II, capital intensity and labour composition, the technological background, as Sections III and IV. Location and occurrence—the space and time incidence—and scale of organization (the structural middle-ground) appear as Sections V, VI, and VII, government as Section VIII. The main lines of this logic appear in Table III (Chapter I), and are discussed in that chapter. Facts grouped under the very first and two later sections and subsections require, however, some further explanation.

Section I A

The British Standard Industrial Classification, adopted in 1948, contains twenty-four orders, of which two are for extractive industries (I) agriculture, forestry and fishing, and (II) mining, fourteen (III to XVI) are manufacturing, two (XVII and XVIII) building and public utilities, and six (XIX–XXIV) are services. The manufacturing orders with which the Table deals contain between them 115 industries. Their sizes in number employed, as stated in the first section of Table XV range from 603 to 538,477; but in subsequent sections industries are cited only from the 100 employing over 5,000. Many of the larger industries could have been split up further. The United States Census of 1947 in fact distinguished 453 manufacturing industries. On the other hand, in some of the sources used as data (*see* footnotes to the table) many of these census industries are lumped together in just a few groups.

Section VI

Growth is not measured in value of output, since prices changed so considerably between 1935 and 1951, but by taking these two census of production years, it is possible for most industries to supplement growth in numbers employed by change in horse-power-a-worker. Thus weight is given to growth in mechanical as well as labour power.

Section VIII C

Most industries have some central organ for advisory or research purposes, collective bargaining, or public relations. To that extent there is practical recognition of an industry as the sociologists' "association" with a measure of self-government.

So much for the main sections. Most of the subsectional measures lettered *A*, *B*, *C*, etc., are sufficiently explained in the Table itself. VII *B* attempts to measure whether there is in reality any representative size of plant before stating the size of that plant. One subsection and one section have *several* measures marked (i), (ii), etc. These are alternative methods of measuring the importance of materials (I *B*) and the degree of capital intensity (III). Elsewhere (69, pp. 90–3) I have considered in detail the pros and cons of six measures of investment or capital intensity. Four measures, in-

cluding (i) horse-power per worker, appear in the Table below.
They were chosen partly because of their availability in censuses,
partly because of their popularity in textbooks, partly because of
their comparability between times and places, and partly because
of their freedom from ambiguity. Unfortunately, availability and
popularity are often associated with incomparability and ambiguity. The values of net output per worker and the values of
fixed assets per worker (iii), the most popular and available of all
plausible indices of capitalization, cannot, because their numerators
are expressed in money and their denominator in men, be compared
between countries or between times when the value of money has
changed. Moreover, net output-a-worker is ambiguous in its
indications. Industries with high net output-a-worker tend to be
industries not only with high capital but also with high staff-ratios
and with more highly paid wage-earners than average (i.e., with
skilled craftsmen rather than unskilled labourers and women
workers). The *Production Census* of 1951 measures these (scientifically
speaking) "disturbing" factors of staff salaries and highly paid
craftsmen by giving for each industry the percentage that wages
and salaries form of the net output. Taking (ii) the percentage of
net output that remains after subtracting wages and salaries, a
residue devoted largely to depreciation and profit, we get nearer to
the pure cost of the capital. In short, crude net value of output-a-
worker will not be used unless, as in most underdeveloped countries,
there is no neater measure of capital intensity. The fourth measure
(iv) given in the Table is connected more directly with the fundamental notion of capital intensity as a relation between fixed capital
(indicated in fixed assets) and output. Since both numerator and
denominator are expressed in money values, this measure is fairly
comparable between times and places; but the valuation of fixed
assets has always been rather arbitrary.

The alternative indices or indicators presented as measures of
capital intensity are far from agreeing upon the industries that show
extreme results. Rosenbluth (165, p. 43) finds a rank-correlation of
no more than 0·74 between power-a-worker and fixed capital-a-
worker, a disagreement which stresses the need for the alternative
measures. Each has its limitations. For instance, horse-power-a-
worker is unduly influenced by the sheer weight of the materials
worked upon. The five industries (at Section I B) with the greatest
tons per worker have a power-a-worker ranging from 4·3 to 14·0;
for the five industries with least tons the range is 0·4 to 1·7. The
value-of-net-output type of measures, on the other hand, may be
influenced by manufacturers' selling costs or use of skilled labour, as
much as by capital costs. For each industry we could quote more
traits which are now measured and significant enough for some
industries' structure, though, perhaps, less so than the traits actually
given. Instances are water required, or coal and coke used, per
worker; or the proportion of youths, or old men employed.

Though the final tracing of any association between traits must wait on a complete set of measures for all industries and not just the extreme cases, causal trains are suggested in the Table by the frequent reappearance as extreme cases of certain particular industries. The two industries appearing most frequently to be extreme cases are dressmaking and tailoring or the clothing group (fifteen times) and iron and steel melt and roll, blast furnaces or primary metal group (twelve times). Both rank high in total size, but are never otherwise at the same extreme. They show opposite extremes in capital intensity (by three tests) large as against no representative size of plant, linkage (with some other industry as market) and cyclical fluctuation. Where the association of such opposite values of a trait repeat in enough industries (for instance high capital intensity with large size of plants, low intensity with small plants) some causal relations between the traits may be supposed.

In the detailed Table XV that follows, the several characteristics are measured and illustrated from *manufacturing* industries

TABLE XV

RANGE OF MEASURABLE CHARACTERISTICS OF MANUFACTURES: GREAT BRITAIN

All industries cited after Section I A employ over 5,000 workers

Characteristics	Industries with Lowest Indices	Industries with Highest Indices
I. MATERIALS AND MARKETS; WORK DONE A: *Size of Industry* * (No. employed, *Census of Production*, 1951)	Ice 603; incandescent mantles 769; wholesale slaughtering 853; flax processing 1,387; manufactured fuel 1,448; fellmongery 1,657; roofing felts 1,909	Iron and steel melt and roll 204,897; shipbuilding 207,788; radio and telecommunication 240,315; electrical engineering 292,485; motor and cycles 361,227; tailor and dressmaking 410,334; mechanical engineering 538,477
B: *Materials*— (i) Weight (tons per worker) (*b*)	Tobacco 2·6; cotton weaving 3·7; lace 4·8; linen 5·0; needle 5·0; wool 5·1	Cattle, etc., food 231; seed crush 251; fertilizer 287; iron and steel 330; grain mill 357; coke 1,680
(ii) Percentage of total cost (*b*)	Brewing 18; chinaware 25; starch 28; machine tool 30; glass 30	Wholesale bottling 75; butter, margarine 75; tobacco 77; seed crushing 79; bacon curing 81
C: *Products*— Weight (tons per £1,000 value) (*b*)	Tobacco 0·8; lace 1·1; silk and art silk 1·2; needle 1·8; wool 2·2	Cattle, etc., food 114; grain milling 118; brewing 161; fertilizer 200; coke 628
D: Percentage total imported requirements of final industrial output ((*f*) Table E, row 47): Industry groups (Import-content)	Coke-ovens 4; china and glassware 5; mechanical engineering 8; shipbuilding and marine engineering 9; textile finish and pack 9; building materials 9; aircraft 10; printing and publishing 10; motor and cycle 11	Cotton and man-made fibres 31; timber and furniture 34; nonferrous metals 36; leather and fur 40; cereal foodstuffs 41; woollen and worsted 48; oils and greases 53; mineral oil refine 80

TABLE XV—*continued*

Characteristics	Industries with Lowest Indices	Industries with Highest Indices
I. MATERIALS AND MARKETS; WORK DONE *E:* Percentage exported of total supply ((*f*) Table B, col. 48/col. 51): Industry groups	Textile finish and packing 0; timber and furniture 1; cereal foods 1; oils and greases 3; clothing 4; food not cereal 4; coke-ovens 5	Electrical engineering 21; woollen and worsted 21; mechanical engineering 23; precision instruments 24; drugs and perfumery 25; tinplate and tubes 28; motors and cycles 31
F: Elasticity of (working class) demand in respect of income (*g*) Food products Products not food	Margarine −0·25; condensed milk −0·22; flour 0·07; bread 0·12; tinned meat 0·23 Shoes 0·52; soap 0·69; men's clothing 0·81; newspapers 0·87; women's clothing 1·04	Cakes 0·56; biscuits 0·68; tinned fruit 0·69; tinned fish 0·70; sweets 0·79 Draperies 1·76; gas fittings 1·93; cosmetics, tooth powder, etc. 2·11; miscellaneous household equipment 2·30; carpets 2·36
II. LINKAGE WITH WORK OF OTHER INDUSTRIES *A: With another Industry as Source*— Highest percentage of final output value from any other home industry group ((*f*)Table E)	Mineral oil refine 2·1; oils and greases 2·3; non-ferrous 2·5; drink and tobacco 2·6; paper and board 4·1; timber and furniture 4·3; wool 4·4; radio, etc. 4·9	Printing (from paper) 20·0; paint and plastic materials (from chemicals and dyes) 20·1; clothing (from cotton, etc.) 21·5, (from wool) 21·5; railway rolling stock (from iron and steel melt) 22·8; hosiery (from cotton and man-made fibre) 28·9; boot and shoe from leather 32·5; manufactured foods not cereal (from agriculture) 41·9; tinplate and tubes (from iron and steel melt) 49·7; coke-ovens (from coal) 58·9
B: With other Industries as Market— Percentage of total supply for further production, i.e., intermediate output ((*f*) Table B, Col. 47/col. 51)	Boots and shoes 5; clothing 10; drugs and perfumery 10; hosiery and lace 10; drink and tobacco 11	Non-ferrous metals 90; iron and steel melt and roll 92; coke-ovens 93; oils and greases 98; textile finish and pack 100
III. CAPITAL INTENSITY OF PROCESSING (i) Horse-power per worker (*c*) 1951	Tailor and dressmaking 0·2; glove 0·3; made-up household textiles 0·3; leather goods 0·3; hosiery 0·6; toilet preparations 0·6; bread 0·7; shoes 0·7; motor repairs 0·7; canvas 0·7; preserved fruit and vegetables 0·7	Marine engineering 7·8; mineral oil refining 9·9; general chemicals 10·2; fertilizer 10·4; paper and board 11·5; iron and steel 12·5; spirit distil 18·8; cement 25·4
(ii) Percentage of net output not wages or salaries (*a*)	Loco shops 14·8; railway carriage 20·8; explosives 22·4; shipbuilding 23·9; motor repairs 25·4	Cement 66·8; brewing 67·9; paper and board 71·1; tobacco 74·4; bottling 74·8; toilet preparations 72·5
(iii) Fixed assets (£) per person employed 1954 (*i*) Industry groups	China 590; clothing, fur and leather 670; biscuit 780; wood and cork 860; shipbuilding 860; vehicles not motors 950; precision instruments and miscellaneous metal goods 1,050; electrical 1,050; glass 1,140; bread, etc. 1,170	Cement 2,950; iron and steel 3,480; drink 3,800; rayon, etc., production 4,340; paper and pulp 4,460; grain milling 4,690; chemicals and plastics 5,000; sugar and glucose 5,150; coke-ovens 8,450; mineral oil refine 12,680

TABLE XV—*continued*

Characteristics	Industries with Lowest Indices	Industries with Highest Indices
III. CAPITAL INTENSITY OF PROCESSING (iv) Capital (fixed) assets ÷ output (i) (The Capital coefficient)	Tobacco 1·0; china 1·2; biscuit 1·3; drugs 1·3; paint 1·3; wood and cork 1·3; clothing leather, fur 1·4; electrical engineering 1·4; shipbuilding 1·4	Drink 2·7; rayon, etc. 2·7; non-ferrous metal 2·7; iron and steel 3·2; grain milling 3·6; paper and pulp 3·9; other textiles 4·0; sugar 4·1; general chemicals 4·3; coke-ovens 7·7; mineral oil refine 7·9
IV. LABOUR COMPOSITION A: *Employment of Women*— Percentage women to total employed (a)	Coke-ovens 2; blast furnace 4; shipbuilding 4; railway carriage 4; marine engineering 5; cement 5; railway locomotive 5; steel sheets 5; motor repair 5	Canvas 67; linen 67; toys and games 67; gloves 69; narrow fabrics 69; toilet preparations and perfumery 70; hosiery 71; tailor and dressmaking 81; made-up household textiles 87
B: Percentage of total of workers on piece wages (e)	Wallpaper 2; shop and office fitting 2; mineral oil refining 2; grain milling 2; milk products 3; print and publish news 3; brewing 3; wholesale bottling 4; motor repair 5; bread and flour confectionery 6	Stationary engines 61; electric wire and cables 61; iron and steel melting and rolling 62; textiles and telephone apparatus 62; tinplate 64; rayon production 64; carpets 64; linoleum 67; hosiery 69; batteries 75
V. LOCATION PATTERN (Place Incidence) Coefficient of (Regional) Localization 1951 (c)	Mechanical engineering repair 0·07; motor repair 0·10; building materials 0·11; bread 0·11; brewing 0·11; timber 0·12	Cotton weaving 0·71; lace 0·72; cotton spinning 0·74; china 0·77; linen 0·84; jute, tinplate 0·89
VI. OCCURRENCE (Time-Incidence) A: Growth and decline 1935–51 in employed and (brackets) in horse-power-a-worker 1935 = 100 (a)	Hats and caps 45 (180); musical instruments 70 (93); lace 74 (114); jewellery 74 (178); seed crush 75 (111)	Radio and telecommunication 235 (n.a.); watch and clock 280 (300); machine tools 330 (n.a.); aircraft 439 (476); plastics materials 512 (n.a.)
B: *Seasonal Fluctuations*— Maximum range of monthly variation in *un*employed as percentage (m) of insured 1927–32	Drink 2·6; printing 2·8; bread 3·0; laundries 3·1; cardboard box, stationery 3·4	Tailoring 10·8; pottery 11·0; cotton 11·9; shipbuilding 12·0; linen 17·6
C: Cyclical slump in 1932 from level of employment 1929–35 (l)	Printing +1; bread −1; tailoring −1; electric cables −7; furniture −9	Motor vehicles −20; engineering −22; iron and steel −35; shipbuilding −46
VII. ORGANIZATION A: Staff (or employer) ratio per 100 operatives and staff (a Table 3)	Cotton 6; jute 7; tinplate 8; china 9; wool 9; tailor and dressmaking 10; brick 10; gloves 10; shipbuilding 11; shoes 11	Drugs 31; toilet preparations 31; aircraft 31; plastics 33; polishes 36; dyes 37; newspapers 39; oils and greases 43; paint 43; publishing 71
B: *Size of Plant*— How far average representative? Highest percentage of workers in any two *consecutive* size classes (1,000 + counts as two) (c)	Motor repairs 33; printing and binding 36; scientific instruments 36; jewellery 39; tailor and dressmaking 40; drugs 41	Cotton spinning 67 (M); cotton weaving 70 (M); radio 71 (L); marine engineering 73 (L); aircraft 78 (L) (h)

TABLE XV—*continued*

Characteristics	Industries with Lowest Indices	Industries with Highest Indices
VII. ORGANIZATION B: *Size of Plant—* If representative, percentage of workers in plants of over 500 (*c*) industries employing over 20,000 workers	Wood containers 0; timber 4·3; milk products 10·0; soft drinks 10·3; brick 11·2; brass manufacturing 11·6; furniture 12·0; bread 14·8; grain mill 15·2	Rubber 67; electrical engineering 73; shipbuilding 74; motor and cycle 77; iron and steel 80; radio 82; electric wire and cable 83; marine engineering 84; aircraft 87
C: Specialization (as against Integration) by Plants Percentage of sales of its principal products to total sales by the plants the Census allocated to the industry (*a*)	Fertilizer 63; preserved meat 69; linen 73; electric wires 75; electric light accessories 78; soft furnishing 79; brass manufacturing, railway locomotives 80; coke-ovens, electric engineering, glue, etc. 81	China, film production, grain milling, lace, leather, milk products, scrap metal, tailoring and dressmaking, wallpaper 99; tobacco, 100
D: *Size of Firm—* Large Companies (Assets £2·5m. +) per 100,000 workers (*d*)	Wood and cork 0·3; clothing 1·3; leather and fur 1·3; print and publishing (not newspapers) 1·5; Vehicles 2·6	Paper 12·9; newspaper 13·8; oil refining 15·4; cement 20·0; drink 30·9
VIII. GOVERNMENT A: *Quoted Joint Stock Companies—* Percentage they employ (*n*) of all workers in industry	Clothing 21; food 34; wool 35; building materials 36; pottery and glass 36; other metals 36	Electrical engineering 74; tobacco 85; metal (primary) 70; vehicles 70; drink 62
B: Concentration in three largest percentage businesses of net output (*j*) (Census Industries only)	Cotton weaving 4; motor, etc., repairs 4; tailoring and dressmaking 5; wood containers 5; leather 7; wool and worsted 8; printing 8; canvas 8; lace 8	Precious metal refining 84; margarine 85; wallpaper 86; dyes 89; starch 89; cement 89; explosives and fireworks 91
C: Central Organs for Industry	Majority with trade associations only	Furniture Development Council; wages councils (*see* industries listed, and Florence, *Industry and State*). Iron and Steel Board

Notes: Sources of Data

* After Section I A, the industries cited from the full list of the *Census of Production* are those employing over 5,000. But other official sources have shorter lists. In the input–output tables for 1954, the smallest manufacturing group distinguished was mineral oil refining employing 16,000, the largest mechanical engineering employing 929,000. In my *Investment, Location and Size of Plant*, I omitted all the *Census of Production* industries employing less than 4,000.

(*a*) *U.K. Census of Production* 1951
(*b*) FLORENCE, *Investment, Location and Size of Plant*, 1948, Appendix I
(*c*) FLORENCE, *Post-War Investment, Location and Size of Plant*, 1961
(*d*) FLORENCE, *Ownership, Control and Success of Large Companies*, 1961
(*e*) *Ministry of Labour Gazette*, April 1956 and June 1958
(*f*) *Input–Output Tables*, 1954. Division into 37 specific manufacturing industries
(*g*) PRAIS and HOUTHAKKER, *The Analysis of Family Budgets*, pp. 104–5, 1955
(*h*) M = Medium percentage employing between 100 and 1,000; L = Large percentage employing over 1,000
(*i*) BARNA, *Statistical Journal*, 1957, Part I, p. 24
(*j*) EVELY and LITTLE, *Concentration in British Industry*, 1960, Appendix B.
(*k*) This industry was subdivided in the Census of 1935 and 1930
(*l*) FLORENCE, *Labour*, 1948, p. 159
(*m*) SAUNDERS, *Seasonal Variations*
(*n*) National Institute of Economic and Social Research, *Company Income and Finance*, 1949–53

R

only, since industry in this strict sense is the subject of this book. But contrasts, probably still wider contrasts, and associations could also be measured between the manufacturing as a whole and the other main "sectors" of economic activity. Examples would include the large plant and high capital intensity associated in mining and public utilities, and the opposite small plant and low capital association in trade and building; or the association between the small *firms* and relatively few *companies* in agriculture, building, road transport, trading, and other services and the corresponding association of large firms and much company employment (in America) or nationalization (in Britain) in mining, rail and air transport, public utilities.

BIBLIOGRAPHY

In alphabetical order of authors' names except for eleven additional references (208–18) to recent publications 1961–3. Numbered references as in brackets in text. The page of the text where the reference occurs is given in the index under the name of the author.

Abbreviations

British Association: British Association for the Advancement of Science

E.J.: Economic Journal
I.L.R.: International Labour Review
J.I.E.: Journal of Industrial Economics
J.R.S.S.: Journal of the Royal Statistical Society

1. ACTON SOCIETY TRUST, *Size and Morale* (1953).
2. ACTON SOCIETY TRUST, *Management Succession* (1956).
3. ALLEN, G. C., *The Structure of Industry in Britain* (1961).
4. ANDIC, S. and PEACOCK, A. T., International Distribution of Incomes, *J.R.S.S.*, Part 2 (1961).
5. ANDREWS, P. W. S., *Manufacturing Business* (1949).
6. ANDREWS, P. W. S. and BRUNNER, ELIZABETH, Business Profits and the Quiet Life, *J.I.E.* (Nov., 1962).
7. BAIN, J. S., *Industrial Organization* (1959).
8. BALDAMUS, W., Type of Work and Motivation, *Brit. Jl. of Sociology* (March, 1951).
9. BARNA, T., Replacement Cost of Fixed Assets in British Manufacturing Industries, *J.R.S.S.* (Part I, 1957).
10. BARNA, T., *Investment and Growth Policies in British Industrial Firms* (1962).
11. BAUER, P. T. and YAMEY, B. S., *The Economics of Underdeveloped Countries* (1957).
12. BEESLEY, M., The Birth and Death of Industrial Establishments, *J.I.E.* (Oct., 1955).
13. BEHREND, HILDE, *Absence under Full Employment. Studies in Economics and Society*, University of Birmingham (1952).
14. BERLE, A. A., *Twentieth-Century Capitalist Revolution* (1955).
15. BERLE, A. A. and MEANS, G., *The Modern Corporation and Private Property* (1934).
16. BERTRAM, G. C. L., *Population Trends and the World's Biological Resources*, Eugenics Society (1949).
17. BEVERIDGE, LORD, Valedictory Address, The Place of the Social Sciences in Human Knowledge, *Politica* (Sept., 1938).
18. BEVERIDGE, LORD, *Full Employment in a Free Society* (1944).

19. BLACKETT, P. M. S., Presidential Address, British Association (1957).
20. BOHR, K. A., Investment Criteria for Manufacturing Industries in Underdeveloped Countries, *The Review of Economics and Statistics* (May, 1954).
21. BOSWELL, J., *Life of Samuel Johnson* (1791).
22. BRITISH ASSOCIATION FOR THE ADVANCEMENT OF SCIENCE, *Report of Committee on Scientific Research on Human Institutions* (1943).
23. BROWN, A. J., Inflation and the British Economy, *E.J.* (Sept., 1958).
24. BROWN, J. A. C., *Social Psychology of Industry* (1954).
25. BROWN, W., *Exploration in Management* (Foreword by E. L. Trist) (1960).
26. BRUNI, L., *Aspetti Strutturali delle Industrie Italiane* (1961).
27. BURNHAM, J., *The Managerial Revolution* (1941).
28. BURNS, A. F., *The Frontiers of Economic Knowledge* (1954).
29. BURNS, A. R., *Comparative Economic Organization* (1955).
30. CAIRNCROSS, A., *Introduction to Economics* (1944).
31. CALDER, R., The Mathematics of Hunger, *J.R.S.S.*, Part 3 (1962).
32. CARR-SAUNDERS, Sir A., FLORENCE, P. S. and PEERS, A., *Consumers' Co-operation in Great Britain* (1938).
33. CARTER, C. F. and WILLIAMS, B. R., *Investment in Innovation* (1958).
34. CARTER C. F. and WILLIAMS, B. R., The Characteristics of Technically Progressive Firms, *J.I.E.* (March, 1959).
35. CATLIN, G. E. G., Systematic Politics, *Elementa Politica et Sociologica* (1962).
36. CHARLES, ENID, *The Changing Size of the Family in Canada. Census of Canada* (1948).
37. CHENERY, H. B. and BRUNO, M., Development Alternatives in an Open Economy. The Case of Israel, *E.J.* (March, 1962).
38. CLAPHAM, SIR J., Of Empty Economic Boxes, *E.J.* (Sept., 1922).
39. CLARK, COLIN, *The Conditions of Economic Progress* (1951).
40. CLARK, COLIN, *The Economics of 1960* (1942).
41. CLARK, COLIN, New Light on Population, *Listener* (26th March, 1953).
42. COALE, A. J., Population Growth (A Review), *Science* (22nd Sept., 1961).
43. COPEMAN, G. H., *Leaders of British Industry* (1957).
44. CUMPER, G. E., Tourist Expenditure in Jamaica 1958, *Social and Economic Studies* (Sept., 1959).
45. DAVISON, J., FLORENCE, P. S., GRAY, BARBARA, and ROSS, N. S., *Productivity and Economic Incentives* (1958).
46. DEAN, J., *Managerial Economics* (1950).

47. EDWARDS, R. S. and TOWNSEND, H., *Business Enterprise* (1958).
48. ENGLAND AND WALES, *Preliminary Reports*, Census of Population (1951), (1961).
49. ENGLAND AND WALES, *Industry Tables*, Census of Population (1951).
50. EVELY, R. and LITTLE, I. M. D., *Concentration in British Industry* (1960).
51. FIRTH, R., *Elements of Social Organization* (1951).
52. FISHER, A. G. B., *The Clash of Progress and Security* (1935).
53. FISHER, G. R., Some Factors Influencing Share Prices, *E.J.* (March 1961).
54. FISHER, R. M. (Ed.), *The Metropolis in Modern Life* (1955).
55. FLEW, A., The Structure of Malthus's Population Theory, *Australian Journal of Philosophy* (May, 1957).
56. FLORENCE, LELLA. S., *Progress Report on Birth Control* (1956).
57. FLORENCE, P. S., *Economics of Fatigue and Unrest* (1924).
58. FLORENCE, P. S., *Over-Population, Theory and Statistics* (1926).
59. FLORENCE, P. S., *Economics and Human Behaviour* (1927).
60. FLORENCE, P. S., *The Statistical Method in Economics and Political Science* (1929).
61. FLORENCE, P. S., *Uplift in Economics* (American Edition, *Sin and Sociology*) (1929).
62. FLORENCE, P. S., A Statistical Contribution to the Theory of Women's Wages, *E.J.* (March, 1931).
63. FLORENCE, P. S., *Logic of Industrial Organization* (1933).
64. FLORENCE, P. S., The Method and Content of Political Science, *Proceedings of the Aristotelian Society* (1934).
65. FLORENCE, P. S., An Index of Working-Class Purchasing Power in Great Britain 1929–35, *Journal of Political Economy* (Oct., 1936).
66. FLORENCE, P. S., Science and the Social Relations of Industry, *Sociological Review* (Jan., 1939).
67. FLORENCE, P. S., The Selection of Industries suitable for Dispersion into Rural Areas, *J.R.S.S.*, Part II (1944).
68. FLORENCE, P. S., The Statistical Analysis of Joint Stock Company Control, *J.R.S.S.*, Part I (1947).
69. FLORENCE, P. S., *Investment, Location and Size of Plant* (1948).
70. FLORENCE, P. S., *Labour* (1948).
71. FLORENCE, P. S., Patterns in Recent Social Research, *The British Journal of Sociology* (Sept., 1950).
72. FLORENCE, P. S., *Logic of British and American Industry* (1953).
73. FLORENCE, P. S., *Industry and the State* (1957).
74. FLORENCE, P. S., The Reward for Risk-bearing by Shareholders in Large Companies, *J.I.E.* (May, 1957).

75. FLORENCE, P. S., New Measures of the Growth of Firms, *E.J.* (June, 1957).
76. FLORENCE, P. S., A Note on the Ratio of Staff to Wage-earners *E. J.* (Sept., 1957).
77. FLORENCE, P. S., Tests of the Validity of Some Stock Exchange Folk-lore, *Three Banks Review* (March, 1958).
78. FLORENCE, P. S., *Ownership, Control and Success of Large Companies* (1961).
79. FLORENCE, P. S., *Post-war Investment, Location and Size of Plant* (1962).
80. FLORENCE, P. S., *The Future of the Conurbations* (Town-planning Institute, 1963).
81. FLORENCE, P. S., Economia Realistica e Problemi dell' Industria Brittannica attuale, *La Scuola in Azione* (1963).
82. FLORENCE, P. S., Basic English for the Social Sciences (in *Basic English as an International Language for Science*) (Evans Bros., 1963).
83. FREUD, S., *Group Psychology*, translated J. Strachey (1959).
84. GALBRAITH, K., *American Capitalism* (1952).
85. GLAISYER, JANET, BRENNAN, T., FLORENCE, P. S. and RITCHIE, W., *County Town (A Survey of Worcester)* (1946).
86. GLASS, D. V., How many can climb the Social Ladder? *Listener* (5th April, 1951).
87. GLASS, D. V., Population Prospects and their Implications (contribution to *Hunger*) (British Association, 1961).
88. GOODRICH, C. *et al.*, *Migration and Economic Opportunity* (1936).
89. GORDON, R. A., *Business Leadership in the Large Corporation* (1945).
90. GRAHAM, B. and DODD, D. L., *Security Analysis* (1951).
91. HAGUE, D., Economic Theory and Business Behaviour, *Review of Economic Studies* (May, 1949).
92. HALL, R. and HITCH, C. H., Price Theory and Business Behaviour, *Oxford Economic Papers* (1939).
93. HANEY, L. H., *Business Organization and Combination* (1913).
94. HENDERSON, SIR H., *Supply and Demand* (1922).
95. HIMES, N. E., *Medical History of Contraception* (1936).
96. HOBSON, J. A., *Evolution of Capitalism*, Rev. Ed., (1916).
97. HOOVER, E. M. and VERNON, P., *Anatomy of a Metropolis* (1959).
98. HOSELITZ, B. F., *Sociological Aspects of Economic Growth* (1960).
99. HUTCHISON, T. W., *The Significance and Basic Postulates of Economic Theory* (1938).
100. INTERNATIONAL LABOUR ORGANIZATION, The Size of Industrial Establishments, *I.L.R.* (Oct., 1955).

101. INTERNATIONAL LABOUR ORGANIZATION, Incidence of Industrial Disputes, *I.L.R.* (Sept., 1956).
102. JAQUES, E., *Measurement of Responsibility* (1956).
103. KATONA, G. T., *Psychological Analysis of Economic Behaviour* (1951).
104. KAY, H. D., What Limits Food Production in *Hunger* (British Association, 1961).
105. KERR, C., Changing Social Structures, in Moore and Feldman, *Labor Commitment and Social Change in Developing Areas* (1960).
106. KERR, C. and SIEGEL, A., The Interindustry Propensity to Strike in *Industrial Conflict*, Ed. Kornbaurer, Dubin and Ross (1954).
107. KEYNES, DR. J. N., *Scope and Method of Political Economy*, 4th ed. (1917).
108. KEYNES, LORD, *A Treatise on Money* (1930).
109. KEYNES, LORD, *The General Theory of Employment, Interest and Money* (1936).
110. KILBRIDGE, M. D., Statistical Indicators of the Continuing Effectiveness of Wage Incentives, *J.I.E.* (Nov., 1960).
111. KUZNETS, S., Toward a Theory of Economic Growth in Lekachman *National Policy for Economic Welfare at Home and Abroad*, (1955).
112. KUZNETS, S., *Notes on the Study of Economic Growth*, "*Items*" (Social Science Research Council, 1959).
113. LABOUR, MINISTRY OF, Earnings of Administrative, etc. Employees, *Gazette* (Sept., 1960).
114. LABOUR, MINISTRY OF, Payments by Results, *Gazette* (Aug., 1961).
115. LABOUR, MINISTRY OF, The Family Expenditure Survey, *Gazette* (Oct., 1961).
116. LABOUR, MINISTRY OF, Membership of Trade Unions— 1960, *Gazette* (Dec., 1961).
117. LAVINGTON, F., *The English Capital Market* (1921).
118. LEKACHMAN, R., The Non-Economic Assumption of J. M. Keynes, in *Common Frontiers of the Social Sciences*, ed. Komarovsky (1957).
119. LENIN, V. I., The Teachings of Karl Marx 1914, *A Handbook of Marxism* (1936).
120. LENIN, V. I., Imperialism 1917, *A Handbook of Marxism* (1936).
121. LEWIS, A., *The Theory of Economic Growth* (1955).
122. LINTON, D. L., Population and Food in the Tropical World, *The Advancement of Science* (Nov., 1961).
123. LONG, JOYCE, Labour Turnover under Full Employment, *Studies in Economics and Society* (University of Birmingham, 1951).

124. LYDALL, H. and LANSING, J. B., Distribution of Personal Income and Wealth, *American Economic Review* (March, 1959).
125. MACKINTOSH, A., *The Development of Firms* (1963).
126. MADGE, C., *War-Time Patterns of Saving and Spending* (1943).
127. MALTHUS, T. R., *Essay on the Principle of Population*. 2nd ed. (1803).
128. MARCH, J. G. and SIMON, H. A., *Organizations* (1958).
129. MARSHALL, A., *Principles of Economics*, 6th ed. (1910).
130. MARSHALL, A., *Industry and Trade* (1920).
131. MARX, K., *Capital* (English Translation ed. Engels) (1919).
132. MASON, E. (Ed.), *The Corporation in Modern Society* (1959).
133. MAYO, E., *The Social Problems of an Industrial Civilization* (1949).
134. McGREGOR, D. H., *Enterprise, Purpose and Profit* (1934).
135. McIVER, R. M. and PAGE, C. H., *Society* (1950).
136. MEANS, G., *Pricing Power and the Public Interest* (1962).
137. MEHTA, M. M., *Structure of Cotton-mill Industry of India* (1949).
138. MELMAN, S., *Dynamic Factors in Industrial Productivity* (1956).
139. MILWARD, G. E. (Ed.), *Large-scale Organization* (1950).
140. MITCHELL, W., Business Cycles, in *Business Cycles and Unemployment* (National Bureau of Economic Research 1923).
141. MORGAN, T., Income Distribution in Ceylon, Puerto Rico, U.S., and U.K., *E.J.* (Dec., 1953).
142. MUMFORD, L., *The Culture of Cities* (1938).
143. MYRDAL, G., *An International Economy* (1956).
144. NORTHCOTT, C. H., *African Labour Efficiency Survey* (Colonial Office, 1949).
145. NURKSE, R., *Problems of Capital Formation in Underdeveloped Countries* (1952).
146. PARKINSON, C., Parkinson's Law (Original Statement), *The Economist* (Nov. 1955).
147. PARSONS, T., *The Structure of Social Action* (1937).
148. PENROSE, EDITH, *Theory of the Growth of the Firm* (1959).
149. PIGOU, A. C., *The Economics of Welfare* (1920).
150. PRAIS, J. and HOUTHAKKER, O., *The Analysis of Family Budgets* (1955).
151. PREST, E. J., National Income of the United Kingdom 1870–1946, *E.J.* (March, 1948).
152. RAMANADHAM, V. V., Certain Aspects of the Industrial Structure of India, *J.I.E.* (June, 1958).
153. REDDAWAY, W. B., *The Development of the Indian Economy* (1962).

154. REDDAWAY, W. B., The Economics of Underdeveloped Countries, *E.J.* (March, 1963).
155. RICARDO, D., *Principles of Political Economy and Taxation* (1817).
156. ROBERTS, B. C., *National Wages Policy in War and Peace* (1958).
157. ROBERTSON, SIR D., *The Control of Industry* (1927).
158. ROBERTSON, SIR D., Increasing Returns and the Representative Firm, *E.J.* (March, 1930).
159. ROBINSON, E. A. G., *Structure of Competitive Industry* (1931).
160. ROBINSON, E. A. G., The Changing Structure of the British Economy, *E.J.* (Sept., 1954).
161. ROBINSON, E. A. G. (Ed.), *The Economic Consequences of the Size of Nations* (1961).
162. ROBINSON, JOAN, Imperfect Competition Revisited, *E.J.* (Sept., 1953).
163. ROBINSON, JOAN, *Economic Philosophy* (1962).
164. ROETHLISBURGER, F. J. and DICKSON, W. J., *Management and the Worker* (1939).
165. ROSENBLUTH, G., *Concentration in Canadian Manufacturing Industries* (1957).
166. ROSKILL, O., *Who Owns Whom?* (1959).
167. ROSTOW, W. W., *The Process of Economic Growth* (1953).
168. ROSTOW, W. W., *The Stages of Economic Growth* (1959).
169. RUSSELL, LORD, *The Analysis of Matter* (1927).
170. SARGANT, W. L., *Recent Political Economy* (1867).
171. SAUNDERS, C., Consumption of Raw Materials in the United Kingdom, 1851–1950, *J.R.S.S.* (Part III, 1952).
172. SCHUMPETER, J., *The Theory of Economic Development* (1934).
173. SMITH, A., *Wealth of Nations* (1776).
174. SMYTH, R. L., Economics for the Uninitiated, *The Advancement of Science* (May, 1961).
175. STEINDL, J., *Small and Big Business* (1945).
176. STRACHEY, ALIX, *The Unconscious Motives of War* (1957).
177. STYKOS, J. M., *Family and Fertility in Puerto Rico* (1955).
178. SUKHATME, P. V., The World's Hunger and Future Needs in Food Supplies, *J.R.S.S.* (Part IV, 1961).
179. TAWNEY, R. H., *Equality* (1931).
180. TEW, B. and HENDERSON, R. E., *Studies in Company Finance* (1959).
181. TROUGHTON, F., The Teaching Concerning Cost Functions in Introductory Economics, *J.I.E.* (March, 1963).
182. U.K. CENSUS OF PRODUCTION, *Summary Tables* (1951).
183. UNITED NATIONS, *Demographic Yearbooks*.

184. UNITED NATIONS, *Patterns of Industrial Growth*.
185. UNITED NATIONS, *Statistical Year Books*.
186. U.S. FEDERAL TRADE COMMISSION, Divergence between Plant and Company Concentration (1950).
187. U.S. FEDERAL TRADE COMMISSION, Report on Changes in Concentration (1954).
188. U.S. NATIONAL RESOURCES PLANNING BOARD, *Industrial Location and National Resources* (1943).
189. U.S. PUBLIC HEALTH SERVICE, *Bulletin 106*, Comparison of an Eight-hour Plant and a Ten-hour Plant (1920).
190. U.S.S.R. ECONOMY, *A Statistical Abstract* (1957).
191. VEBLEN, T., *The Theory of the Leisure Class* (1899).
192. VEBLEN, T., *The Theory of Business Enterprise* (1904).
193. VEBLEN, T., *Engineers and the Price System* (1923).
194. VILLARD, H., Some Notes on Population and Living Levels, *Review of Economics and Statistics* (May, 1955).
195. VILLARD, H., *Economic Performance* (1959).
196. WALKER, G., Road and Rail Competition, *E.J.* (June, 1933).
197. WALLAS, G., *Human Nature in Politics* (1916).
198. WEST MIDLAND GROUP, *English County (Herefordshire)* (1943).
199. WEST MIDLAND GROUP, *Conurbation (Birmingham and the Black Country)* (1948).
200. WHEELWRIGHT, E. L., *Ownership and Control of Australian Companies* (1957).
201. WHYTE, W. H., *The Organization Man* (1957).
202. WINSTEN, C. and HALL, MARGARET, The Measurement of Economies of Scale, *J.I.E.* (July, 1961).
203. WOOLF, L., *After the Deluge* (1931)
204. WOOTTON, LADY, *The Social Foundations of Wage Policy* (1954).
205. WRIGHT, N. C., The Current Food Supply Situation and Present Trends in *Hunger* (British Association, 1961).
206. YOUNG, ALLYN, Increasing Returns and Economic Progress, *E.J.* (Dec., 1928).
207. ZIPF, G. K., *Human Behaviour and the Principle of Least Effort* (1949).

Additional References for 1960–3

208. FARRELL, M. J., On the Structure of the Capital Market, *E.J.* (Dec., 1962).
209. GALBRAITH, J. K., The Language of Economics, *The Advancement of Science* (May, 1963).
210. GORT, M., *Diversification and Integration in American Industry* (1962).
211. GRANICK, D., *The European Executive* (1962).
212. KISER, C. F. (Ed.), *Research in Family Planning* (1962).

213. LABOUR, MINISTRY OF, Age and Regional Analysis of Employees in Great Britain, *Gazette* (June, 1963).
214. LUPTON, T., *On the Shop Floor* (1963).
215. MASSÉ, P., French Methods of Planning, *J.I.E.* (Nov., 1962).
216. NATIONAL ECONOMIC DEVELOPMENT COUNCIL, *Growth of the United Kingdom Economy to 1966* (1963).
217. SANDS, S. S., Changes in Scale of Production in U.S. Manufacturing Industries, *The Review of Economics and Statistics* (Nov., 1961).
218. SMITH, J. H., Sociology and Management Studies *British Journal of Sociology* (June, 1960).

INDEX

254